CW00889075

GABB & COMPANY
SOLICITORS
ABERGAVENNY

Practical Planning: Enforcement

Practical Planning: Enforcement

Shona Emmett, MA (Cantab)

Solicitor, Nabarro Nathanson

General Editor

Charles Mynors, FRTPI, ARICS

Barrister

© Longman Group Ltd 1994

ISBN 075200 0624
Published by
Longman Law, Tax and Finance
Longman Group Ltd
21–27 Lamb's Conduit Street
London WC1N 3NJ

Associated offices
Australia, Hong Kong, Malaysia, Singapore, USA

Printed in Great Britain by Biddles Ltd, Guildford

Contents

Table of Cases

Table of Statutes

Table of Statutory Instruments

Chapter 1

Introduction

1 Background and history

Introduction

The enforcement of planning control has been a key element in the modern planning system since it was introduced by the Town and Country Planning Act 1947. However, those enforcement procedures have not been without criticism, particularly in recent years. As a result, numerous attempts have been made to strengthen and improve the law relating to the enforcement of planning control.

The Town and Country Planning Act 1947

The Town and Country Planning Act 1947 created the basis of the modern planning system that applies today. Provisions relating to the enforcement of planning control were introduced as part of that legislation. Under the 1947 Act, the local planning authority (referred to in the remainder of this book as 'the LPA') could serve an enforcement notice where it appeared to them that a breach of planning control had been committed and that it was expedient to do so, having regard to the development plan and other material considerations.

Enforcement action was entirely a matter for the discretion of the LPA and there was no criminal liability for a breach of planning control. The time limit for enforcement action under the 1947 Act was four years from the date of the breach (except in the case of minerals development where the four-year period ran from the time of discovery). The recipient of an enforcement notice had three options:

    (a) comply with the requirements of the notice;
    (b) apply to the LPA for retrospective planning permission;
    (c) appeal to the magistrates' court.

Once it came into effect, criminal liability arose where the notice required discontinuance of a use of land. Where the notice required steps other than the discontinuance of a use of land, ie, the carrying out of works, the LPA could enter the land, carry out the steps themselves and recover the costs from the owner.

The 1947 Act created difficulties in that it was highly technical and, as it affected private property rights, which were stoutly protected by the courts of the day, the case law that developed required strict adherence to the formalities. As a result, a considerable number of enforcement notices were quashed and regarded as nullities (see for example *East Riding County Council v Park Estates (Bridlington) Ltd* [1957] AC 223).

The Caravan Sites and Control of Development Act 1960

The control of caravan sites became a particular problem in the 1950s, and the enforcement provisions of the Town and Country Planning Act 1947 were reformed by the Caravan Sites and Control of Development Act 1960. The 1960 Act introduced a right of appeal to the Minister against an enforcement notice, who was given the power on appeal to correct any informality, defect or error in the notice that was not considered material. The 1960 Act also introduced criminal liability for failure to comply with the requirements of an enforcement notice, whether relating to the carrying out of works, or to the discontinuance of a use of land.

The 1960 Act alleviated some of the difficulties of a rigid interpretation of the requirements of the legislation. This was recognised by the courts, and in particular by the Court of Appeal in the case of *Miller-Mead v Minister of Housing and Local Government* [1963] 2 QB 196 where Upjohn LJ stated a simple test for the validity of an enforcement notice, 'Does the notice tell (the recipient) fairly what he has done wrong and what he must do to remedy it?'

The Town and Country Planning Act 1968

The provisions of the Caravan Sites and Control of Development Act 1960 were incorporated into the Town and Country Planning Act 1962, but the next major revision of the legislation relating to breaches of planning control occurred with the Town and Country Planning Act 1968.

The 1968 Act applied to all enforcement notices issued after 1 April 1969. One of the major changes introduced by the Act was that the four-year time limit for taking enforcement action against breaches of planning control comprising a material change of use (other than to a use as a single dwellinghouse) was replaced by the removal of any immunity period for uses that were begun after the end of 1963. The four-year time limit remained for operational development and breaches of related conditions.

In addition, the 1968 Act introduced 'established use certificates' for uses that could be shown to be immune from enforcement action, and 'stop notices' by which the LPA could prohibit the continuation of operational development. If the enforcement notice on which the stop notice was based was subsequently overturned, the LPA were liable to pay compensation.

The Town and Country Planning Act 1971

The Town and Country Planning Act 1971, Part V consolidated the previous legislation, and provided the central core of planning control for almost 20 years. It was subject to subsequent amendment by two main pieces of legislation. The Town and Country Planning (Amendment) Act 1977 extended the scope of the stop notice procedure to a wider range of development, and set a 12-month time limit for its use. It also strengthened the powers of the LPA to obtain information. The Local Government and Planning (Amendment) Act 1981 introduced a number of minor amendments clarifying the enforcement provisions. These reflected the recommendations for improving the enforcement system made in the report by George Dobry QC in 1975.

The Town and Country Planning Act 1990

The Town and Country Planning Act 1990 consolidated planning legislation; the enforcement provisions are contained in Part VII. This Act now contains the current legislation as it relates to the enforcement of planning control, as amended substantially by the Planning and Compensation Act 1991. The 1990 Act (as amended) is referred to in the remainder of this book as 'the TCPA 1990', and unless stated otherwise, all statutory references are to this Act. Where relevant, reference is made to the provisions of the Planning and Compensation Act 1991.

2 The Carnwath Report

Introduction

The most recent changes for the enforcement of planning control have been introduced by the Planning and Compensation Act 1991. These were based on the recommendations resulting from a review of the legislative provisions relating to the enforcement of planning control carried out by Robert Carnwath QC, whose report 'Enforcing Planning Control' (referred to in the remainder of this book as 'the Carnwath Report') was presented, in February 1989, to the Secretary of State for the Environment (referred to in the remainder of this book as 'the Secretary of State').

Carnwath had been given the task of reviewing the scope and effectiveness of the legislative provisions relating to the enforcement of planning control. After carrying out a series of consultations and drawing on existing information, he identified three primary objectives which an effective enforcement system should seek to achieve:

    (a) bringing an offending activity within planning control;
    (b) remedying or mitigating its undesirable effects; and
    (c) punishment or deterrence.

In achieving these, the system must be seen to operate fairly and, as far as possible, it should aim for speed, clarity and cost-effectiveness.

A number of recommendations were made by the Carnwath Report with these objectives in mind. Most of the recommendations made were accepted by Parliament and given effect in the Planning and Compensation Act 1991.

These are described below, and referred to at appropriate points throughout the book. However, not all were accepted; those that were not are referred to on p 7.

Preliminary procedures

It was considered that existing powers to enter land were too narrow for enforcement purposes. The LPA should be able to obtain accurate information as a basis for enforcement action. Carnwath accordingly recommended that rights of entry be extended

> to allow entry on any land at all reasonable hours on production of appropriate authority, for the purposes of investigating any alleged breach on that land or on immediately adjoining land, for determining the nature of any remedial action, or generally for the purpose of the exercise of the authority's enforcement functions. (Carnwath Report, para 2.1)

This recommendation was accepted by Parliament and is now incorporated in the legislation in ss 196A–C (*see* Chapter 12). Enforcement action is now excluded from the purposes for which more general rights of entry are conferred by s 324(1)(*c*).

The existing powers to obtain information under the planning legislation were also relatively limited. The Carnwath Report therefore recommended that provision be made for a new optional statutory procedure for serving a 'contravention notice' to enable LPAs to obtain information and to secure co-operation without recourse to enforcement action. This was accepted by Parliament and ss 171C and 171D now contain provision for the service of a planning contravention notice (*see* Chapter 3).

Immunities

The Carnwath Report identified a clear need to clarify and rationalise the existing law on immunity from enforcement. It was recommended that an amendment be made to the legislation to the effect that the general period of immunity from enforcement should be a period of ten years prior to the issue of an enforcement notice. The Report also recommended that the four-year protection period given to breaches of condition be removed and that where development has become immune from enforcement action, planning permission should be deemed to have been granted immediately prior to commencement.

These recommendations were enacted in s 171B. Operational development and the change of use of any building to use as a single dwelling house retain the four year immunity period. Other material changes of use and breaches of condition are subject to a rolling ten-year immunity period (*see* Chapter 5).

Enforcement notices

The technicality and complexity associated with the drafting of enforcement notices was an area that came in for considerable criticism in the Carnwath

Report. A series of recommendations were made to reduce this technicality and to introduce more flexibility in enforcement notices. These were accepted by Parliament, and incorporated into ss 172 and 173A (*see* Chapter 6).

Appeals

The Carnwath Report contained recommendations to amend the grounds of appeal against an enforcement notice so that these would tie in with other recommendations made in the Report. These were accepted by Parliament and included in s 174(2) and (3) (*see* Chapter 9).

More significantly, the Report considered the widespread practice of exploiting the considerable opportunities for delay under the existing enforcement procedures, as exemplified by the case of *R v Kuxhaus et al* [1988] JPL 545. The effect of an enforcement notice was suspended pending the final determination of an appeal against the notice, which could include an appeal to the High Court (and beyond) on a point of law. As a result, unauthorised uses continued while the enforcement action was concluded. This led to both public and professional concern about the effectiveness of the whole enforcement system.

The Carnwath Report recommended that an appeal to the High Court should not be brought other than by leave of the court, and that where the court allows an appeal, it shall have power to give directions as to:

(a) the operation of the notice in the period prior to any further decision of the Secretary of State; and

(b) the effect of any proceedings previously take pursuant to the notice.

These recommendations were accepted by Parliament and incorporated into s 289 (*see* Chapter 11).

Determining lawful uses

Under the pre-1991 law, there were somewhat unsatisfactory procedures relating to established use certificates and the determination of the planning status of a proposed use. The grant of an established use certificate did not make a use lawful, it merely rendered it 'established', that is immune from enforcement action. As a result, there were difficulties for the layman in ascertaining the planning status of land. There was also a mechanism to find out whether a proposed operation or change of use would require a planning application; it too suffered from limitations.

The Carnwath Report recommended that both the existing procedures be repealed and replaced by a single procedure whereby the LPA could be invited to issue a certificate that any specified use or operation (whether or not instituted before the application) can be carried on without planning permission. In addition, provision should be made to enable a use to be described by reference to a class of use in a use classes order and to enable the form of application and the supporting evidence required to be regulated by a development order. There would be a right of appeal to the Secretary of State.

These recommendations were wholly accepted by Parliament and were incorporated into the legislation as ss 191–196 (*see* Chapter 13).

Breaches of condition

The existing procedures did not provide a prompt remedy for breaches of certain conditions. To provide a swift and more effective procedure, the Carnwath Report made a recommendation that provision be made for a new procedure for summary enforcement of breaches of condition, without any right of appeal.

This recommendation was accepted by Parliament and is enacted as s 187A (*see* Chapter 8).

Stop notices

The Carnwath Report identified the failure to use the stop notice procedure effectively as one of the main reasons for criticism of the present system. The position for compensation also needed to be clarified. A recommendation was made that no compensation should be awarded for any use or operation which was or would have been in breach of planning control, and that the assessment of compensation should take into account any failure to respond to a planning contravention notice.

A second recommendation was made to extend the limit of stop notices for unauthorised uses from 12 months to four years, and to leave out of account any period covered by a planning permission, to repeal the exception in respect of residential caravans, and to allow immediate effect in special cases.

All these recommendations were accepted by Parliament and led to a revision of the statutory powers relating to stop notices as set out in ss 183, 184 and 186 (*see* Chapter 7).

Injunctions

There was no existing back-up to the statutory system of enforcement control that LPAs could turn to in difficult cases. As a result, the Carnwath Report recommended that

> there be an express power for authorities exercising planning functions to apply to the High Court or County Court for an injunction to restrain any threatened or actual breach of planning control (whether or not an enforcement or stop notice has been served) where they consider it necessary or expedient in order to prevent serious damage to amenity or otherwise to supplement the powers available under the Act. (Carnwath Report, para 10.4)

A power to apply to the High Court for an injunction was introduced by the Planning and Compensation Act 1991 and can be found s 187B (*see* Chapter 12).

Default action

The Carnwath Report recognised that default action by the LPA was a last resort power, but that it could be strengthened by making it available for any steps carried out under an enforcement notice, including works for alleviating injury to amenity or the discontinuance of a use. It was also recommended that there should be an offence of wilfully obstructing the exercise of the power and that regulations should be created to enable expenses to be made a charge on the land.

These recommendations were accepted by Parliament and are now incorporated in s 178 (*see* Chapter 12).

Criminal penalties

It was considered that the courts should be given powers to impose penalties that would act as a real deterrent, and that the statutory provisions relating to criminal liability should be reviewed generally. In particular:

    (a) the maximum penalties should be increased, and financial benefit taken into account in assessing penalties, provision being made for the prosecution's estimates of such benefit to be binding unless disproved;

    (b) the range of potential defendants should be extended;

    (c) the date when an offence arises following first conviction should be clarified, and it should be made clear that there may be further offences following a second conviction.

These recommendations were largely accepted by Parliament and incorporated into the TCPA 1990, primarily in s 179 (*see* Chapter 12).

Review of guidance

The Carnwath Report was critical of existing policy guidance relating to the enforcement of planning control, and recommended that the policy guidance in current Circulars should be clarified. In particular, the policy guidance should emphasise that:

    (a) the LPA have primary responsibility for the enforcement of planning control;

    (b) where persuasion fails, that it is legitimate to use enforcement powers as a means of bringing an unauthorised development within planning control, even where development is broadly acceptable; and

    (c) where enforcement action is necessary, that the authority should not allow negotiations to delay the preparation of the legal groundwork.

Two new Department of Environment Circulars have now been issued. Circular 21/91 (WO Circular 76/91) provides advice on the implementation of the main enforcement provisions introduced by the Planning and Compensation

Act 1991. Circular 17/92 (WO Circular 38/92) provides advice on the implementation of the remaining provisions introduced by the Planning and Compensation Act 1991, that is the breach of condition notice, the revised immunity rules, and lawful development certificates. The DoE and Welsh Office have also introduced planning policy guidance in the form of PPG 18, 'Enforcing Planning Control'. Reference is made to this policy guidance throughout the book where relevant.

Recommendations that were not implemented

The Carnwath Report recommended that a new procedure to obtain information by a planning contravention notice supersede the powers to serve information notices conferred by s 330. This recommendation was not accepted by the Government and the powers under s 330 thus remain, to be used in addition to a planning contravention notice.

Some of the recommendations in the Carnwath Report which related to a reduction in the technicalities associated with the drafting of enforcement notices were not incorporated into the legislation. These included widening the Secretary of State's powers to vary an enforcement notice on appeal and making it a statutory provision that an enforcement notice should not be invalid because of a misdescription of the breach.

The general power conferred on the Secretary of State by the TCPA 1990 to vary the contents of an enforcement notice is subject to the limitation that it can only be used where there will be no injustice to either party. The Carnwath Report considered that this limitation was unnecessary and should be removed. This recommendation was not accepted, however, and the 'without injustice' test thus remains.

Lastly, the Carnwath Report recommended that magistrates' courts should have power to order compliance with the requirements of a breach of condition notice. This was not however incorporated into s 187A.

Practice manual

In view of the paucity of Government guidance on the enforcement of planning control, the Carnwath Report recommended that consideration should be given to the preparation of a practice manual for LPAs on all aspects of enforcement work. This recommendation was not rejected by the Government, but the manual has not yet appeared.

3 Transitional provisions

Enforcement notices served under earlier legislation

Various transitional provisions apply to enforcement notices served under previous legislation relating to planning control. These are as follows:

Enforcement notices served before 29 August 1960 are subject to the provisions of the 1947 Act, by virtue of Sched 3, para 3 to the Planning (Consequential Provisions) Act 1990.

Enforcement notices served between 30 August 1960 and 1 April 1969 are subject to the provisions of the 1968 Act, by virtue of Sched 3, para 3 to the Planning (Consequential Provisions) Act 1990.

Enforcement notices served between 2 April 1969 and 27 July 1981 are subject to the provisions of the 1971 Act, by virtue of Sched 3, para 10 of the Planning (Consequential Provisions) Act 1990. Enforcement notices served after 27 July 1981 are subject to the provisions of the 1971 Act as substituted by the Local Government and Planning (Amendment) Act 1981, by virtue of the Interpretation Act 1978, s 17(2)(*b*).

Breaches of planning condition prior to the 1991 Act

Any immunity that attached to a breach of planning condition under the Town and Country Planning Act 1971 and the TCPA 1990, prior to the implementation of the provisions of s 171B is not affected by that section. This is explained in more detail in Chapter 5.

Chapter 2

Development

1 Introduction

The enforcement system relating to breaches of planning control is a self-contained system set out in the TCPA 1990, Part VII. The power conferred on LPAs to take enforcement action only arises in circumstances where a breach of planning control has taken place. The TCPA 1990, s 57(1) states that planning permission is required for the carrying out of any development of land, and development carried out other than in accordance with a grant of planning permission is unauthorised development against which enforcement action may be taken.

There are no direct criminal sanctions against the development of land without planning permission (and their introduction was firmly resisted in the Carnwath Report), the planning enforcement machinery provides the option of sanctions for breaches of planning control.

The definition of a breach of planning control is contained in s 171A(1). It is either carrying out development without the required planning permission, or failing to comply with any condition or limitation subject to which planning permission has been granted. This chapter concentrates on the first limb, unauthorised development. The second limb, failure to comply with a condition or limitation, is referred to at various stages throughout the remainder of this book and, in particular, in Chapter 8.

It is necessary to understand when development has taken place without planning permission, and therefore what constitutes development, in order to know when a breach of planning control has taken place. In this context, reference needs to be made to the provisions of the TCPA 1990 and the 1988 GDO.

The term 'development' is defined in s 55(1). It may take one of two forms:

    (a) the carrying out of building, engineering, mining or other operations in, on, over or under land (operational development); or

    (b) the making of any material change in the use of any buildings or other land (material change of use).

These two forms of development are distinct; this is clarified by the definition of 'use' in relation to land (contained in s 336(1)) as excluding 'the use of land for the carrying out of any building or other operations on it'.

This book is primarily concerned with the specific topic of enforcement. The question of what constitutes development, which has been the subject of much litigation over many years, is therefore only dealt with in outline. For further details, the standard text books (or the *Encyclopaedia*) should be consulted.

2 Operational development

Introduction

The first limb of the definition of development refers to operational development. Four types of operation are expressly included: building, engineering, mining and other operations. In addition, various categories of operations are specifically excluded from the definition of development.

Building operations

The term 'building operations' is now defined in s 55(1A). It includes:
- (a) demolition of buildings;
- (b) rebuilding;
- (c) structural alterations of or additions to buildings; and
- (d) other operations normally undertaken by a person carrying on business as a builder.

This definition is not exhaustive, as indicated by the use of the word 'includes'. However, the fourth part of the definition is expressed in broad terms and would cover general forms of building operation, in particular, the erection of an entirely new building which is not specifically mentioned.

Certain building operations are specifically excluded from the definition of development by s 55(2). In addition, building operations may have the benefit of a grant of planning permission under the 1988 GDO. These exceptions are set out on pp 13 and 14.

The meaning of the word 'building' is also relevant to this type of operational development. The term 'building' is defined to include 'any structure or erection, and any part of a building, as so defined, but does not include plant or machinery comprised in a building' (s 336(1)). This is a broad definition, and the precise meaning of the definition has been the subject of litigation. A number of cases give some indication of what is meant by the term 'building'.

Firstly, the permanence of a particular development is a factor that the courts have considered when determining if a building operation has taken place. Thus in *James v Brecon County Council* (1963) 15 P & CR 20, a battery of six swing boats erected at a fairground, which could be dismantled by six men in half an hour, was held not to have sufficient permanency to be a structure or erection, and its erection therefore did not constitute development. In *Cheshire County Council v Woodward* [1962] 2 QB 126 a coal hopper and conveyor were installed on land, the hopper being mounted on wheels in order to be mobile and to fulfil the function of delivering coal to lorries. The court declined to accept that this was development. Lord Parker CJ stated that 'There is no one test; you look at the erection, equipment, plant, whatever it is, and ask: in all the circumstances is it to be treated as part of the realty?' Physical attachment of itself is inconclusive.

However, in a subsequent case, the court considered a large crane which ran on a steel track permanently fixed in concrete as development, despite the fact that it could be dismantled and re-erected over the course of several days (*Barvis Ltd v Secretary of State for the Environment* (1971) 22 P & CR 710).

These cases illustrate the difficulty in determining whether or not an erection or structure is development, and it is often a fine balancing exercise for the LPA or the Secretary of State, as no hard and fast rules apply.

Secondly, a building can be a development even when it is on a small scale. In *Buckinghamshire County Council v Callingham* [1952] 1 All ER 1166, a model village and railway was held to constitute a structure or erection and was therefore a building. However, insignificant or *de minimis* operations are likely to be outside of development control, eg, boundaries marked out by metal pegs.

Engineering operations

There is little guidance in the TCPA 1990 about engineering operations, although s 336(1) provides that the term includes the formation or laying out of means of access to highways. It is now generally recognised that an operation which would normally require the skills of an engineer, would come within this category of development (*Fayrewood Fish Farms Ltd v Secretary of State for the Environment* [1984] JPL 267). This would include the work of civil, traffic or other specialist engineers.

The placement or assembly of a tank in any part of any inland waters for the purpose of fish farming is now explicitly defined as an engineering operation by virtue of s 55(4A), and is therefore operational development. However, such activity is permitted development under Sched 2 to the GDO 1988 when carried out on land outside National Parks, subject to a prior notification procedure.

Mining operations

There is no statutory definition of mining operations as such. Relevant definitions are set out in Chapter 15, which deals briefly with the enforcement of minerals planning control.

It might appear that mining operations are more akin to the use of land rather than either building operations or engineering operations in that they constitute a continuing activity that may take place over a considerable length of time, and is of a destructive rather than a constructive nature. However, for the general purposes of the TCPA 1990, and in particular planning enforcement, it is to be treated as operational development.

'Other' operations

Not every operation constitutes development. Although most fall within the definition of 'building, engineering or mining operations', Parliament envisaged that some would not. The reference to 'other operations' is intended to include those operations that are of a sufficiently significant nature to constitute development, but that are not dealt with in any of the other specified categories.

The scope of the category of 'other operations' is uncertain. In *Coleshill and District Investment Co Ltd v Minister of Housing and Local Government* [1969] 1 WLR 746 the House of Lords held that 'other operations' were distinct from building, engineering and mining operations, although there must be some restriction on its meaning and it must be construed by reference to building, engineering and mining. It was possible that 'other operations' would denote an activity similar to building, engineering or mining operations.

The Court of Appeal considered the matter in *Cambridge City Council v Secretary of State for the Environment* (1991) 89 LGR 1015, with reference to the demolition of houses. The court considered whether the work constituted an 'other operation' on land, and concluded that it did not. Other operations did not mean *all* other operations, they had to be '... at least of a constructive character, leading to an identifiable and positive result', or be '... similar to building operations or to engineering operations'.

Demolition is now defined in s 55(1A) as a building operation (*see* above, p 11). However, the circumstances in which demolition will constitute development are limited by the Town and Country Planning (Demolition—Description of Buildings) (No 2) Direction 1992 (issued as an Annex to Circular 26/92 (WO Circular 57/92)). The permitted development rights (subject to prior approval) that are contained in the 1988 GDO, Sched 2, Part 31 also limit the circumstances in which demolition will constitute development.

Excluded operations: minor works

The carrying out for the maintenance, improvement or other alteration of any building of works which affect only the interior of the building, or do not materially affect the external appearance of the building, does not constitute development (s 55(2)(*a*)). Therefore works that are purely works of internal alteration or conversion do not constitute development.

This exclusion applies in the case of internal works or works of conversion to a listed building as in any other case. However, it should be borne in mind that such works normally require listed buildings consent by virtue of the Planning (Listed Buildings and Conservation Areas) Act 1990, s 8.

In addition, minor or internal works that are incidental to the making of a material change of use may be the subject of an enforcement notice. This can require that incidental operational works of this nature be undone, even though they do not of themselves constitute development (*Somak Travel Ltd v Secretary of State for the Environment* [1987] JPL 630, *see* Chapter 5, p 53).

Excluded operations: public works

The carrying out on land within the boundaries of a road by a local highway authority of any works required for the maintenance or improvement of a road does not constitute development (s 55(2)(*b*)).

This exclusion is limited to highways authorities. Improvement of the road falls under the Highways Act, Part V, which confers a broad improvement power and a series of specific powers and includes the erection, maintenance, alteration and removal of traffic signs.

Unconditional planning permission is conferred on whoever undertakes these works by virtue of Sched 2, Part 9 to the 1988 GDO.

Similarly, the carrying out of works to inspect, repair or renew any sewers, mains, pipes, cables or other apparatus does not constitute development (s 55(2)(*c*))

This exclusion is restricted to local authorities and statutory undertakers as defined in s 262. Unconditional planning permission is conferred on whoever undertakes these works by virtue of Sched 2, Part 10 to the 1988 GDO.

Excluded operations: demolition

Finally, the demolition of any description of building specified in a direction given by the Secretary of State is not development(s 55(2)(*g*)).

This exclusion was inserted by the Planning and Compensation Act 1991, alongside the inclusion of demolition within the definition of a building operation contained in s 55(1A). The Secretary of State has directed in the Town and Country Planning (Demolition—Description of Buildings) (No 2) Direction 1992 (issued as an Annex to Circular 26/92 (WO Circular 57/92)), that the demolition of certain descriptions of buildings is not to be taken to involve development. In addition, there is an automatic planning permission conferred by Sched 2, Part 31 to the 1988 GDO for building operations constituting the demolition of all buildings not excluded by the direction, subject to a prior notification procedure. The one exception to this is a building which has been made unsafe or uninhabitable, either through deliberate action or neglect and where the building cannot be made safe through temporary repairs or support.

The net result of this highly complex set of provisions is that planning permission is only rarely required for demolition works.

3 Material change of use

Introduction

The second limb of the term development is 'material change of use'. Apart from the exclusionary definition of 'use' contained in s 336(1) which is referred to above at p 10, there is no statutory definition of material change of use.

Section 55(3) does however provide that, for the avoidance of doubt, a material change of use occurs when a building, previously used as a single dwelling is converted into two or more separate dwellings. The deposit of refuse or waste materials on land involves a material change of use, notwithstanding that the land is comprised in a site already used for that purpose, if the area or the height of the deposit is extended and exceeds the level of the adjoining site.

A substantial body of case law has developed that provides some guidance as to what is a material change of use. The most important rule is that a change of use is only development if it is 'material'. It is primarily a matter of fact and degree for the LPA (or the Secretary of State on a call-in or an appeal) as to whether, in a particular set of circumstances, a material change of use has occurred. A change must be material from a planning point of view, so that, for example, a change in the use of a yard from the storage of coal to the storage of cars (both for onward transport by rail) was held not to be material (*see East Barnet Urban District Council v British Transport Commission* [1962] 2 QB 484). Further, a change is not material if it is *de minimis*. The court is unable to interfere with a finding on such a matter, unless the LPA or Secretary of State could not properly have reached the conclusion that they did (*ibid*).

Intensification of use

A use may have the benefit of the grant of planning permission, and be acceptable in planning terms. However, the extent of the use may intensify, and thereby become unacceptable. In such circumstances, it could be argued that there has been a material change of use and therefore development.

There are cases where the courts refused to recognise that intensification could of itself constitute a material change of use. These culminated in the case of *Royal London Borough of Kensington and Chelsea v Secretary of State for the Environment* [1981] JPL 50 where Donaldson LJ said that 'it had to be clearly understood by all concerned that intensification which did not amount to a material change of use was merely intensification and not a breach of planning control.'

It is now generally accepted that, to constitute development, there must be intensification of such a degree as to amount to a material change in the character of a use. For example, a change in the part-time use of a garage for car repairs to repairing cars on a full-time basis (*Peake v Secretary of State for Wales* (1971) 22 P & CR 889).

The planning unit

The extent of the land involved must be ascertained in order to determine whether a material change of use has taken place. What may not amount to a material change of use on a large site could be a material change of use on a much smaller site. The extent of the land involved in terms of planning is referred to as 'the planning unit'. Generally, this will be the whole site, nomally the whole of the area in the same ownership or the same occupation.

Criteria used to determine the correct planning unit were set out in the case of *Burdle v Secretary of State for the Environment* [1972] 1 WLR 1207.

(1) Whenever it is possible to recognise a single main purpose of the occupier's use of his land to which secondary activities are incidental or
ancillary, the whole unit of occupation should be considered.

(2) Where the occupier carries on a variety of activities and it is not possible to say that one is incidental or ancillary to another, the entire unit of
occupation should be considered.

(3) Where two or more physically separate and distinct areas within a single unit of occupation are occupied for substantially different and un-
related purposes, each area used for a different main purpose (together
with its incidental and ancillary activities) ought to be considered as a
separate planning unit.

On the basis of these criteria, the LPA or the Secretary of State should be
able to determine the area of land against which to assess the materiality of
change, and decide, as a matter of fact and degree, whether a material change
of use has taken place. Other factors to be considered in determining the appropriate planning unit are:

(a) the unit of occupation;
(b) composite uses;
(c) functional separation;
(d) physical separation;
(e) subdivision of the planning unit; and
(f) dual and recurrent uses.

In some of these cases a new planning unit may be created and this would
affect the assessment of whether a material change of use had taken place.

Primary and ancillary uses

To assess whether a material change of use has taken place, it is necessary to
determine the primary use of land and the uses that are ancillary to it. It is an
accepted principle in planning law that the right to use land for a primary
purpose includes the right to use it for an ancillary purpose. Although the Use
Classes Order provides that uses which fall within the same class do not constitute development (*see* below p 17), and there is no need to look beyond the
general category of use, there may be cases where it is necessary to consider
the position more closely.

Once the planning unit has been established, the character of the main use
of that unit will dictate every part of the unit, even if a small part is devoted to
some separate ancillary use, eg, storage ancillary to the main use of land as a
haulage depot. The substitution of one ancillary use for another, or the relocation, or addition of an ancillary use will not be a material change of use, so
long as the ancillary link remains. In the above example, the site used for
storage could be relocated within the planning unit without involving a material change of use, as long as it remained ancillary to the main use.

A material change of use will have taken place where an ancillary use changes
in character and becomes a primary use in its own right, eg, where land and
buildings had been used for boat hire purposes including boat manufacturing
as an ancillary use, and the manufacturing use increased to such an extent that

it became a primary use in its own right (*Jillings v Secretary of State for the Environment* [1984] JPL 32).

The assessment of whether a material change of use has occurred where the change relates to a primary and ancillary use requires a subjective judgement of the facts and circumstances surrounding a particular case. Again, no hard and fast rules can be applied to determine if a material change of use has occurred in any development of the land.

Excluded changes of use: dwellinghouses

As with operational development, certain changes of use are specifically excluded from the definition of 'development'. The first of these is the use of any buildings or other land within the curtilage of a dwellinghouse for any purpose incidental to the enjoyment of the dwellinghouse as such (s 55(2)(*d*)). This exclusion will only apply where the material change of use occurs within the curtilage of a dwellinghouse *and* the new use is for any purpose incidental to the enjoyment of the dwellinghouse. It was considered by the Court of Appeal in *Wallington v Secretary of State for Wales* [1991] 1 PLR 87, which held that factors to be considered included:

    (a) the location and size of the dwellinghouse;

    (b) the nature of the activity; and

    (c) the disposition and character of the occupier.

As to the extent of the 'curtilage', this is a matter of fact and degree.

It should be noted that s 55(2)(*d*) does not authorise any operational development within the curtilage of a dwellinghouse, although such development may be given planning permission by virtue of Part 1 of Sched 2 to the 1988 GDO.

Excluded changes of use: agriculture and forestry

The use of any land for the purposes of agriculture or forestry and the use for any of those purposes of any building occupied together with land so used does not constitute development (s 55(2)(*e*)).

The term 'agriculture' is comprehensively, but not exclusively, defined in s 336(1). This exclusion applies to a material change of use of land from a non-agricultural use to a use for the purpose of agriculture or forestry. Land and buildings requisite for the agricultural use of land or for forestry purposes also benefit from a planning permission (subject to certain limitations) by virtue of Part 6 of Sched 2 to the 1988 GDO.

Use classes

In the case of buildings or other land within a use class contained in the Use Classes Order, the use of the buildings or other land for any other purpose of the same class does not constitute development (s 55(2)(*f*)). This reflects art 3(1) of the Use Classes Order 1987, which provides that 'where a building or other land is used for a purpose of any class specified in the Schedule, the use of that building or that other land for any other purpose of the same class shall not be taken to involve development of the land'. The order itself should be consulted for details of the various classes; see also Circular 13/87.

4 Permitted development rights

Introduction

Planning permission for development may be granted (by the LPA or the Secretary of State) as the result of an application for planning permission made to the LPA by the Secretary of State in a general or special development order, or, in certain very limited circumstances, it may be deemed by the TCPA 1990 to be granted. Permitted development rights reflect the permission granted by a general development order for certain classes of development.

Article 3(1) of the 1988 GDO provides that 'planning permission is hereby granted for the classes of development described as permitted development in Schedule 2'. There are 31 separate Parts to Sched 2, each dealing with a particular class of development that may be undertaken on land without an application needing to be made to the LPA. The GDO is likely to be amended and consolidated in 1995-96, but these classes are unlikely to change substantially.

The classes of development permitted by the 1988 GDO are generally in the following categories:

      (a) minor building etc operations associated with certain categories of land use (eg, residential, agricultural, industrial);

      (b) other minor operations;

      (c) certain works by statutory undertakers and other public or quasi public developers (eg, drainage bodies, airport operators, English Heritage);

      (d) certain changes of use (eg, from industrial to office).

Where there are permitted development rights conferred on a particular development, such development will be lawful and cannot therefore be subject to enforcement action. However, it is important to note the various restrictions imposed on these rights by the GDO 1988 (*see* below) as, where these apply, the LPA will be in a position to take enforcement action where they consider it expedient to do so.

Restrictions on permitted development rights

There are five main restrictions on permitted development rights. Where these restrictions apply, development will be unauthorised, unless benefiting from a grant of planning permission. In these circumstances the LPA are empowered to take enforcement action for a breach of planning control. The five restrictions are as follows:

      (1) Permitted development rights may only be exercised in relation to an existing building or use of land, if construction of the building or the

use is lawful (art 3(4A) of the 1988 GDO). This now includes land and buildings that are immune from enforcement action by virtue of the passage of time (*see* Chapter 5).

(2) Any permission granted by art 3(1) of the 1988 GDO is subject to any relevant exception, limitation or condition specified in Sched 2. These can relate to the size of the development permitted by one of the classes in Sched 2, (eg, Part 1, Class A—the enlargement, improvement or other alteration of a dwellinghouse) or the external appearance of the development permitted, (eg, Part 8, Class B—development carried out on industrial land for the purposes of an industrial process). Development that is in contravention of these exceptions, limitations or conditions does not have the benefit of permitted development rights and would be unauthorised development against which the LPA could take enforcement action.

(3) Permitted development rights may be restricted by a direction made by the LPA and approved by the Secretary of State under art 4 of the 1988 GDO. Such a direction may be made if they are satisfied that it is expedient that development specified in one of the classes in Sched 2 (other than certain mineral exploration and removal of material from mineral-working deposits) should not be carried out unless permission is granted for it on an application. These 'article 4 directions' are common in conservation areas.

(4) Planning permission granted by art 3 of the 1988 GDO does not permit development contrary to any condition imposed by any planning permission granted or deemed to be granted under the TCPA 1990, Part III. It is common for a grant of planning permission to contain conditions restricting the scope of development which would otherwise be permitted under the 1988 GDO. The LPA or Secretary of State may consider that this is required as the development permitted as a result of the application is the maximum that should be allowed on the site. It is necessary for the condition to exclude the permitted development rights in express terms (*Dunoon Development v Secretary of State for the Environment* (1992) NPC 22).

(5) There are also restrictions on permitted development in relation to 'article 1(5) land'. This is defined in Part 1 of Sched 1 to the 1988 GDO as land within a national park, an area of outstanding natural beauty, a conservation area, and an area specified by the Secretary of State for the purposes of the Wildlife and Countryside Act 1981, s 41(3). In these areas, the permitted development rights are significantly limited, eg, as to the size of extensions to dwellinghouses.

Chapter 3

Information Gathering

1 Introduction

The taking of enforcement action is a discretionary power exercised by the LPA. In order to be able to assess whether that discretion should be exercised, LPAs need to be appraised of the facts relating to the use or development of land, or the activities taking place on land. There are established statutory methods for obtaining information about interests in land and these are contained in TCPA 1990, s 330 and the Local Government (Miscellaneous Provisions) Act 1976, s 16. However, these rights are limited, as explained below.

There is now a wider power to obtain information about activities on land for enforcement purposes which was introduced by the Planning and Compensation Act 1991. LPAs may serve what is known as a 'planning contravention notice' requiring such information. This power supplements the existing methods for obtaining information referred to above which LPAs may still use if they prefer. The service of a planning contravention notice does, however, enable the LPA to do more than merely obtain information, and it will therefore normally be the first procedure used. It is considered fully below.

In addition, there are now specific powers (in ss 196A–C) enabling an authority to enter onto land in relation to forthcoming enforcement action, to ascertain by direct observation whether there has been any breach of control, and what to do about it (see p 28 below).

2 Planning contravention notices

Objectives

The planning contravention notice was introduced by the Planning and Compensation Act 1991 following a recommendation in the Carnwath Report. It was perceived that the procedure would achieve four main objectives outlined by Carnwath.

These are that:

    (a) it would act as a formal warning of the prospect of an enforcement or stop notice, as the receipt of a formal document may concentrate the mind in some cases and produce results, and it would provide authorities with a means of responding immediately to complaints of contravention, without affecting the policy approach that actual enforcement should be 'a last resort' (*see* Chapter 4);

(b) it would require the recipient to confirm at an early stage the facts as to what is happening on the land, and the legal justification, if any, for it;

(c) it would give the authority the opportunity (in cases where the development is broadly acceptable) of encouraging either the submission of a planning application or the making of some other undertaking (such as a planning obligation); and

(d) the response, or lack of it, would provide the authority with a firmer basis to decide whether to support any enforcement notice with a stop notice.

Power to require information

The statutory power to require information for enforcement purposes is contained in s 171C. Where it appears to the LPA that there may have been a breach of planning control in respect of any land, they may serve a planning contravention notice requiring information. This does not affect any other power exercisable for any breach of planning control (s 171C(7)).

It is an investigative procedure and it need only 'appear' to the LPA that there 'may' have been a breach of planning control. The LPA may serve a planning contravention notice where it suspects that a breach of planning control has occurred: they need not have *prima facie* evidence that a breach has occurred. A complaint from a neighbour may be sufficient for the LPA to exercise the power.

The LPA cannot use the power contained in s 171C to obtain general information about the use of a site. The planning contravention notice may *specify* a use, operation or activity (s 171C(3)(*a*)), and the recipient of the notice must provide information on that use, operation or activity. The LPA must therefore have formed a view as to the suspected breach before serving the notice. They cannot undertake 'a fishing expedition' about the use of the land.

Procedural arrangements

The power to serve a planning contravention notice is suitable for delegation to a single officer or sub-committee (*see* Chapter 4). It may constitute an initial response to a complaint regarding the use of land made by a neighbour or some other third party affected. A complaint may be made via a committee member, in which case the LPA can be seen to be acting on such a complaint by the service of a planning contravention notice. The committee, and in particular the relevant member, should be kept informed of the result of any action taken by the LPA. Alternatively, a complaint may be made direct to a planning or enforcement officer, who can then take immediate action without the need to obtain authority from the committee, where the power to serve a planning contravention notice has been delegated.

The response given to a planning contravention notice can be used in the preparation of a report to committee, where enforcement action is being considered and authority to take such action is being sought from the committee.

If the matter is dealt with by delegated powers there can be a quicker response in relation to a suspected breach of planning control, and as the committee procedure does not have to be repeated, eg, once to seek authorisation to serve the planning contravention notice and again to seek authorisation to take enforcement action once the response to the planning contravention notice has been considered, the ultimate sanction of enforcement action will not be unduly delayed. This may be critical where the time limits relating to the breach of planning control are about to expire (*see* Chapter 5).

Service of a planning contravention notice

A planning contravention notice may be served on any person who is the owner or occupier of the land or has any other interest in it; or is carrying out operations on, in, under or over the land or is using it for any purpose (s 171C(1)). The options relating to the parties that may be served will ensure that the LPA obtain as much information as possible about the activities being carried out on land. For commentary as to who is the 'owner' and who is the 'occupier' of the land, *see* Chapter 6, p 58.

To obtain a full picture of the activities being carried out, the LPA may serve notices on more than one person, eg, the owner, who can provide information on the planning history of the site, and a current occupier, who can inform the LPA what the site is being used for at the present time.

LPAs are advised in para 7 of Annex 1 to Circular 21/91 that when serving persons who have an interest in the land, they should try to ensure, as far as is practicable, that any known mortgagees of the land are served with the relevant notice. This is because a mortgagee in possession will need to be made aware of the situation, where the owner of the land is a defaulting mortgagor, and the LPA cannot locate him.

The service of a planning contravention notice has two purposes. First, it enables the LPA to be properly informed about activities being carried out on land, and to obtain that information directly from the person who is most involved and therefore has direct knowledge about those activities (*see* below). Secondly, it enables the LPA to seek the co-operation of the owner or occupier of the land, so as to avoid the necessity for taking any enforcement action

It should be noted that the service of a planning contravention notice is entirely optional. It is not a pre-requisite to taking enforcement action (the LPA may already have all the necessary information to enable it to initiate action), nor does it constitute 'taking enforcement action' as defined in s 171A(2). The fact that a planning contravention notice was not served before an enforcement action was taken is not a valid basis for an award of costs on any appeal against an enforcement notice (para 3 of Annex 1 to Circular 21/91).

The mechanism for the service of a planning contravention notice is set out in s 329. Service may be effected by delivering the notice personally, by leaving it at the usual or last known place of abode of the person on whom it is being served, or by sending it in a pre-paid registered letter or by recorded delivery. For further commentary on the mechanics of service, *see* Chapter 6, p 59.

Information that may be sought by a notice

The statute prescribes the information that a planning contravention notice may require from the person on whom it is served. The information required by the LPA need only be the information that is required for enforcement purposes, and as such the notice may be very specific as to the information being sought.

A planning contravention notice may require information as to:

(a) any operations being carried out on the land, any use of the land and any other activities being carried out on the land; and

(b) any matter relating to the conditions or limitations subject to which any planning permission in respect of the land has been granted (s 171C(2)).

In addition, a planning contravention notice may require the person on whom it is served, *so far as he is able*, to:

(a) state whether or not the land is being used for any purpose specified in the notice or any operations or activities specified in the notice are being or have been carried out on the land;

(b) state when any use, operations or activities began;

(c) give the name and address of any person known to him to use or have used the land for any purpose or to be carrying out, or have carried out, any operations or activities on the land;

(d) give any information he holds as to any grant of planning permission or any reason for planning permission not being required;

(e) state the nature of his interest in the land, and the name and address of any other person known to him to have an interest in the land (s 171C(3)).

A model planning contravention notice for use by LPAs is appended to Annex 1 to Circular 21/91 and is reproduced in Appendix 1. Different information may be required from different parties, and some information for which provision is made in the model planning contravention notice may not be required at all by the LPA, eg, details of a planning permission or other information that is already in their possession. In such cases, it should be made clear on the face of the notice what information is required. This can be achieved by deleting those sections of the notice for which information is not required from a particular recipient, and by enclosing a covering letter with the planning contravention notice explaining that the deleted sections do not require a response.

The opportunity to make representations

Following a recommendation in the Carnwath Report, in addition to the LPA's ability to obtain information, a mechanism enabling them to seek the co-operation of an owner, occupier or user of land can be secured. The LPA has a statutory power to extend an invitation to the recipient of a planning contravention notice to meet with officers of the LPA to discuss the means by which any suspected breach of control may be remedied. This could include the submission of a retrospective application for a conditional planning permission; or the carrying out of remedial works, eg, reducing the amount of on-site storage, or changing the hours of working, or ceasing certain operations or activities.

The planning contravention notice may give notice of a time and place at which the person on whom the notice is served can make an offer to the LPA concerning an application for planning permission, the cessation of operations or activities, or the carrying out of remedial works, or make any other representations about the notice (s 171C(4)). It is open to the recipient of a planning contravention notice to initiate a meeting with the LPA, if no invitation is made by the LPA in the planning contravention notice.

Paragraph 10 of Annex 1 to Circular 21/91 provides that such opportunity may be given to the recipient of a notice by the LPA 'where they consider it appropriate'. It does not have to be given on every occasion. Where it is considered that enforcement action may be avoided, an invitation to the recipient of a notice to negotiate can be extended by means of the planning contravention notice, and as a result, it may be possible to remedy the situation by means other than enforcement action. However, where it is considered that no useful purpose would be served by discussion with the recipient of the notice, the LPA can use the planning contravention notice for the limited purpose of obtaining information they require to decide whether to initiate formal enforcement action.

Response to a planning contravention notice

Any requirement of a planning contravention notice shall be complied with by giving information in writing to the LPA (s 171C(6)). There is a statutory duty to respond to a planning contravention notice within 21 days of the service of the notice. However, it is recognised in para 13 of Annex 1 to Circular 21/91 that 'a person who is served with a planning contravention notice cannot reasonably be expected to provide information he does not possess or could not reasonably find out'. For example, a corporate owner of a site may not know the precise details of the actual use of a site by a tenant at a particular time and therefore could not supply the LPA with the appropriate information.

The planning contravention notice must inform the recipient of the likely consequences of his failing to respond to the notice, in particular, that enforcement action may be taken, and of the effect of s 186(5)(b) (s 171C(5)). This is a mandatory requirement, whereas the other requirements of a planning contravention notice are optional (*see* above). Section 186(5)(*b*) relates to the financial compensation payable in the event of a stop notice being served on a claimant who was required to provide information under s 171C. No compensation is payable for any loss or damage which could have been avoided if the recipient of the notice had provided the required information, or had co-operated with the LPA when asked to do so (*see* Chapter 7, p 88). This warning is included as part of the text of the model planning contravention notice (*see* Appendix 1).

The LPA will consider the factual information given in response to a planning contravention notice when deciding if a breach of planning control has occurred, and whether to proceed with enforcement action and subsequently serve a stop notice. If the reply to a notice creates doubt, a site inspection will usually be essential to ensure that any subsequent enforcement decision is well-founded. To this extent the powers of entry contained in ss 196A–C can be exercised (*see* below p 28 and Chapter 12).

Non-compliance with a planning contravention notice

The recipient of a planning contravention notice has a period of 21 days, beginning with the day on which it was served on him, to comply with the requirements of the notice. Non-compliance with any requirement of a notice within that period is an offence (s 171D(1)). On summary conviction, the maximum penalty is a fine not exceeding 'level 3' on the standard scale (currently £1,000). There is a continuing offence where compliance with the requirements of the notice remain outstanding, and a second and subsequent offence is charged by reference to any period of time following the preceding conviction.

There is a statutory defence for a person charged under s 171D(1), contained in s 171D(3), to prove that he had reasonable excuse for failing to comply with the requirement of a planning contravention notice. The burden of proof lies with the defendant. Where the information required is not known to the recipient of the notice, there is no positive duty upon him to discover such information. If he can show that he did not hold the information, or have the requisite knowledge to comply with the requirements of the notice then he can rely on the statutory defence.

In some instances, the necessary information may already be known to the LPA, or be readily accessible from another source. In such circumstances, the LPA should not seek to charge the offence under s 171D(1). Instead they should use their power to be selective about the information required by the notice, or to serve another party who has the requisite knowledge or information with a planning contravention notice.

A separate offence is created by s 171D(5) where any person makes any statement purporting to comply with a requirement of a planning contravention notice which he knows to be false or misleading in a material particular or recklessly makes such a statement which is false or misleading in a material particular. The maximum penalty on summary conviction for this offence is a fine not exceeding 'level 5' on the standard scale (currently £5,000).

Validity

The validity of a planning contravention notice may be challenged either by application for judicial review, or by way of defence to prosecution under s 171D. There is no statutory bar to any such challenge afforded by s 285 as there is for enforcement notices. In this respect planning contravention notices are similar to stop notices (*see* Chapter 7) and breach of condition notices (*see* Chapter 8).

Registration

There is no requirement to enter a planning contravention notice in the enforcement register maintained by the LPA pursuant to s 188. Nor is the notice a legal charge on the land. Therefore, it will not be revealed in a search. However, in cases of doubt, a direct question could be made to the LPA.

3 Other powers to require information

TCPA 1990, s 330

Section 330 gives the LPA, and the Secretary of State, the power to require information as to interests in land. It is a general power that may be exercised for the purpose of enabling the LPA, or the Secretary of State, to make any order or issue or serve any notice or other document under the TCPA 1990. This will include orders, notices and documents under Part VII which deals with enforcement powers.

The power to require information is exercised by a notice in writing served on the occupier of any premises and any person who receives rent from it. The notice may specify that the recipient give information as to any of the following matters such as the:

(a) nature of the interest in the premises of the person on whom the notice is served;

(b) name and address of any other person known to him as having an interest in the premises;

(c) purpose for which the premises are being used;

(d) time when that use began;

(e) name and address of any person known to the person on whom the notice is served as having used the premises for that purpose;

(f) time when any activities being carried out on the premises began.

The recipient of a notice served under s 330 may be required to specify the use of the land. To this extent, the information that can be obtained is arguably wider than that obtainable by a planning contravention notice, which may only require the giving of 'such information as to any use of the land as may be specified in the notice' (s 171C(2)(*a*)). Therefore, where the LPA are uncertain about what the land is being used for, a notice served under s 330 may be of more use in providing them with the necessary information. It is always open to the LPA to serve both notices, either together, or one as a result of the response given to the other.

Time limit

The recipient of a notice served under s 330 must respond to the notice within 21 days of the date on which it is served, or such longer time as may be specified in it, or as may be allowed (s 330(3)).

Offences

Failure to comply with the requirements of the notice without reasonable excuse is an offence under s 330(4). On summary conviction the maximum penalty is a fine not exceeding 'level 3' on the standard scale (currently £1,000). It is also an offence, triable either way, knowingly to make a misstatement in response to a notice (s 330(5)). The maximum penalty on summary conviction is a fine not exceeding the statutory maximum (currently £20,000); on conviction on indictment, the maximum penalty is an unlimited fine, or two years' imprisonment, or both.

A failure to respond to the requirements of a notice or to co-operate with the LPA when responding to it are also factors that may be taken into account in assessing the liability of the LPA to make financial compensation for the use of the stop notice procedure (s 186(5), *see* Chapter 7, p 88).

The service of a notice under s 330 is also the only way in which the Secretary of State may obtain information before taking enforcement action under s 182, since he has no power under s 171C or under the 1976 Act.

The Local Government (Miscellaneous Provisions) Act 1976, s 16

Section 16 empowers LPAs to obtain particulars of persons interested in land. It is more restricted than the power contained in s 171C or s 330. Under s 16, a notice may be served on:

    (a) the occupier of land;

    (b) any person who has an interest in the land; and

    (c) any person authorised to manage or let the land, requiring the recipient to state:

        (i) the nature of his interest in the land; and

        (ii) the name and address of each person whom the recipient of the notice believes is the occupier of the land, or has an interest in the land, or is authorised to manage or let the land.

This information must be supplied within a period specified in the notice, which must be more than 14 days from the date of service of the notice. It is an offence not to comply with the requirements of a notice, or to make a statement which is false in a material particular, or to recklessly make a statement which is false in a material particular (s 16(2)). On summary conviction the

maximum penalty in either case is a fine not exceeding 'level 5' on the standard scale (currently £5,000).

It will be noted that the penalty for offences in connection with a notice
under the 1976 Act is less than with a notice under s 330, but that the time for
furnishing information can be as little as two weeks, rather than three. The
only other notable difference between the two procedures is that the power
under s 16 of the 1976 Act can be exercised in respect of any function of any
local authority, and is not restricted to powers under the TCPA 1990. It may be
useful for the LPA to serve a notice under s 16 where they need to ascertain
who should be the recipient of a planning enforcement notice, and therefore
may be served prior to the service of a planning contravention notice.

Rights to enter land

The LPA have statutory rights to enter onto land, with or without warrant,
specifically for enforcement purposes. These rights are conferred by ss 196A–
C. The right may be exercised to ascertain whether there is or has been any
breach of planning control on the land, or on any other land, to determine
whether and how any of the enforcement powers should be exercised, or to
ascertain whether there has been compliance with any requirements imposed
as a result of the exercise of enforcement powers. The right of entry in relation
to enforcement purposes is dealt with in detail in Chapter 12.

Chapter 4

Power to Take Enforcement Action

1 Introduction

The TCPA 1990 (s 171A(2)) defines 'taking enforcement action' as the issue of an enforcement notice or the service of a breach of condition notice. The broader scope of enforcement action, however, includes the service of planning contravention notices and stop notices, and the determination of applications for certificates of lawfulness.

Both the Secretary of State and the LPA are empowered by statute to issue an enforcement notice (*see* Chapter 6) or to serve a stop notice (*see* Chapter 7) or a breach of condition notice (*see* Chapter 8); but it is in practice virtually always the LPA which actually takes action. It is also the sole function of the LPA to serve planning contravention notices (*see* Chapter 3) and to determine applications for a certificate of lawfulness (*see* Chapter 13).

In considering who has the power to take enforcement action — including for these purposes, the broader function of the LPA to enforce — it is necessary to determine which local authority is 'the local planning authority' and then to determine who has the power to discharge the functions of the LPA.

2 The local planning authority

The scheme of the 1990 legislation

The consolidation legislation of 1990 provides some clarification on the allocation of functions under the town and country planning legislation. There is a distinction between the enforcement functions of the local authority as local planning authority, and the local authority as mineral planning authority. The 'mineral planning authority' have enforcement powers in respect of minerals planning (*see* Chapter 15), and the 'local planning authority' have enforcement powers for all other areas of development control.

Section 1 of the TCPA 1990 identifies the local planning authority and mineral planning authority for the three categories of county in England and Wales. These are summarised below. Further provisions then set out the arrangements applying in certain special cases (*see* below). With the restructuring of local government currently being mooted, these categories may change in the near future with the introduction in some areas of unified authorities. The legislation that will be required to introduce the changes will however contain specific provisions relating to the allocation of planning functions.

Non-metropolitan counties

In a non-metropolitan (or shire) county there are two local planning authorities: the county council is the county planning authority and the district council is the district planning authority. The county planning authority is also the mineral planning authority in a non-metropolitan county (s 1(4)(a)). All functions conferred on local planning authorities under the planning acts may in principle be exercised by both (s 1(3)).

Schedule 1 to the TCPA 1990 specifies the distribution of the functions of the LPA. Schedule 1, para 3, provides that the determination of an application for a certificate under s 191 or s 192 shall be exercised by the district council except where the application relates to a 'county matter', when it shall be exercised by the county council.

For other enforcement powers, namely the power to issue an enforcement notice, or to serve a planning contravention notice or stop notice or breach of condition notice, Sched 1, para 11 provides that, in general, they shall be exercisable solely by the district council (para 11(1)). However, where they relate to county matters they can be exercised either by the county council (para 1(3)), or by the district council after consulting with the county council (para 1(2)). In relation to minerals development, the county council alone shall exercise the functions of the LPA in their capacity as mineral planning authority (para 1(4)).

Section 286(2) provides that the validity of an enforcement notice, stop notice or planning contravention notice issued or served under the TCPA 1990 cannot be challenged in any legal proceedings on the grounds that, in the case of a notice issued or served by the district planning authority, they failed to consult the county planning authority; or in the case of a notice issued or served by the county planning authority, that they had no power to issue it because it did not relate to a county matter. This provision relates only to the relationship between counties and districts in non-metropolitan areas.

Metropolitan counties

The metropolitan district council is both the only local planning authority and the mineral planning authority for its area (s 1(2)(4)(b)).

Greater London

The council of each of the London boroughs (including the Common Council of the City of London) is both the only local planning authority and the mineral planning authority (s 1(2)(4)(b)).

National parks

Joint planning boards may be established by the Secretary of State as the county planning authority for the areas or parts of two or more county councils, or as the district planning authority for the area or parts of two or more district councils. Joint planning boards have been established to date in two designated national parks. These are the Lake District Special Planning Board and the Peak Park Joint Planning Board. These have the function of an LPA under the Act. However, under s 2(7), they may be deprived of such functions if an enterprise zone, urban development corporation or housing action trust is established in its area.

In the other national parks, the functions of the LPA are undertaken by the metropolitan district council (in metropolitan counties) and by the county planning authority outside these areas. The Government has proposed that all national parks should in future be placed on the same footing as the Peak District and the Lake District, and be administered by independent national park authorities, rather than county or metropolitan district councils. Again, the legislation that will be necessary to implement this proposal will clarify the responsibility for planning functions.

The Broads

For land in the Broads, the sole LPA is the Broads Authority, which was established pursuant to the Norfolk and Suffolk Broads Act 1988. Its functions include the power to take enforcement action under the TCPA 1990, (s 5).

Other special cases

In enterprise zones, a designation order may provide that the enterprise zone authority shall be the LPA for such purposes and for such kind of development which may be specified in the order (s 6). For all of the nearly 70 zones designated so far, the enterprise zone authority has in each case been the district council or urban development corporation, which accordingly remains as the LPA.

Where an urban development area is declared under the Local Government, Planning and Land Act 1980, the urban development corporation may be specified in an order made under s 149(1) of the 1980 Act as the LPA for the urban development area concerned for such purposes and for such kinds of development as may be specified in the order (s 7). Every urban development corporation created to date, with the exception of Cardiff Bay, has been designated as the LPA for its area for all purposes, including enforcement.

In housing action trust areas, designated under the Housing Act 1988, the housing action trust specified in an order made under s 67(1) of the 1988 Act is the LPA for such area, for such purposes and in relation to such kinds of development as may be so specified in the order (s 8(1)).

Finally, where an area is designated under s 170 of the Leasehold Reform, Housing and Urban Development Act 1993, the Urban Regeneration Agency (also known as English Partnerships) may be designated as the LPA.

3 Decision taking within the planning authority

Delegation of functions

The Local Government Act 1972, Part VI provides for the discharge of functions by local authorities. Sections 101 and 102 of the 1972 Act determine if the functions of the LPA have been exercised properly. The council of a local authority may (and in practice always does) arrange for the discharge of any of their functions by a committee, a sub-committee, an officer of the authority, or by any other local authority. In addition, the committee empowered to discharge any functions of a local authority may delegate the discharge of those functions to a sub-committee or an officer of the authority and a sub-committee empowered to discharge the functions of the local authority may delegate the discharge of those functions to an officer of the authority. Both powers are

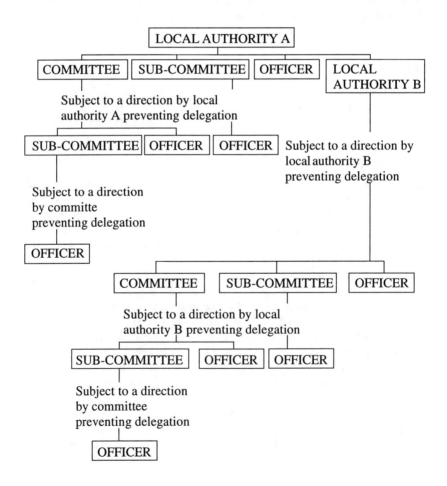

subject to a direction by the local authority or the committee, as relevant, preventing such delegation.

One local authority may also arrange for the discharge of any of its functions by another local authority. That authority may, subject to the terms of such arrangement, delegate in turn to a committee, sub-committee or officer of theirs and the further delegation referred to above also applies (Local Government Act 1972, s 101). In all these circumstances the existence of a delegation arrangement does not prevent the delegating authority from exercising the delegated function itself.

Committees (see diagram opposite)

The Local Government Act 1972, s 102 empowers the local authority to appoint a committee or sub-committee for the purpose of discharging any function in pursuance of arrangements made under s 101. The development control functions of a local authority may therefore be discharged by a committee or a sub-committee appointed under s 102. It is normally the standing orders of the local authority which constitute the 'arrangements' under s 101.

The Local Government Act 1972 provides (in s 99 and Sched 12) that 'a local authority may make standing orders for the regulation of their proceedings and business and may vary or revoke any such orders'. A model set of standing orders has been published for the guidance of local authorities, the most recent edition, entitled 'Model Standing Orders Contracts' was published by HMSO in 1983. The actual form and operation of the standing orders regulating the affairs of any particular local authority are under its own control, and they can be rescinded or suspended by a simple majority decision in accordance with the Local Government Act 1972, Sched 12, para 39. The standing orders of a local authority are available for examination by members of the general public, and proof of the delegation of powers should be found in those standing orders.

A committee meeting should be convened in accordance with the standing orders of the local authority. Three days public notification of committee meetings must be given (Local Government Act 1972, s 100B(4)). In *R v Swansea City Council, ex parte Elitestone* (1993) EGCS 87, the Court of Appeal held that the committee meeting agenda had to be open for at least three clear days before the meeting, excluding the date of publication of the notification and the day of the meeting itself. However, it seems that it is possible to hold a committee meeting by telephone conference (*R v Secretary of State for Environment, ex parte Bickenhall Parish Council* [1987] JPL 773).

Delegation to officers

The situation relating to the exercise of functions is not always clear cut, in particular where action is taken by a single person. Although the Local Government Act 1972, s 101(1)(*a*) expressly provides for a local authority to arrange for the discharge of their functions by an officer of the authority, there have been a number of cases where the courts have looked carefully at the circumstances to determine whether such arrangements exist or can be implied.

Enforcement action can be taken by an officer or the staff of an officer to whom power has formally been delegated under s 101. The legislation does not require the personal exercise of the delegated function by the nominated officer (*Cheshire County Council v Secretary of State for the Environment* [1988] JPL 30).

In this case, an appeal against several enforcement notices was made to the Secretary of State. He refused to determine the appeal, forming the view that the enforcement notices were nullities because the decision to issue them had been taken by a solicitor employed by the LPA who was not empowered to make that decision. The local authority's standing orders provided that the County Secretary and Solicitor had power, in consultation with the County Planner, to issue enforcement and stop notices. Although there was no delegation in writing, the court held that such power could be exercised by a member of the County Secretary and Solicitor's staff. The council relied on a combination of standing orders and practice and had arranged for the discharge of their functions for the issue of the enforcement notices by solicitors in the employ of the council. The court applied the case of *Provident Mutual Life Assurance Association v Derby City Council* [1981] 1 WLR 173, which involved an assistant to the treasurer of the council who filled in a typed completion notice served under the General Rate Act 1967. The House of Lords held that this arrangement was valid.

Although the arrangements for the discharge of functions do not need to be made in writing (s 101), the need for the courts to consider such issues indicates that local authorities would be advised to make formal arrangements for the delegation of functions rather than relying on past delegations.

Delegation involving elected members
The power to arrange for the discharge of the LPA's functions under the Local Government Act 1972, s 101 does not authorise the delegation of the functions of a local authority to a single elected member of that authority, as opposed to an officer.

Thus in *R v Secretary of State for the Environment, ex parte Hillingdon London Borough Council* [1986] 1 WLR 192, a case similar to the *Cheshire* case, the Secretary of State refused to consider appeals against enforcement notices served by the council on the grounds that the notices were nullities. The service of the enforcement notices had been authorised by the chairman of the council's planning committee. The council's standing orders purported to permit delegation to a chairman. The court held that standing orders *regulate* the proceedings and business of the local authority. The provisions to make standing orders cannot authorise the delegation of what otherwise is not authorised. The only relevant statutory provision as to delegation in the ordinary way is s 101 and this does not specifically state that there could be delegation to the chairman of the committee or a single elected member. The court rejected the concept of a committee of one and held that the action of the chairman was unauthorised and *ultra vires*.

On the other hand, a decision taken by a duly authorised officer pursuant to s 101 in consultation with the elected chairman would be valid. Thus in *Fraser v Secretary of State for the Environment* (1987) 56 P & CR 386 the court held that standing orders could require the officer to obtain the approval of a member of the council, such as the planning committee chairman, before exercising the delegated power. This supported a view expressed by the court in the *Hillingdon* case that there were circumstances where urgent matters had to be dealt with which could not go before an elected committee or sub-committee but where it was undesirable for a single officer to take sole responsibility. This is in practice a common arrangement, and is sometimes referred to (misleadingly) as 'chairman's action'.

Subsequent ratification of an officer's action
There may be circumstances where action is taken by an officer of the local authority, where that officer did not have authority to discharge that function. The council cannot convert such action into action of the authority.

In *Co-operative Retail Services Ltd v Taff-Ely Borough Council* (1979) 39 P & CR 223, the House of Lords held that the council was not bound by the actions of its clerk who was not authorised to take such action. The case involved two competing sites for superstores, one to be developed by Tesco, the other by the Co-op. The application for the Tesco site was considered by the planning committee of the district council on 6 July 1976. The planning officer recommended that outline planning permission be granted, subject to a referral to the county council who had objected to the scheme. The solicitors for the owner of the Tesco site subsequently wrote to the council threatening proceedings for *mandamus* if the formal permissions granted were not issued as they asserted that the council had resolved to grant planning permission for the Tesco site on 6 July 1976. The clerk to the council erroneously took the view that the resolution of the council amounted to a grant of planning permission for the Tesco superstore. He accordingly issued the formal permission despite the fact that he had received no authority from the council to do so. On 14 December 1976, the council resolved to confirm the action of the clerk in issuing the permission. The House of Lords upheld the Court of Appeal decision that the council's resolution of 6 July 1976 had not amounted to a grant of planning permission, that the action of the clerk could not have converted what was not a planning permission into a planning permission, and that the council's resolution of 14 December 1976 had done nothing more than to convert the council's unauthorised action into an authorised action. Planning permission had not been granted.

This ruling is supported by the case of *Barnard v National Dock Labour Board* [1953] 2 QB 18, which made it clear that there can be no ratification of a decision made by a person who has no power to delegate.

Nor is it possible to ratify an *ultra vires* resolution of a local authority. Thus in *R v Rochester-upon-Medway City Council, ex parte Hobday* (1989) 58 P & CR 424, which involved the use of land as a market, the council had delayed taking enforcement action, although they had resolved to do so immediately after a 14 day period, in the belief that the owners were entitled by virtue of the provisions of the GDO to use the land as a market for 14 days. However, prior to the expiry of the 14 day period, the council resolved to issue an enforcement notice and serve a stop notice after receiving legal advice that, where the evidence suggested that the use was not temporary, but permanent, the benefit of the GDO was not available. The enforcement notice and stop notice were subsequently served, and an application for judicial review of the stop notice was made.

The application was dismissed. The court held that the first resolution of the council was *ultra vires* as, at that time, the council did not believe that a breach of planning control had taken place. That *ultra vires* resolution could not be ratified by the subsequent resolution of the council. However, the subsequent resolution was of itself valid as it included a fresh decision to issue an enforcement notice and to serve a stop notice.

A council may on the other hand ratify action taken by an officer on behalf of the local authority where that officer has not been formally authorised to take such action. So, for example, in *Warwick Rural District Council v Miller-Mead* [1963] Ch 441, the evidence showed that the action of the officer did reflect the actual intention of the council, despite the fact that such intention had not been expressed in a formal resolution until after the action had been taken.

Conclusions

From the above decisions, it is clear that the normal practice of local authorities to discharge their functions through a single officer of the authority or through a member of the staff of that officer, possibly after consultation with an elected member, is entirely legitimate. It is however not lawful for action to be authorised solely by a committee chairman or other elected member or an officer who had no authority to discharge that function (subject to the right to ratify that action in circumstances such as in the *Warwick* case).

The principles in this section should be borne in mind in the context of enforcement appeals and prosecutions, as a notice issued unlawfully will be a nullity.

4 The decision to take enforcement action

The planning authority's discretion

Parliament has made it clear that enforcement action should remain within the LPA's discretion. The legislation therefore provides for local authorities to take enforcement action when they regard it as expedient. Parliament gave the LPA's the exclusive right to take enforcement action and rejected proposed amendments to the Planning and Compensation Bill which would have imposed a general duty on LPAs to take such action. In addition, it exclusively reserved the right to take enforcement action to the LPA: there is no private right of enforcement of a breach of planning control.

If the LPA refuses to take enforcement action, this decision cannot be challenged in the courts, unless it is shown to be capricious or arbitrary. In *Perry v Stanborough (Developments) Ltd* (1977) 244 EG 551, planning permission had been granted on the condition that an access to an adjoining site be constructed. The LPA refused to enforce the condition, considering that the matter was best dealt with by negotiation between the developers concerned.

The LPA may serve a planning contravention notice where it appears to them that there may have been a breach of planning control in respect of any land in their area (s 171C; *see* Chapter 3). The LPA may issue an enforcement notice where it appears that there has been a breach of planning control and that it is expedient to issue the notice, having regard to the provisions in the development plan and to any other material considerations (s 172). Where the LPA consider it expedient that the relevant activity should cease before the expiry of the period for compliance with an enforcement notice, they may serve a stop notice (s 183). The LPA may serve a breach of condition notice if any of the conditions attached to the grant of a planning permission are not complied with (s 187A).

The common denominator of all these powers is that there should be a breach of planning control and, for enforcement notices and stop notices, that the LPA consider it expedient to take enforcement action.

Breach of planning control

The first issue to be determined is whether or not there has been a breach of planning control. This expression is defined in s 171A as 'carrying out development without the required planning permission, or failing to comply with any condition or limitation subject to which planning permission has been granted'. The distinction between these two limbs is important as an enforcement notice must state within which of these limbs the breach falls, in the opinion of the local authority, ie, whether it is unauthorised development or a breach of condition or limitation (*see* Chapter 6, p 63). The local authority only have to be satisfied that there appears to be a breach of planning control, and to believe that a breach of planning control has taken place, they do not have to be satisfied that it has actually occurred. As in the *Hobday* case (*see* above p 35), the council could take enforcement action before the expiry of the 14 day period as all the evidence indicated that there was an intention to use the land permanently as a market. The breach of planning control had not actually taken place, as the 14 day period had not expired at the time when the resolution to issue the enforcement notice was made.

In determining whether or not there has been a breach of planning control, the decision making committee or officer should consider the following:

(1) Has any development taken place – either operational development or a material change of use? In this context, reference should be made to s 55 (*see* Chapter 2).

(2) If there has been development, was planning permission required? For

example, a lawful use of land may be resumed without planning permission once a temporary permission has expired or ceased to be relied upon. Planning permission would not be required for the resumed use. In addition, land may without permission revert to its lawful use where an enforcement notice has been issued in respect of unauthorised development (s 57).

(3) Did any development fall within permitted development rights under the GDO (or any other development order which was in force at the relevant time)? This includes permitted changes of use within the Use Classes Order (*see* Chapter 2).

Expediency

If it appears to the LPA that there has been a breach of planning control, it must then exercise its discretion in considering whether it is expedient to issue an enforcement notice and possibly a stop notice.

In exercising their discretion as to whether it is expedient to take enforcement action, the LPA must look at the provisions of the development plan and any other material considerations (s 172(1)(*b*)). These indicate the planning considerations which underlie the taking of enforcement action. Since it is necessary to have regard to the development plan, it will be necessary for the LPA to determine whether or not to take enforcement action 'in accordance with the plan unless material considerations indicate otherwise'—by virtue of s 54A. The requirement specified in s 172(1)(*b*) nevertheless reflect the discretionary aspect of taking enforcement action.

PPG 18 on the enforcement of planning control provides guidance for LPAs on the general approach they should adopt to enforcement. It acknowledges that LPAs have a general discretion to take enforcement action, when they regard it as expedient, and then goes on to set out five considerations to be taken into account. These are that:

(a) Parliament has given LPAs the primary responsibility for taking whatever enforcement action may be necessary in the public interest in their administrative area (the private citizen cannot initiate planning enforcement action);

(b) the local ombudsman has held that there is maladministration if the authority fail to take effective enforcement action which was plainly necessary and has occasionally recommended a compensatory payment to the complainant for the consequent injustice (*Local Government Ombudsman Reports, Complaint No 90/B/1742* [1993] JPL 693 and *Complaint No 88/B/1560* [1994] JPL 69);

(c) the decisive issue for the LPA when considering whether or not to take enforcement action should be whether the breach of planning control would unacceptably affect public amenity or the existing use of land and buildings meriting protection in the public interest;

(d) the enforcement action should always be commensurate with the breach of planning control to which it relates; and

(e) where the LPAs initial attempt to persuade the owner or occupier of the site voluntarily to remedy the harmful effects of unauthorised development fails, negotiations should not be allowed to hamper or delay whatever formal enforcement action may be required to make the development acceptable on planning grounds, or to compel it to stop. A reminder is given as to the statutory limits for taking enforcement action.

These are the underlying considerations and can serve as reminders to LPAs when exercising their discretion as to whether or not it is expedient to take enforcement action. To that extent, they act as a check list in circumstances where it appears to the LPA that there has been a breach of planning control and the authority are considering whether or not to take enforcement action, and the form that such action should take.

5 Policy guidance on specific situations

Introduction

The remaining substance of PPG 18 deals with a number of specified scenarios, and provides guidance on the approach to be taken in each. This structure provides a good practical guide to LPAs on the issues to be considered in each of those scenarios. It also gives an indication to owners and occupiers upon whom an enforcement notice is served of the issues to be considered by the LPA when exercising their discretion to take enforcement action. In circumstances where the LPA patently fail to consider such issues, there may be grounds for appeal (*see* Chapter 9). The following sections of this chapter summarise the advice in PPG 18. The advice is directed at the LPA.

Where development is carried out without permission (PPG 18: paras 6 and 7)

(1) Where it is likely that unconditional planning permission would be granted for development which has already taken place, suggest to the person responsible for the development that he submit a retrospective planning application.

(2) Consider the use of the planning contravention notice (*see* Chapter 3) to establish what has taken place on the land and persuade the owner or occupier to seek permission for it, if permission is required.

(3) Tell the owner or occupier of the land that, without a specific planning permission, he may be at a disadvantage if he subsequently wishes to dispose of his interest in the land and has no evidence of any permission having been granted for development.

Where unauthorised development can be made acceptable by the imposition of conditions (PPG 18: paras 8 and 9)

(1) Invite the owner or occupier of the land to submit a planning application.

(2) Advise the person concerned that the authority have a public duty to safeguard amenity by ensuring that development is carried out, or continued, within acceptable limits.

(3) If the owner or occupier of land refuses to submit a planning application, consider whether to issue an enforcement notice stating clearly what injury to amenity, or damage to the site has been caused by the unauthorised development and how a conditional grant of planning permission will effectively remedy it (*see* Chapter 6).

Where the unauthorised development is unacceptable on the site but relocation is feasible (PPG 18: paras 10 and 11)

(1) If the LPA are aware of a suitable alternative site as part of their economic development functions, suggest it and encourage the removal to it of the unauthorised development. However, it is not the LPA's responsibility to seek out an alternative site.

(2) Make it clear to the owner or occupier of the site that where an alternative site is available, he is expected to relocate either to that site or to an acceptable alternative.

(3) Set a reasonable time limit within which such relocation should be completed.

(4) If the time limit is ignored, issue an enforcement notice specifying what the LPA regard as a reasonable time period for relocation.

Where the unauthorised development is unacceptable and relocation is not feasible (PPG 18: para 12)

(1) Inform the owner or occupier of the land that the LPA are not prepared to allow the operation or activity to continue at its present level of activity, or (if this is the case) at all.

(2) Advise the owner or occupier how long the LPA are prepared to allow before the operation or activity must stop or be reduced, and seek to agree a period of time. The LPA should beware of the possibility of the expiry of the statutory period for enforcement action (*see* Chapter 5).

(3) If no agreement can be reached, take enforcement action allowing a realistic compliance period for the unauthorised operational activity to cease, or its scale to be acceptably reduced.

Where the unauthorised development is unacceptable and immediate remedial action is required (PPG 18: para 13)

In these circumstances the LPA should normally take vigorous enforcement action if they are of the view that unauthorised development has been carried out and the breach of control took place with full knowledge that planning permission was needed, the person responsible for the breach will not submit a planning application for it, despite being advised to do so, and the breach is causing serious harm to public amenity in the neighbourhood of the site.

Unauthorised development by small businesses or self-employed people (PPG 18: paras 14 to 17)

(1) Consider whether or not the owner or operator of a small business or a self-employed person has carried out unauthorised development in good faith, believing that no planning permission is needed for it.

(2) Consider whether the cost of responding to enforcement action might represent a substantial financial burden on the small business or self-employed person.

(3) Discuss with the owner or occupier or operator the possibility of the business continuing to operate on the site and suggest ways of overcoming the planning objections to the current operation of the business. This may result in a mutually acceptable planning permission.

(4) If the site's owner or occupier is at first reluctant to negotiate, serve a planning contravention notice.

(5) If formal enforcement action is essential, it should be preceded by informal discussion about possible means of minimising harm to local amenity caused by the business activity, and possible relocation to another site.

(6) If relocation is a possibility, the LPA should aim to agree a timetable for relocation which will minimise disruption to the business and, if possible, avoid any permanent loss of employment as a result of the relocation.

(7) A reasonable compliance period, or an extension of the initial period should be considered when taking enforcement action against businesses.

Unauthorised development by private householders (PPG 18: para 18)

(1) Bear in mind that independent professional advice about whether planning permission was needed for the development may sometimes not have been readily available or affordable.

(2) Where a householder may have relied on permitted development rights in the 1988 GDO, but exceeded a specified limit discuss with the householder the extent of the permitted development rights and suggest ways to secure compliance or to remedy the breach and where appropriate invite an application for planning permission.

(3) Where the householder fails to take satisfactory steps to regularise the development, despite being allowed adequate time to do so, a breach of condition notice should be served and should include a full explanation of the alleged unauthorised development. Unless this has been done, prosecution under s 187A(9) for failure to secure compliance with the limitation imposed on a grant of planning permission by virtue of the 1988 GDO will be inappropriate (*see* Chapter 8, p 104).

(4) Enforcement action should not normally be taken in order to remedy only a slight variation in excess of what would have been permitted by the GDO provisions, for example, where the owner of a detached dwellinghouse has constructed an extension whose volume is 15.5 per cent that of the main house.

6 Exercise of the Power

Policy guidance

Breaches of planning control may come to light as a result of a planning officer or an enforcement officer of the LPA becoming aware of development that is unauthorised or which has been carried out not in accordance with approved plans and any conditions imposed. More often, they come to the attention of the LPA as a result of a complaint by a neighbour, or other member of the public, or an amenity group. The effect of unauthorised development on the amenity and the local neighbourhood are indeed emotive issues that lead to many complaints to LPAs. In particular, the length of time taken to achieve compliance in some instances (usually well publicised) can lead to public dissatisfaction. The performance of the LPA is therefore not only governed by policy guidance, but also subject to the increased awareness of the public who expect high standards of service. In addition, with the publication of the National Planning Forum's Guide for Development Control, there is a need for the administrative procedures of the authority to be clear.

Central Government policy (notably PPG 18) deals largely with the planning considerations underlying enforcement action (*see* above). In terms of administrative procedures, PPG 18 advises (in para 22) that 'all authorities should ensure that there is a close and co-operative working relationship between the Planning Department and the Solicitor's (or Secretary's or Chief Executive's) Department'. This is important in terms of effective action in the event of a breach of planning control.

In terms of enforcing the planning law and regulations, the Development Control Charter Guide is also relevant. It sets out three principles:

(1) The council's policy on enforcement will be published. It will explain the council's enforcement procedures and practice.

(2) When an alleged breach of planning control is reported or suspected, the site or premises will be inspected and other information sought to establish the facts. Where a breach of planning control is established, the person responsible for the breach will be informed of what is wrong and what action should be taken to correct it. A time limit will be given and the consequences of not taking the appropriate action will be explained.

(3) Complaints about alleged breaches of planning control will be treated confidentially within the council so far as practicable. They will be acknowledged within five working days. The complainant will be notified in writing within 15 working days of receipt of the complaint of

how the council intends to pursue the matter. The complainant will be further notified in writing of the decision to take enforcement action within ten working days of that decision being made. If the council decides not to take action the reason will be explained.

Administrative procedures

In the light of the above guidance, LPAs should endeavour to have clear administrative procedures for dealing with breaches of planning control. Some suggestions for procedures that can be instituted by LPAs to improve performance in relation to the exercise of the power to take enforcement action are listed below:

(1) Set target dates for each stage of the enforcement procedure along the lines set out in the Charter Guide. These could include the following
    (a) acknowledgement of any complaint;
    (b) investigation and negotiation;
    (c) initial decision on complaint;
    (d) service of planning contravention notice;
    (e) assessment of information obtained;
    (f) report to committee;
    (g) drafting and issue of enforcement notice; and,
    (h) where required service of a stop notice.
(2) Set up a programme of regular meetings between the enforcement officer and solicitor to obtain legal advice where a case raises difficult issues of law.
(3) Report any breach of planning control to the committee at the first available opportunity, even if this is merely to appraise the committee of the current situation. Often complaints from the public will come through members, and an updating system on particular cases to members can prove to be invaluable in terms of public relations.
(4) Keep any complainant informed of the authority's actions throughout.
(5) Maintain a clear structure of delegated powers. Routine matters can be delegated to officers, eg, planning contravention notices, with the power to issue enforcement notices, stop notices, and breach of condition notices left with the committee. However, it may be expedient to delegate such powers to officers in consultation with the committee chairman in significant cases (*see* the cases of *Hillingdon* and *Fraser* detailed above pp 34 and 35).
(6) All forms and letters should be in clear understandable English and should reflect the position of the person supplying the information or receiving the letter, not just that of the LPA.

7 Estoppel

Introduction

The principles of private law are generally inapplicable to a statutory system such as that governing development control. However, to protect the public interest, the courts have on occasion applied the principle of estoppel to planning law, usually in circumstances which prevent the LPA from taking enforcement action.

An LPA will thus be unable to take enforcement action where:

(1) it has tried unsuccessfully to do so before, and nothing has changed ('issue estoppel'; see below); or

(2) its officers have stated that planning permission is not required for the development concerned ('estoppel by representation'; see below).

The second of these is now only applicable in relatively limted circumstances.

Issue estoppel

Where an issue has already been determined, and a final decision made, as in an enforcement appeal, the principle of issue estoppel applies. For example, where an appeal is successful, the principle of estoppel would prevent the LPA from taking further enforcement action in circumstances where there has been no material change in fact relating to the activities concerned (*Thrasyvoulou v Secretary of State for the Environment et al* [1988] JPL 689). There must however be a sufficient identity of issue in the circumstances under consideration (*RJ Williams Le Roi v Secretary of State for the Environment and Salisbury District Council* [1993] JPL 1033). In the *Thrasyvoulou* case, the Court of Appeal also held that the burden of proving that issue estoppel arises lies with the party who claims to be protected by the estoppel.

Estoppel by representation

Generally, the principle of estoppel by representation has no place in planning law. Officers of an authority may make representations to a member of the public. Such representations are usually stated to be the personal view of the officer and not the formal view of the authority. Statements to this effect will be posted in council offices and often appended as a standard paragraph to letters from the council.

The courts have however allowed this principle of estoppel to apply where:

(1) an officer acted with ostensible authority in making a planning determination; and

(2) that determination was relied upon.

In *Lever Finance Ltd v Westminster (City) London Borough Council* [1971] 1 QB 222, the court held that any person dealing with the LPA is entitled to assume that all the necessary resolutions have been passed. That case involved a planning officer advising an architect that variations to plans that were the subject of a planning permission were immaterial and therefore permitted within the terms of the planning permission.

However, since the *Lever Finance* case the courts have endeavoured to restrict the principle. In *Western Fish Products v Penwith District Council and Secretary of State for the Environment* (1978) 38 P & CR 7, the Court of Appeal held that, for an estoppel to arise, there had to be some evidence that justified the person dealing with a planning officer thinking that a representation by him would bind the LPA. In this context, the type and scale of the development was relevant. A planning officer is less likely to have powers delegated to him to determine an application for planning permission or even a variation to an existing permission, for a larger scale development. The principle, as stated by Megaw LJ, was that 'An estoppel cannot be raised to prevent the exercise of a statutory discretion or to prevent or excuse the performance of a statutory duty'.

As a result of the *Western Fish* case there are now only two circumstances in which estoppel by representation can arise in planning law:

Firstly where the LPA, acting as such, delegate powers to their officers to determine specific questions, and there is evidence that justified the person relying on the determination and thinking that the officers actions would bind the LPA. This includes circumstances where it is accepted practice for planning officers to approve immaterial variations to plans that are the subject of a grant of planning permission, as in the *Lever Finance* case (a case decided by the Court of Appeal). This circumstance was applied recently in the case of *London Borough of Camden v Secretary of State for the Environment and Barker, ex parte Motion* [1993] JPL 1049. This case fell within the *Lever Finance* category. An architect relied upon a planning officer's confirmation that amendments to a plan were 'minor variations' and therefore would not constitute development requiring planning permission. The court held that the planning officer had conveyed ostensible authority. Evidence to this effect arose from the general practice of LPAs that immaterial variations could be approved without the formal grant of planning permission.

Secondly where the LPA waived a procedural requirement relating to any application made to it for the exercise of its powers, such waiver applying to what was then s 53, for a determination as to whether planning permission is required for a proposed development. This provision is now effectively superseded by the new procedure to apply for a certificate of lawfulness of a proposed use or development under s 192 (*see* Chapter 13).

In a subsequent High Court case, *Graham v Secretary of State for the Environment and East Hampshire District Council* [1993] JPL 353, the Deputy Judge recognised that since the *Western Fish Products* case, the scope for estoppel in the general area of planning law was very limited, citing the two circumstances set out above. The reason for such a narrow scope to the ambit of estoppel for enforcement action was that the LPA should not be estopped by anything its officers might say from exercising the powers and duties bestowed on it by Parliament.

Other instances of estoppel

Three other circumstances in which estoppel may appear to arise in planning law are:

    (a) permission issued by mistake (*Norfolk County Council v Secretary of State for the Environment* [1973] 1 WLR 1400);

   (b) forgery; and

   (c) where a determination is outside the powers of the LPA itself (*Co-operative Retail* case—*see* above p 35).

In each of these cases, an apparent permission wrongly issued by the authority cannot prevent it from subsequently taking enforcement action.

Chapter 5

Time Limits

1 Introduction

The LPAs power to take enforcement action has some restrictions. One of the main restrictions is the time limit within which such action can be taken for a breach of planning control, before it becomes 'immune' from such action. A breach of planning control is defined in TCPA 1990, s 171A as 'carrying out development without the required planning permission; or failing to comply with any condition or limitation subject to which planning permission has been granted'. 'Development' is in turn defined in s 55(1) as 'the carrying out of building, engineering, mining or other operations' in relation to land—operational development; or 'the making of any material change in the use of any buildings or other land'—a material change of use (*see* Chapter 3). The 'change of use' category is further divided according to whether or not the new use is use as a single dwellinghouse. Each of these categories is protected by a different time limit within which the LPA can take enforcement action. In summary, the time limits that apply (set out in s 171B) are as follows:

(1) Operational development — 4 years
(2) Change of use to a single dwellinghouse — 4 years
(3) Any other change of use — 10 years
(4) Breach of condition —10 years

Each of these is now considered in more detail.

2 Operational development

General rule

This is the first limb of the definition in s 55(1). A breach of planning control consisting of the carrying out without planning permission of all forms of operational development is protected by a time limit of *four years* from the date on which the operations were substantially completed (s 171B(1)). This means that after four years, such operational development will be immune from enforcement action.

The requirement for operational development to be 'substantially complete' before the four year period starts to run is contained in the statute. It is usually quite clear when a particular operation is substantially complete. However, Circular 21/91 states that what is substantially complete must always be decided as a matter of fact and degree. It is not possible to define precisely what is meant by the term 'substantially completed'. To assist LPAs, para 46 of Annex 2 to the Circular provides that:

> All the relevant circumstances must be considered in every case. A decision on the date of substantial completion is unlikely to be overturned by the Secretary of State, or the Courts, if it is clear that the LPA have timed their enforcement action after taking all such relevant matters into account and not reached a perverse decision because no reasonable authority could have taken it, on the relevant facts.

Although the four year time limit for taking enforcement action for operational development begins with the date on which the operations were substantially completed, the LPA are entitled to take enforcement action on the commencement of the operational development (s 172). It is at that time that the breach of planning control takes place, the LPA does not have to wait until the operation has been substantially completed before taking enforcement action. The legislation therefore applies different dates for different purposes. This means that the LPA has considerably longer than four years from the commencement of the operation to take enforcement action. However, given the policy advice contained in PPG 18, the LPA should use the time differential to negotiate with the owner or occupier of the site prior to taking the step of enforcing against him (see Chapter 4).

Self-contained operations

The terms 'substantial completion' and 'practical completion' are familiar in standard construction contracts, and, it should be possible, in cases of self-contained operational development, for such contracts to be used as an aid to interpretation.

The case of *Ewen Developments Ltd v Secretary of State for the Environment* [1980] JPL 404 established that, in the case of a single operation (here the construction of an embankment), the four year period does not begin to run until the whole operation is substantially complete. Where an operation is self contained, it will usually be clear when the operation is substantially completed. Difficulties arise when the operation is ongoing, such as in the case of mining, or where the development is an integral part of a larger operation.

Ongoing operations

An example of the application of the 'substantially complete' test in relation to an ongoing operation was considered by the court in the case of *(Thomas) (David) (Porthcawl) Ltd v Penybont Rural District Council* [1972] 1 WLR 1526. This case concerned an enforcement notice served in relation an area of land within which two small areas were being worked for the extraction of sand and gravel. Some of these workings had occurred more than four years before the service of the enforcement notice. The notice was upheld on appeal.

The court dismissed an appeal by the operator against that decision, on the basis that, in the case of mining operations, each shovelful is an operation in itself, and where there is no planning permission, is a separate breach of planning control. In the case of *Robert Reginald Howes v Secretary of State for the Environment and Devon County Council* [1984] JPL 439, the court made a clear distinction between mining, building and engineering operations. Hodgson J stated that 'An operation of building or an operation of engineering had a definable end, when the operation was completed, whereas mining had no discernible end'.

Integral operations

Where the operation is an integral part of a larger operation it will not always be clear when a single operation that is in breach of planning control is substantially complete. In these circumstances the appearance of the building involved will normally be critical (*Worthy Fuel Injection v Secretary of State for the Environment* [1983] JPL 173).

Additional works

The four year period will not be affected by any additional works of a minimal nature carried out after the operations have been substantially completed, eg, fitting out work or internal plastering or decorating or external decorating work, particularly where the building has already been put to its intended use.

3 Change of use to a single dwellinghouse

General rule

The time limits for taking enforcement action for a material change of use differ depending on the change of use involved. In the case of a change of use of any building to a single dwellinghouse, no enforcement action may be taken after *four years* from the date of the breach (s 171B(2)).

Paragraph 9(2) of Annex 1 to Circular 17/92 provides that the four year time limit applies, either where the change to use as a single dwellinghouse involves development without planning permission, or where it involves a failure to comply with a condition or limitation subject to which planning permission has been granted.

Development without planning permission would involve operational development as dealt with above, and would already have protection from enforcement action after four years by virtue of the provisions of s 171B(1). The effect of s 171B(2) is that a change of use of any building to a single dwelling house has the same four year protection period.

As a change of use to a single dwellinghouse is given special protection by the legislation, it is important to determine when a building is being used as a single dwellinghouse. The term dwellinghouse has no statutory definition. However, para 47 of Annex 2 to Circular 21/91 advises that 'If no reasonable person would look at a particular structure used as a dwellinghouse and identify it as such, it is justifiable to conclude, as a matter of fact, that it is not a dwelling house.'

The distinction between what is a dwellinghouse and the use of a building as a dwellinghouse is important. Although the *use* of a building as a dwelling house might be immune from enforcement action, due to the lapse of time, it may not be a dwellinghouse as such, and it would not therefore have the benefit of permitted development rights under the 1988 GDO (*Deitsch and Deitsch v Secretary of State for the Environment and Richmond-upon-Thames LBC* [1993] JPL 579, a case involving the use of premises as both a dwellinghouse and as a solicitors office). A flat would be excluded from enjoying the benefits of permitted development rights, as it is excluded from the definition of a dwellinghouse for the purposes of the 1988 GDO. However, it will be immune from enforcement action after four years where it is being *used* as a single dwellinghouse (see the Court of Appeal decision in the *Van Dyck* case detailed below).

Policy guidance

Guidance is provided by para 47 of Annex 2 to Circular 21/91 on the criteria for determining use as a single dwellinghouse. First it is necessary to determine the planning unit (*see* Chapter 2), then to consider both the physical condition of the premises and the manner of use:

> Is it designed or adapted for residential purposes, containing the normal facilities for cooking, sleeping and eating associated with use as a dwellinghouse?

> Is it used as a dwelling, whether permanently or temporarily, by a single person or more than one person living together as, or like, a single family?

Where both questions are answered in the positive, such premises can properly be regarded as being in use as a single dwellinghouse. On the basis of the above criteria, a bed-sitter, where some communal facilities are shared, or a building in use for the purposes of multiple residential occupation, could not be regarded as a single dwellinghouse, and would not be protected by the four year period.

Case law

There has been some confusion as to whether the conversion of a single dwelling house into flats involves a material change of use protected by the four year period that applies to a change of use of any building to use as a single dwelling house or the ten year period that applies to other material changes of use. Section 55(3)(*a*) provides that the use of a single dwellinghouse as two or more separate dwelling houses involves a material change in the use of the building, and of each part of it. That change is protected by the four year rule. However, the change of use of the whole building would be subject to the ten year rule. There were three conflicting High Court judgements on this issue that all arose at about the same time. Fortunately, the issue was taken to the Court of Appeal and the position was clarified.

In *Van Dyck v Secretary of State for the Environment and Southend on Sea Borough Council and Doncaster Borough Council v Secretary of State for the Environment and Dunhill* [1993] JPL 565, the Court of Appeal considered both of the named cases and the High Court judgment in *Worthing Borough Council v Secretary of State for the Environment and Breach* [1992] JPL 353. All three cases involved similar facts, the conversion of a large dwelling house into two or more separate flats, without planning permission. The issue to be decided by the Court of Appeal was, whether the four year immunity rule applies equally to a breach of planning control consisting of an unauthorised change of use from a single dwellinghouse into two or more separate dwelling houses, as it does to an unauthorised change of use of any building to use as a single dwellinghouse. Simon Brown LJ held that the four year rule did apply to residential subdivisions and that s 172(4)(*c*) (now s 171B(2)) was capable of being construed and applied so as to benefit all new separate residences after four years. In coming to this conclusion Simon Brown LJ considered the definition of 'building' in s 336(1). As that definition included *any part of a building*, it included that part which became a flat following subdivision, and the flat itself became a separate and accordingly a 'single' dwellinghouse.

As a result, it appears that flat conversions are protected by the four year rule, notwithstanding the status of the building as a whole. As long as the criteria for a 'single' dwellinghouse is satisfied, a material change of use involving a change to a single dwellinghouse has the benefit of the four year immunity period. The four year period runs from the date of occupation of the dwellinghouse, as it is this which constitutes the change of use, rather than the conversion works.

4 Other material change of use

General rule

The statutory time limit for taking enforcement action against a breach of planning control involving any material change in the use of land (other than a change to use as a single dwellinghouse) is *ten years* (s 171B(3)).

This provision sweeps away the previously arcane legislative provision where an unauthorised change in use (other than a change to use as a single dwellinghouse) only became immune from enforcement action where it had been undertaken before the beginning of 1964. This provision was criticised in the Carnwarth Report as it was becoming increasingly difficult to establish that such a long period of immunity existed. As Carnwath pointed out, 'Not only is evidence difficult to obtain, but the use is likely to have varied in character and intensity in the meantime.' He favoured the approach of a rolling period of immunity of ten years and this was adopted by Parliament in the Planning and Compensation Act 1991.

This period applies to all breaches of planning control involving any material change in the use of land (other than a change of use to a single dwelling house) occurring after 27 July 1982. This is ten years before s 171B(3) was brought into force from 27 July 1992 by the Planning and Compensation Act 1991 (Commencement No 11 and Transitional Provisions) Order 1992. All breaches of planning control that occurred between the beginning of 1964 and 27 July 1982 became immune from enforcement action on that date.

In order to be able to take enforcement action, LPAs need to detect such breaches of planning control within the ten year period. Following the expiry of this period, the right to take enforcement action lapses and the use of the land becomes lawful (*see* below, p 55).

Intensification of use

It is not always easy to determine the exact date of breach in change of use cases. Often the change is gradual and may come about as a result of an intensification of an existing use. This was the case in *Cheshire County Council v Secretary of State for the Environment* [1972] 222 EG 35. A site that was originally used for the purposes of a small scale haulage business in 1956 had developed over the years, accommodating an increased number of vehicles and handling containers. Two enforcement notices were served by the LPA and were overturned on appeal. The LPA challenged the Secretary of State's decision on the basis that he had failed to consider the period from the end of 1963 through to 1970 as a whole when considering the question of an intensification of use. The court held that he had, and so there had been no error in law. This goes to show that the period for consideration when dealing with an alleged intensification of use is the whole period during which the breach has occurred, either four years or ten years, depending on the category. The test is therefore a comparison between the present use and the use in the base year, ie, either four or ten years.

Ancillary operational development

In cases where operational development is ancillary to a material change of use, it will not be protected by the four year period of immunity (*see* above p 47). Provided that the operational development forms an integral part of the material change of use of land, the LPA have the power to enforce against that operational development for the ten year period. The power to enforce against any material change of use includes the power to require the land to be restored to its former use (*see* Chapter 6, p 67). This may involve the removal of ancillary operational development, to which the ten year rule applies.

In *Burn and Others v Secretary of State for the Environment* (1971) 219 EG 586, enforcement notices had been served alleging a breach of planning control involving development of a site by a material change of use from agricultural use to the use of storing motor vehicles. The notices required the applicants to discontinue the use of the land for the storage of vehicles and to restore it to its condition before development. The applicants had laid hardcore on the site and claimed that the four year immunity period applied to that operational development. The court held that it was open to the LPA to proceed either for the development by change of use *or* for the development by building operations when issuing the enforcement notices.

Operational development would not be a breach of planning control had it been carried out as an independent operation from a material change of use. However, it will not be immune from enforcement action by virtue of the lapse of four years where it is incidental or ancillary development to a material change of use. In *Murfitt v Secretary of State for the Environment and East Cambridgeshire District Council* (1980) 40 P & CR 254, the appellant laid hardcore as part of an agricultural haulage business. The hardcore was laid more than four years before the service of the enforcement notice. The LPA served an enforcement notice directed at the change of use of land and buildings and required the removal of the hardcore. The court held that such a requirement was authorised under the Act as the hardcore was ancillary to the change of use of the land and buildings.

Integral building works as part of material change of use

Works that do not require planning permission in themselves, eg, internal works of conversion, may also be subject to enforcement action as part of a material change of use which constitutes a breach of planning control. In *Somak Travel v Secretary of State for the Environment* [1987] JPL 630, the breach of planning control alleged involved the unauthorised conversion of the upper floor of a building from residential to office use. An internal staircase had been built as part of that development. This constituted conversion works which did not require planning permission. The whole works were held as breach of planning control, being a material change of use. A requirement in the enforcement notice for restoration of the land to its condition prior to the making of the change of use, could include the removal of the internal staircase as an incidental operation.

In the case of *Hereford City Council v Secretary of State for the Environment and Davies* [1994] JPL 448, the court held that there was no general test that could be derived from the *Somak* case for works that were integral to a material change of use. It was a question of fact if a particular physical change was integral to a change of use. It was a matter for the Secretary of State's discretion whether or not such physical change was something that could be the subject of a rectification or restoration requirement in an enforcement notice.

5 Breaches of condition

There is no specified time limit for taking enforcement action against a failure to comply with any condition or limitation, subject to which planning permission has been granted. However, by virtue of s 171B(3), the ten year rule applies, as this applies to any other breach of planning control not specified in the earlier part of s 171B. Therefore, no enforcement action may be taken against a breach of condition after the end of the period of *ten years* beginning with the date of the breach.

The four year rule will still prevail in the case of a breach of condition preventing the change of use of any building to use as a single dwellinghouse, as this is protected by s 171B(2).

Under the previous legislation, there was some confusion about the time limits that applied when taking enforcement action for breaches of condition. This was thought to have been resolved by the court in *Peacock Homes v Secretary of State for the Environment* [1984] JPL 729 who held that a time limit of four years applied to a breach of condition, whether it related to operational development or use. This was subsequently endorsed by the Court of Appeal in *Harvey v Secretary of State for Wales* [1990] JPL 420. However, the Court of Appeal have now held, in the case of *Newbury District Council v Secretary of State for the Environment* [1994] JPL 137, that the four year rule does not apply to the breach of an agricultural occupancy condition as opposed to a condition relating to the carrying out of building operations, as in the *Harvey* case.

Under s 171B(3) the immunity period for a breach of condition or limitation is extended from four years to ten years. As a result, there could be circumstances where a breach of condition was immune under the previous legislation, but would now fall within the ten year period for breaches of condition. In order to protect any immunity that has already accrued, the Planning and Compensation Act 1991, s 4(2) provides that enforcement action cannot be taken for any breach of planning control for which the time for issuing an enforcement notice has expired before s 171B(3) came into force, that is 27 July 1992.

The *Newbury* decision is still of practical effect, as the breach of an agricultural occupancy condition will not have acquired immunity from enforcement action by virtue of the Planning and Compensation Act 1991, s 4(2) where the breach took place more than four years, but less than ten years before the new ten year immunity period for a breach of condition came into force on 27 July 1992.

The LPA may serve a breach of condition notice under s 187A (*see* Chapter 8) and an enforcement notice for the same breach of planning control and a breach of condition notice may be served where an enforcement notice for the breach is already in effect (s 171B(4)(*a*)). This provision is intended to cater for the situation where an enforcement notice is already effective for a breach of control, and the LPA wish to strengthen its effect with a breach of condition notice for the same breach (Annex 1, para 13, Circular 17/92).

Section 171B(4) states that the preceding subsections of s 171B do not prevent a breach of condition notice being served where an enforcement notice is in effect. No time limit is imposed on the power to serve a breach of condition notice in these circumstances, so this enforcement action can be taken outside of the normal time limits.

6 Mining operations

Special provisions apply to non-compliance with any condition or limitation subject to which permission for mining operations was granted. Regulation 4 of the Town and Country Planning (Minerals) Regulations 1971 (SI 1971 No 756) modifies s 171B in its application to mining operations. An enforcement notice for non-compliance with any condition or limitation attached to planning permission for mining operations may only be issued within *four years* of the non-compliance *becoming known to the LPA*. Effectively, this means that the four year period runs from the time when such non-compliance comes to the attention of the LPA, not when it actually occurs. Chapter 15 deals in detail with enforcement powers in relation to mining operations.

7 Immunity

The status of the immunity conferred by the time limits for taking enforcement action was considered to be unsatisfactory by Carnwarth in his report on enforcing planning control. Under the old legislation, immunity from enforcement action did not render an unlawful use lawful and therefore did not confer lawful status. In other words, a breach of planning control that was immune from enforcement action because of the lapse of time, did not become a lawful use of land. Carnwarth referred to the creation of 'a "limbo" state described as "unlawful but immune".'

This 'unlawful but immune' use of land caused certain difficulties in the application of planning legislation and regulations. Such a use could not benefit from rights under the 1988 GDO, or be a use to which land could revert after subsequent changes of use (s 57(4)). Parliament took heed of Carnwarth's concerns and accepted his recommendation that, where development has become immune from enforcement action, planning permission should be deemed to have been granted immediately prior to the commencement of the operation or the change of use.

With effect from 27 July 1992, a breach of planning control that has become immune from enforcement action as a result of the lapse of time, is included as one of the categories of lawful development contained in the legislation. This is achieved by s 191(2) and (3) which effectively puts development that is immune from enforcement action on the same footing as a permitted use. It means that operational development, material changes of use and non-compliance with conditions or limitations that are immune from enforcement action are also lawful for planning purposes.

8 Further enforcement action

The legislation specifically provides for enforcement action to be taken outside of the normal time limits in certain circumstances. Where the LPA has already taken or has purported to take enforcement action for any breach of planning control, they have power to take further enforcement action for that same breach, during the period of four years ending with that action being taken (s 171B(4)(*b*)).

This is intended to deal with the situation where earlier enforcement action has been taken, within the relevant time limit, but has subsequently proved to have been defective or requires reinforcement. Section 171B(4)(*b*) empowers the LPA to rectify the situation notwithstanding the fact that the normal time limit for taking enforcement action has since expired. They have a further four years, after their initial, or last unsuccessful, enforcement action, in which to take further enforcement action. A developer can no longer benefit from the lapse of time that occurs while the LPA are defending an enforcement appeal which may be successful due to a technicality. Within a four year period the LPA can serve a fresh notice notwithstanding the fact that the normal time limit has expired. This provision is prevented from operating retrospectively by art 5(2) and (3) of the Planning and Compensation Act 1991 (Commencement No 5) Order 1992 (SI No 2905).

The four year periods are cumulative, so if an LPA repeatedly serve defective enforcement notices, they can rely on the provisions of s 171B(4)(*b*). However, on an appeal, the Secretary of State or the courts are likely to take a dim view of enforcement notices which are repeatedly defective.

Chapter 6

Enforcement Notices

1 Introduction

The technicality and complexity of planning enforcement was one of the principle criticisms of the Carnwath Report. At the root of this is the nature of case law and practice relating to the drafting and service of enforcement notices. It is not surprising therefore that the statutory provisions of the TCPA 1990 relating to the issue of an enforcement notice and the contents and effect of an enforcement notice have been substantially and significantly redrafted and re-enacted by the Planning and Compensation Act 1991, nor that the rules nevertheless remain complex, and the subject of continuing litigation.

2 Issue of an enforcement notice

It is made clear in s 171A(2)(*a*) that it is the issue of an enforcement notice that constitutes taking enforcement action. It is not until the enforcement notice is issued that the LPA have formally instigated the action, regardless of any reports made by the planning officer or the enforcement officer, discussions in committee, or even any informal approach to the person concerned.

The power of the LPA to issue an enforcement notice is contained in s 172(1). As explained in Chapter 4, the power may be exercised where it appears to the LPA 'that there has been a breach of planning control; and that it is expedient to issue the notice, having regard to the provisions of the development plan and to any other material considerations.'

There is a clear distinction between the issue of an enforcement notice and the service of an enforcement notice. The concept of *issuing* comes from the Local Government and Planning (Amendment) Act 1981, and the word 'issue' is of procedural significance. The express reference to the issuing of an enforcement notice is to ensure that the notice comes into effect at the same time for all the recipients. This has the advantage of providing for uniformity for the time limits for appeal.

Paragraph 14 of Annex 2 to Circular 21/91 states that 'The requirement to "issue" a notice is interpreted as meaning that the LPA should prepare a properly authorised document and retain it in their records.' It is at the point where an enforcement notice has been drafted following a recommendation of the relevant committee, or the exercise of properly delegated authority, that enforcement action has been taken for the purposes of the TCPA 1990.

3 Service of an enforcement notice

Importance of serving correctly

Having issued an enforcement notice, the LPA is then required to serve a copy of the notice in accordance with s 172(2). The parties to be served are, the owner and the occupier of the land to which the enforcement notice relates, and any other person having an interest in the land 'being an interest which, in the opinion of the authority, is materially affected by the notice.' (s 172(2)(b)).

The requirement to serve the correct parties is onerous, as it must not be forgotten that an enforcement notice forms the basis for potential criminal liability. The LPA must accurately identify those parties that must be served, as it is a defence to a prosecution for an offence under s 179, that a person charged with an offence under that section has not been served with a copy of the enforcement notice and it is not contained in the appropriate register and he can show that he was not aware of the existence of the enforcement notice (s 179(7)). The power to obtain information, and in particular, the power contained in s 171C to issue a planning contravention notice, will assist LPAs in identifying the parties that must be served (*see* Chapter 3).

The owner of the land

The term 'owner' is defined in s 336(1) as:

> a person, other than a mortgagee not in possession, who, whether in his own right or as a trustee for any other person, is entitled to receive the rack rent of the land, or, where the land is not let at a rack rent, would be so entitled if it were so let.

The owner is liable in relation to enforcement action as he is entitled to receive the rack rent as a measure of the value of the premises to an occupier, and ought to be responsible for discharging any liability to which the premises, by reason of their situation or condition, 'give rise' (*Pollway Nominees v Croydon LBC* [1986] 2 All ER 849, a case dealing with liability under the Housing Act 1957, to carry out repairs).

The occupier of the land

The term 'occupier' denotes physical occupation and may be exercised by right under the terms of a lease or licence which grants an interest in the land to which an enforcement notice relates. Occupation may also occur through acquiescence, oral permission given by the owner, or without any right at all, eg, squatters. There is no statutory definition of the term occupier in the Act, and there has been litigation on the point, particularly in relation to caravan dwellers and whether they can be regarded as occupiers.

In *Stevens v Bromley London Borough Council* [1972] 1 All ER 712, it was held that, for a person to be an occupier and entitled to the service of an enforcement notice, he does not have to have a legal or equitable interest in the land. In appropriate circumstances, licensees were capable of being occupiers. Consideration should be given to the length of time of occupation, and the nature of the persons licence to be there. In *Scarborough Borough Council v Adams* (1983) 47 P & CR 133, an enforcement notice was served on the defendants as occupiers in relation to two caravans parked on a lay-by. The court held that for the length of time that the defendants had been on the lay-by, the use to which they had put it, and the exclusive nature of their occupancy, the defendants were 'occupiers' of the land for the purposes of the 1971 Act.

The issue of occupation has now received some clarification by the re-enactment of s 179. A person can only be guilty of an offence of non-compliance with the requirements of an enforcement notice under s 179(4) if he has 'control of or an interest in the land to which the enforcement notice relates.' Section 179(4) specifically applies to persons in control of the land which would include an occupier. An owner will have control of and will have an interest in the land to which an enforcement notice relates, but is specifically excluded from the provisions of s 179(4). Section 179(1) provides that the owner is in breach of the enforcement notice where the notice is not complied with (*see* Chapter 12).

A person can be considered as an occupier if he has a degree of control over the state of the land to which the enforcement notice relates or over the activities carried out on it.

Any other person having an interest

This category provides the LPA with some protection where there is doubt as to whether a person is an owner or an occupier. The fact that a notice must be served on any other person having an interest in the land means that the LPA can ensure that those parties who may have some interest in the land receive a copy of the enforcement notice, even where this interest is not clearly that of an owner or occupier.

There is a qualification set out in s 172(2)(*b*) that the interest of that person should be an interest which, in the opinion of the authority, is materially affected by the notice. It is intended to include mortgagees or persons with the benefit of an easement or restrictive covenant, or other equitable interest as persons upon whom an enforcement notice should be served.

4 The mechanics of service

Alternative methods of service

The mechanism for the service of an enforcement notice is set out in s 329. There are four alternative methods of service:
   (a) by delivering the notice to the person on whom it is to be served;
   (b) by leaving the notice at the usual or last-known place of abode of

that person or at his address for service;

(c) by sending the notice by pre-paid registered letter or recorded delivery; or

(d) in the case of a corporate body, by delivering the notice or sending it to the secretary or clerk at its registered or principal office.

Personal service

Personal service may carry risks in certain cases. In the light of the murder of Harry Collinson, the principal planning officer at Derwentside District Council, in June 1991, care should be taken when personally serving enforcement notices in controversial cases. In some cases it may be advisable for officers to seek local police help. Threats and violence may result from delicate and controversial situations, and alternative means of service may be preferable.

Service by post

Service by post is governed by the Interpretation Act 1978, s 7:

> Where an Act authorises or requires any document to be served by post (whether the expression 'serve' or the expression 'give' or 'send' or any other expression is used) then, unless the contrary intention appears, the service is deemed to be effected by properly addressing, pre-paying and posting a letter containing the document and, unless the contrary is proved, to have been effected at the time at which the letter would be delivered in the ordinary course of post.

Service where the person to be served cannot be identified

Where the LPA cannot find out the name of the person on whom the notice is to be served, it shall be taken to be duly served if it is addressed to him either by name, or by the description of 'the owner' or 'the occupier' of the premises (describing them) and is delivered or sent by one of the means set out in (a), (b) or (c) above (s 329(2)(*a*)).

If it is addressed and marked in such a manner to identify it as a communication of importance, and is sent by pre-paid registered letter or by recorded delivery and is not returned, or delivered to some person on the premises, or affixed conspicuously to some object on those premises, the notice will be taken to have been duly served (s 329(2)(*b*)). The Town and Country Planning General Regulations 1992, reg 13 require the words 'Important—This Communication affects your Property' to be inscribed clearly and legibly on the notice and its envelope.

Where the LPA have made a reasonable attempt to find out the name and address of the person to be served with the enforcement notice, but have been unable to do so, they may post a notice on the land as an alternative to serving it directly (*see* Planning Appeals Decision [1993] JPL 296).

Service where the land is unoccupied

Where it appears that the land to which the enforcement notice relates is unoccupied, the enforcement notice shall be taken to have been duly served if it is addressed to 'the owners and any occupiers' of that part of the land (describing it) and is fixed conspicuously to some object on the land (s 329(3)).

Time limits for service

Section 172(3) requires the notice to be served 'not more than 28 days after its date of issue; and not less than 28 days before the date specified in it as the date on which it is to take effect'. The enforcement notice must specify the date on which it is to come into effect. After that date has passed, the right to appeal against the notice will be lost (*see* Chapter 9).

The two step procedure of the issue of an enforcement notice and service of copies of an enforcement notice can be achieved within a 28 day period. Any person can be served with a copy of the enforcement notice at any time within 28 days from the date of issue of the enforcement notice, and different persons can be served with copies of the same notice on different dates. The second 28 day period allows for time to appeal against the enforcement notice.

5 Failure to serve an enforcement notice

Effect of failure to serve an enforcement notice

Failure to serve a copy of an enforcement notice does not render it a nullity. In *R v Greenwich LBC, ex parte Patel* [1985] JPL 851, the Court of Appeal held that there had been no deliberate disregard of the statutory requirement to serve the owner, nor had the LPA failed to show due diligence. As there was no reason to suppose that the applicant had suffered any real prejudice, the Court of Appeal refused to hold that the failure to serve the enforcement notice rendered it a nullity. It may be that, were there a deliberate disregard of the statutory requirements, or failure to show due diligence, and where the applicant did suffer real prejudice, the courts may be prepared to hold that failure to serve the notice does render it a nullity (*McDaid v Clydebank District Council* [1984] JPL 579).

Where no one is substantially prejudiced by a failure to serve a copy of the enforcement notice, the Secretary of State on appeal may exercise his discretion to disregard that breach of procedure. In Planning Appeals Decision [1993] JPL 297, the LPA made a reasonable attempt to find out the name and address of the operators of a permanent market, but were unable to do so by the time the enforcement notice was served. A copy of the notice was posted on site. The inspector exercised the discretion that he considered was available to him, to disregard this failure to serve, as there was no substantial prejudice, and an appeal against the notice on ground (f) of s 174(2) failed.

In the event that the LPA fail to serve a copy of an enforcement notice the person who should have been served can rely on that failure, either by way of defence to criminal proceedings under s 179, or (in very limited circumstances) as a means of challenging the validity of the notice in the High Court.

Failure to serve as a defence to criminal proceedings

Where a person prosecuted under s 179 for non-compliance with the requirements of an enforcement notice has not been served with a copy of the enforcement notice, it is not contained in the enforcement register, and that person can show that he was not aware of the existence of the notice, there is a statutory defence to prosecution contained in s 179(7). This would preclude the need for such a person to rely on the statutory exclusion contained in s 285, as detailed below.

Where a copy of the enforcement notice was not served on a person prosecuted under s 179, but was entered in the enforcement register (*see* below), that person could not rely on the defence in s 179(7), as he would not be able to satisfy the court that he did not know and could not reasonably have been expected to know that the enforcement notice had been issued.

Failure to serve as grounds for challenge to validity of notice

Section 285 provides that the validity of an enforcement notice cannot be questioned by any legal proceedings on any of the grounds under s 174 on which an appeal to the Secretary of State may be brought. As one of the grounds of appeal is that copies of the enforcement notice were not served as required by s 172 (s 174(2)(*d*)), it would appear that where the LPA have failed to serve an enforcement notice, a challenge in the courts is excluded.

However, s 285(2) specifically permits the validity of an enforcement notice to be questioned in proceedings where those proceedings are brought under s 179 against a person who:

(a) has held an interest in the land to which an enforcement notice relates since before the notice was issued;

(b) did not have a copy of the enforcement notice served on him; and

(c) satisfies the court that he did not know and could not reasonably have been expected to know that the enforcement notice had been issued, and that his interests have been substantially prejudiced by the failure to serve him with a copy of it.

The validity of the enforcement notice can be challenged only as a defence to proceedings taken against a person. If the LPA exercises its powers to enter the land to secure compliance with the requirements of an enforcement notice (*see* Chapter 12), the exception in s 285 does not apply, and the validity of the enforcement notice cannot be questioned in any proceedings.

6 Contents of an enforcement notice

In *Miller-Mead v Minister of Housing and Local Government* [1963] 2 QB 196, Upjohn LJ stated that the recipient of an enforcement notice is entitled to a notice which tells him 'fairly what he has done wrong and what he must do to remedy it'.

The issue of what an enforcement notice should contain, has given rise to prolific and persistent litigation. The Carnwath Report points out that as the enforcement notice must be capable of serving as the foundation for a potential criminal prosecution, 'certain basic requirements of precision and formality must, therefore, be satisfied.' As a result, s 173 was re-enacted by the Planning and Compensation Act 1991, s 5 and the question of what should be contained in an enforcement notice is now specifically set out there.

An enforcement notice must:

(1) state the matters which appear to the LPA to constitute the breach of planning control (s 173(1)(a));

(2) state the paragraph of s 171A(1) within which, in the opinion of the LPA, the breach falls (s 173(1)(b));

(3) specify the steps which the authority require to be taken, or the activities which the authority require to cease, in order to achieve, wholly or partly, certain purposes (s 173(3)), being:

   (a) remedying the breach by making any development comply with the terms (including conditions and limitations) of any planning permission which has been granted for the land, by discontinuing any use of the land or by restoring the land to its condition before the breach took place (s 173(4)(a)); or

   (b) remedying any injury to amenity which has been caused by the breach (s 173(4)(b));

(4) specify the date on which it is to take effect (s 173(8));

(5) specify the period for compliance with the requirements of the notice (s 173(9));

(6) specify such additional matters as may be prescribed (s 173(10)); and

(7) be accompanied by an explanatory note giving prescribed information (s 173(10)).

Section 173(2) provides that an enforcement notice will comply with the requirements set out in (1) and (2) above, namely the requirements of s 173(1), 'if it enables any person on whom a copy of it is served to know what those matters are'. This is an enactment of the classic phrase of Upjohn LJ in the *Miller-Mead* case.

The intention of the re-enactment of s 173 was to simplify and clarify the content of an enforcement notice. Paragraph 5 of Annex 2 to Circular 21/91 advises that this section, together with s 172, 'are intended to reduce the likelihood that a technical defect in drafting the notice will result in its being quashed on appeal, or found to be a nullity'.

From the LPAs point of view, compliance with the requirements as to the content of an enforcement notice as set out in s 173 should ensure that the notice will be valid. However, each aspect must be considered separately, and care taken to ensure that the statutory requirements are satisfied.

Model enforcement notices relating to operational development, change of use, and breach of condition are appended to Annex 2 of Circular 21/91, and are reproduced at Appendix 3. These model notices are intended to cater for most enforcement situations. However, the Circular warns that 'each notice needs to correspond to the specific breach of control it is intended to remedy'.

To a large extent the complexity and technicality associated with the drafting of enforcement notices has been removed by the recent legislation. With the assistance of model notices and the requirements relating to the content of an enforcement notice clearly set out in s 173, LPA solicitors have less to fear when drafting enforcement notices. In addition, the power given to the Secretary of State to vary an enforcement notice on appeal means that it is less likely to fail because of a technical drafting error.

Notwithstanding these assurances, there are still a number of rules that can be derived from case law which deal with issues not specifically addressed in the legislation. Included in this chapter are a number of examples of what can and cannot be done when drafting or serving enforcement notices.

7 Contents of the notice: the breach of control

General rule

The first requirement is that the notice must state the matters which appear to the LPA to constitute the breach of planning control. This element requires a description of the aspects that appear to the LPA to be a breach of planning control. It is a corollary to the discretionary power of the LPA to take enforcement action. The words 'appear to the LPA' are significant, as it is only in circumstances where the LPA consider that a breach of planning control has occurred that enforcement action will be taken. To avoid any risk of challenge, it would be wise for the description of the alleged breach of planning control, which is contained in the enforcement notice, to be identical to any description contained in the report to committee which resulted in the resolution to take enforcement action.

The description in the enforcement notice constitutes alleged fact and is usually referred to as 'the breach of planning control alleged'. It can be a description made in general terms, provided that it is sufficient to identify the activity (*Bristol Stadium v Brown* (1979) 252 EG 803). Under s 173(2) an enforcement notice will only comply with the requirement to state the matters which appear to the LPA to constitute the breach of planning control 'if it enables any person on whom a copy of it is served to know what those matters are'. The model notices appended to Circular 21/91 are in plain English as an aid to completion and comprehension, with the aim of making the notice clear to the recipient.

The Secretary of State has powers when determining an appeal to correct any misdescription in the enforcement notice (s 176(1) — *see* Chapter 9). Therefore, it is not fatal to the validity of the enforcement notice if the description in the notice is inaccurate in some respect, as long as it satisfies the requirements of s 173(2). However, as advised in paragraph 5 of Annex 2 to Circular 21/91, the Secretary of State's powers under s 176(1) do not extend to the correction of notices which are so fundamentally defective any correction would result in a substantially different notice and could cause an injustice to the appellant or to the LPA.

Category of breach

The notice must state the paragraph of s 171A(1) within which, in the opinion of the LPA, the breach falls. Under s 171A, a breach of planning control constitutes carrying out development without the required planning permission, or failing to comply with any condition or limitation subject to which planning permission has been granted. The courts have held that an enforcement notice must inform the recipient of what he has been accused of, and to make it clear whether he has developed the land in question without the grant of planning permission, or whether he has committed a breach of condition subject to which planning permission had been granted. However, the notice need not incorporate the actual words used in the statute (*Eldon Garages Ltd v Kingston-upon-Hull City Borough Council* [1974] 1 All ER 358).

The enforcement notice must state which limb of s 171A applies, in other words the nature of the alleged breach (s 173(1)(*b*)). An enforcement notice which stated that the recipient was 'in contravention of planning control' was held to be invalid because it failed to specify the nature of the alleged contravention (*East Riding County Council v Park Estate (Bridlington) Ltd.* [1956] 2 All ER 669). However, an error in the enforcement notice which puts the breach into the wrong category, will not make the notice a nullity. This may be corrected by the Secretary of State on an appeal under s 176(1) (*Wealdon District Council v Secretary of State for the Environment* [1983] JPL 234, *see* Chapter 9).

More than one breach specified

It is possible to allege more than one breach of planning control in a single enforcement notice without invalidating it? In *Valentina of London Ltd v Secretary of State for the Environment and Another* [1992] EGCS 77, work was started to convert an office building into an hotel and ground floor restaurant. A planning application seeking a change of use was refused on appeal to the Secretary of State. The LPA issued an enforcement notice alleging both a material change of use and operational development in breach of planning control. The notice sought to deal with the change of use from an office to an hotel and restaurant and other unauthorised works, namely an extension at the second floor level of the premises and the installation of vent pipes without planning permission. The court held that the 'composite' approach to the notice did not invalidate it. The LPA could serve an enforcement notice which alleged more than one breach of planning control, there was no need for a separate enforcement notice for each breach. Although the legislation empowering the LPA to serve an enforcement notice referred to 'a breach of planning control', its construction was not restricted to the singular as under the Interpretation Act 1978 the singular included the plural.

In addition enforcement notices can be served in the alternative.Where enforcement notices are served in the alternative, each must be precise and unambiguous in itself, and the fact that they are served in the alternative must be made clear to the person on whom they are served (*Britt v Buckinghamshire County Council* (1962) 14 P & CR 332).

8 Contents of the notice: steps to be taken

General rule

The notice must specify the steps which the authority require to be taken, or the activites which the authority require to cease to remedy the breach or to remedy any injury to amenity which has been caused by the breach. One of the main distinctions between this requirement and those set out above is the need to *specify* the steps or the activities. This is more onerous than merely *stating* the steps or the activities. LPAs must be precise when drafting the requirements of the notice as if they are uncertain or vague, a prosecution brought under s 179 may fail. Where a notice is dubious, it could not be relied on to allege that an offence had been committed (*Warrington Borough Council v David Garvey* [1988] JPL 752). As stated in the Carnwath Report, 'Unless the notice states clearly what the recipient is required to do, he can hardly be convicted of not doing it'.

There may be circumstances where it is difficult for the LPA to be precise in drafting the requirements of the notice, particularly where the alleged breach results from an intensification of use. In the case of *Lee v Bromley London Borough Council* [1982] JPL 778, the LPA served an enforcement notice specifying the activities required to cease in the terms, 'discontinue intensified use of land in connection with scrap metal'. A proviso was added to the effect that the enforcement notice did not apply where the land was used to the same extent and in the same manner as it had been used before 31 December 1963. The court held that the enforcement notice was not so vague as to be unenforceable. Having examined the evidence, the court was able to ascertain the use of the land before 31 December 1963, and was in a position to measure the intensification of use. This case illustrates the difficulty of ensuring that the requirements specified in an enforcement notice are expressed precisely.

In cases where an alleged breach of planning control results from an intensification of use, the LPA must take care not to enforce against any element of the breach that is immune from enforcement action, either through the passage of time, or because the breach alleged benefits from the grant of planning permission, or for any other reason (*see* below p 67). The Secretary of State's powers to correct or vary an enforcement notice under s 176(1) relate to 'any defect, error or misdescription', they do not extend to any uncertainty or vagueness in the notice. Such vagueness in the specification of the required steps may render the enforcement notice a nullity (*Dudley Bowers Amusements Enterprises Ltd v Secretary of State for the Environment* [1986] JPL 689).

It is for the LPA to determine what steps are required to remedy the breach. If the LPA were to impose excessive requirements, there is a right of appeal under s 174(2)(f) (*see* Chapter 9). The Secretary of State will then determine whether the requirements are excessive and if so, whether he can vary the terms of the notice under s 176(1) without causing prejudice to the appellant or to the LPA.

The purpose of the requirements of the enforcement notice

The requirements of the enforcement notice must achieve, wholly or partly, the purposes specified in s 173(4). Those are:

(a) Remedying the breach by making any development comply with the terms (including conditions and limitations) of any planning permission which has been granted for the land
This may be a permission granted on an application or a general permission. Where the alleged breach relates only to a condition or limitation, the LPA may use the breach of condition notice procedure.

(b) Remedying the breach by discontinuing any use of the land or by restoring the land to its condition before the breach took place
A requirement to restore land to its condition before the breach took place may involve the removal of operational development. Where this may be immune from enforcement action had it been carried out as an independent operation, or where it is incidental or ancillary to a material change of use, an enforcement notice may still require its removal (*Murfitt v Secretary of State for the Environment* [1980] JPL 598, *see* Chapter 5).

(c) Remedying any injury to amenity which has been caused by the breach
This may be achieved by steps required to be taken or activities required to cease which would not completely reinstate the land to its previous condition, but would remove the cause of the complaint. Some part of the unauthorised development may be acceptable in planning terms and this purpose gives the LPA flexibility to allow that part of the development to continue.

The wording of s 173(3) provides for *any* of the purposes set out in s 173(4) to be achieved by the requirements of the enforcement notice, and so permits the LPA to seek to achieve any of the above purposes in the alternative, or together where necessary. The purposes may be achieved 'wholly or partly', and so the notice may not require a complete remedy. As suggested above, this may result in the LPA using the notice to remedy that part of an unauthorised development that causes injury to amenity.

The 'Mansi' principle

The terms of an enforcement notice must not go beyond that which is necessary to remedy the alleged breach of planning control. This doctrine was enunciated by the court in *Mansi v Elstree Rural District Council* (1964) 16 P & CR 153. In drafting enforcement notices, LPAs must take care not to enforce against the right to use land for an existing lawful use, an established use, legitimate ancillary uses, or rights conferred by the 1988 GDO or the Use Classes Order.

Some assistance in drafting an enforcement notice is given to LPAs by the case of *R v Hartfield* [1993] JPL 914. Here, the Court of Appeal expressed the view that the enforcement notice was to be read as a whole, in the light of the general presumption that it did not take away any existing permitted use. Words could be used to protect a legitimate ancillary use. In the *Hartfield* case the enforcement notice required the appellant to remove commercial vehicles 'except as may be incidental to the use of the premises as a petrol filling station'. When the enforcement notice was read as a whole, those words protected the ancillary use of the premises from enforcement action.

The application of and limits to the *Mansi* principle in terms of the Secretary of State's power to vary or correct an enforcement notice on appeal are dealt with in more detail in Chapter 9, p 125.

Under-enforcement

The LPA are given power by s 173(11) to under-enforce. Section 173(11) provides that, where all the requirements of an enforcement notice have been complied with, planning permission shall be treated as having been granted for that part of the development or activity, that could have been the subject of the notice, but was not. In other words, where the enforcement notice does not relate to the whole of a development or activity that is in breach of planning control, that part of the development or activity to which it does not relate will be treated as having the benefit of planning permission, as the LPA had the opportunity to require steps to be taken or activities to cease in relation to that part of the breach, but chose not to include those requirements in the notice.

There is no procedure specified in the Act for this 'deemed grant of planning permission'. However, para 8 of Annex 2 to Circular 21/91 suggests that:

> LPAs need only notify the recipient of a copy of an enforcement notice that permission is deemed to have been granted at the time when, in the LPA's view, the requirements of the enforcement notice have been fully complied with. The deemed grant of planning permission might also be entered in the enforcement and stop notice register.

If the LPA do under-enforce, they must correctly state the breach of planning control in the enforcement notice. In *Copeland Borough Council v Secretary of State for the Environment* (1976) 239 EG 503, a planning permission granted for the building of a house required that the roof should be constructed of specified grey tiles. This was not done, and the LPA served an enforcement notice describing the breach of planning control as 'construction of roof of dwelling in ... tiles of a buff colour' and required the tiles to be removed. On appeal, the enforcement notice was quashed because it did not correctly identify the breach. The court held that the breach of control consisted of building a house which did not comply with the plans, not merely the construction of the roof. The LPA could under-enforce. However, if it deliberately chose to do so, it must have correctly stated the breach of control in the enforcement notice first. The court further held that the Secretary of State could not exercise his power to amend the notice, as in this instance, the error was material, and such a fundamental amendment would have produced injustice.

Demolition of a building

The legislation now enables LPAs to enforce for a breach of planning control consisting of the demolition of a building (defined as a 'building operation' in s 55(1A)), and to require the construction of a replacement building (s 173(6)). In constructing a replacement building, the developer is bound by the requirements of s 173(7). However, the LPA may grant planning permission for an application made for an alternative replacement building, or waive or relax any requirement of the enforcement notice under s 173A.

Requirement to commit a criminal offence

An enforcement notice cannot require a party to carry out works that would be a criminal offence.
In the case of *McKay v Secretary of State for the Environment Cornwall County Council and Penwith District Council* (1993) JPL B80, the notice required the appellant to carry out works that would be in breach of s 2 of the Ancient Monuments and Archaeological Areas Act 1979. Such a notice was held to be a nullity and incapable of variation.

Requirement for subsequent approval of LPA

The steps in the enforcement notice cannot require the recipient to submit details of works to the LPA for approval (*Kuidip Kaur v Secretary of State for the Environment and Greenwich London Borough Council* (1990) JPL 814)).

Requirement to make a change of use

In relation to a breach of planning control comprising the making of a material change of use from one dwellinghouse to use as two separate dwellinghouses, it is excessive and unreasonable for an enforcement notice against such a breach to require the positive step to be taken of using the premises as a single dwellinghouse (*Bennett v Secretary of State for the Environment and East Devon District Council* (1993) JPL 134).

9 Contents of a notice: other matters

The enforcement notice must specify a calendar date on which it is to take effect, and as s 172(3)(*b*) provides that the notice shall be served not less than 28 days before the date specified as the date on which it is to take effect, that date must be more than 28 days following service. If an appeal against the notice has been lodged before the date specified, the notice shall not come into effect until the final determination or withdrawal of the appeal (s 175(4))

The period for compliance

The period for compliance with the requirements of the enforcement notice must be specified. The notice may require different periods for different steps or activities specified in the notice (s 173(9)). The compliance period will start to run on the date the notice takes effect. An appeal can be made to the Secretary of State under s 174(2)(*g*) on the ground that the compliance period falls short of what should reasonably be allowed. However, it should be remembered that the Secretary of State can vary the compliance period specified in the notice under s 176(1) if it would not cause injustice to the LPA.

Additional matters

Section 173(10) provides that an enforcement notice must specify such additional matters as may be prescribed.The Town and Country Planning (Enforcement Notices and Appeals) Regulations 1991 made under s 173(10), came into effect on 2 January 1992. Regulation 3 sets out the additional matters to be specified in an enforcement notice.

Firstly every enforcement notice issued by the LPA shall specify the reasons why they consider it 'expedient' to issue the notice. The question of expediency is dealt with in detail in Chapter 4, p 38. The text of the enforcement notice should include the statement of reasons, and the model notices appended to Circular 21/91 provide for this.

Secondly, the enforcement notice shall specify 'the precise boundaries of the land to which the notice relates, whether by reference to a plan or otherwise'. Paragraph 13 of Annex 2 to Circular 21/91 advises that this is always best done by means of a plan (preferably on an Ordnance Survey base with a scale of not less than 1/2500) attached to the enforcement notice, on which the *exact* boundary of the land is clearly identified by a coloured outline. It is also suggested by the Circular that, the plan can be supplemented by a brief written description where necessary.

A description of the land that is entirely verbal satisfies the 1991 Regulations, as it comes within the wording 'or otherwise', as long as the description specifies the precise boundaries of the land (*Wiesenfeld v Secretary of State for the Environment and Brent London Borough Council* [1992] 1 PLR 32). This can be done by giving the address of the premises, ie the street number and the name of the street.

The area of land to be included in an enforcement notice is a matter for the LPA. They may enforce against the whole unit, or a part of it, and they may enforce against the whole unit *and* any part of it. In the case of *Reed v Secretary of State for the Environment and Tandridge District Council* [1993] JPL 249, it was held that where an appeal was made on ground (a) (and presumably, where the Secretary of State is determining a deemed application for planning permission under s 177(5)) there was a duty to consider in the case of *each* notice, whether or not planning permission should be granted for the whole of the land to which the notice related, and this must involve particular consideration of the circumstances for each site. The breach of planning control alleged in each enforcement notice should be considered separately and independently when deciding whether or not to grant planning permission.

The LPA may also direct an enforcement notice to an area larger than the area of occupation (*Rawlins v Secretary of State for the Environment* [1990] 1 PLR 110). In *Ramsay v Secretary of State for the Environment* [1991] 2 PLR 112, a case involving two enforcement notices issued for different parts of the same site, but with an overlap, the court held that 'if any planning authority were to seek to prosecute under both notices in respect of the same alleged contravening activity, it seems ... that it would be unjustified and that it would not be accepted by any court'.

Finally, an enforcement notice must be accompanied by an explanatory note giving 'prescribed information'. Regulation 4 of the Enforcement Notices and Appeals Regulations 1991 requires that every copy of an enforcement notice served by the LPA is accompanied by an explanatory note giving prescribed information as to the right of appeal under s 174. The model notices appended to Circular 21/91 contain an appropriate explanatory note. Paragraph 18 of Annex 2 to the Circular also advises LPAs to enclose a copy of the official explanatory booklet ('Enforcement Notice Appeals—A Guide to Procedure') and two copies of the official appeal form.

10 Defective enforcement notices

Nullity

The concepts of nullity and invalidity are critical to an enforcement notice. They are critical in respect of the power of the Secretary of State to vary or correct notices on appeal (*see* Chapter 9) and the right to apply to the court for relief, rather than appeal against the enforcement notice under the TCPA 1990 (*see* Chapter 11).

An enforcement notice that is a nullity has no legal effect. It cannot be adjudicated upon by the Secretary of State on appeal, nor can it be corrected by him to make it valid and to bring it within his jurisdiction. It can be the subject of other legal proceedings, as s 285 does not apply to a notice that is no notice at all. In *Rhymney Valley District Council v Secretary of State for the Environment* [1985] JPL 27, the court held that, where the enforcement notice had been declared a nullity, the procedure was to apply for judicial review.

A notice will be a nullity where it is defective. If any of the statutory requirements relating to the content of an enforcement notice are not complied with, eg failure to specify a period for compliance, or the date when the notice comes into effect, it will be without legal effect and a nullity.

In Planning Appeals Decision [1993] JPL 1181, an enforcement notice was served relating to the erection of a retaining wall without planning permission. The LPA specified three alternative requirements in the notice. An appeal against the enforcement notice was made to the Secretary of State and the inspector determined that:

(a) the notice failed to indicate which sections of the retaining wall were the subject of the notice, and the appellant was unable to know what matters constituted the alleged breach of planning control as required s 173(1)(a) and (2);

(b) the notice failed to specify separate periods of compliance for each distinct element of the steps required to be taken; and

(c) the requirements specified in the notice for a scheme and calculations to be submitted to and approved by the LPA rendered the notice invalid (*Kuidip Kaur v Secretary of State for the Environment and Greenwich London Borough Council* [1990] JPL 814).

The inspector concluded that the defects in the notice were so significant that the enforcement notice lacked any clarity and was void because of uncertainty. The notice was therefore declared to be a nullity and was quashed.

Invalidity

An invalid enforcement notice can be corrected by the Secretary of State on appeal in certain circumstances. The power contained in s 176(1) empowers the Secretary of State to correct any error, defect or misdescription in an enforcement notice if it would not cause injustice. Therefore, in circumstances where such a correction can be made, an invalid notice can be rendered valid, and the Secretary of State has jurisdiction to determine an appeal. However, the defects may be too fundamental to be corrected without causing injustice. In these circumstances, the notice will be invalid, and, on an appeal, will be set aside. If there is no appeal, the notice will stand. If there is no ground of appeal to the Secretary of State under s 174(2), the notice can be challenged by an application for judicial review.

An enforcement notice may be invalid because the LPA did not have power to issue it (*Cheshire County Council v Secretary of State for the Environment* [1988] JPL 30,or the alleged breach of planning control was wrongly described. In *Francis v Yiewsly and West Drayton UDC* [1957] 3 WLR 919, an enforcement notice which falsely stated that development had been carried out without planning permission (when temporary planning permission had actually been granted, subsequent to the carrying out of the development) proceeded on a wholly false basis of fact and was invalid. However, in many cases such errors can now be corrected by the Secretary of State on appeal under s 176(1) where no injustice would be caused to the appellant or to the LPA.

11 Registration

Every LPA has a statutory requirement to keep a register of enforcement notices which relate to land in their area (s 188). Entries must be made as soon as practicable, but within 14 days of the occurrence to which they relate. The importance of maintaining the register up-to-date and complete is emphasised by the availability of the defence in s 179(7) detailed on p 62.

The information to be maintained in the register is prescribed in art 28 of the 1988 GDO. The register must contain the:

(1) address of the land to which the notice relates or a plan by reference to which its situation can be ascertained;

(2) name of the issuing authority;

(3) date of issue of the notice;

(4) date of service of copies of the notice;

(5) statement or summary of the breach of planning control alleged and the requirements of the notice, including the compliance period;

(6) date specified in the notice as the date on which it is to take effect;

(7) information on any postponement of the date on which the notice is to take effect by reason of an appeal made to the Secretary of State and the date of the final determination or withdrawal of any appeal; and

(8) date, if any, on which the LPA are satisfied that the steps required to remedy any injury to amenity have been taken.

In the event that an enforcement notice is quashed by the Secretary of State or withdrawn, the relevant entry in the register must be withdrawn. Article 28 of the 1988 GDO requires every register to include an index to enable a person to trace an entrance in the register by reference to the address of the land to which the enforcement notice relates.

12 Withdrawal, waiver and relaxation of an enforcement notice

The LPA have the power to withdraw an enforcement notice issued by them, or to waive or relax any requirement of such a notice, and may extend any period specified for compliance with it (s 173A). This power may be exercised whether or not the notice has taken effect. However, it can only be exercised by the LPA who issued the original enforcement notice.

If an enforcement notice is withdrawn, the LPA must notify anyone who has been or was entitled to have been, served with a copy of the enforcement notice. This effectively means any owner, occupier or any person with an interest in the land to which the enforcement notice relates, including a mortgagee.

Where the LPA have withdrawn an enforcement notice they retain the right to issue a further enforcement notice (s 173A(4)). They can only exercise this right where the alleged breach of planning control has not become immune from enforcement action due to the passage of time. However, s 171B(4)(b) empowers the LPA to take further enforcement action within four years of having taken or purported to have taken enforcement action for the same breach of planning control. This can extend the immunity period which is applicable to the relevant alleged breach of planning control (see Chapter 5, p 55).

The power contained in s 173A(4) only applies to the withdrawal of an enforcement notice. It does not extend to any waiver or relaxation of any requirement contained therein. Once the LPA has waived or relaxed such a requirement, it is likely that they would be estopped from reimposing it. They would also have difficulty in showing that it was necessary to reimpose the requirement to remedy the breach of planning control alleged.

If the LPA realise that there is some defect in the notice that cannot be corrected, or that the procedure for the taking action has not been complied with, it may be prudent for them to withdraw the enforcement notice and to issue a replacement. It does not matter if the withdrawal takes place first as two enforcement notices can be issued for the same site (although there may be some difficulty if the LPA ultimately sought to prosecute under both notices (*Ramsay v Secretary of State for the Environment* [1991] 2 PLR 112).

The power to withdraw an enforcement notice enables the LPA to remove a notice that no longer has any practical effect, eg, where planning permission has been granted for the breach of planning control. This can then be removed from the planning register and the planning title of a site cleared.

The power to waive the requirements of the notice is valuable. The LPA can, for example, use the power to accurately reflect the outcome of negotiations with a developer. As an alternative, the LPA can grant planning permission for the whole or part of the development, where an application is submitted to them as a result of negotiations. In such circumstances, the enforcement notice would cease to have effect, so far as inconsistent with that permission (s 180) (*Dudley Borough Council v Secretary of State for the Environment* [1980] JPL 181). The power contained in s 173A is additional to the power vested in the Secretary of State to correct or vary the enforcement notice on appeal. The LPA can serve one enforcement notice relating to the site as a whole and enforcement notices relating to specific parts.

Enforcement by the Secretary of State

The Secretary of State has a residual power to issue an enforcement notice where it appears to him to be expedient (s 182). However, before serving an enforcement notice, he must consult with the relevant LPA. An enforcement notice issued by the Secretary of State pursuant to this residual power shall have the same effect as a notice issued by the LPA.

13 LPAs Checklist for issuing enforcement notice

Preliminary

(1) Investigate any complaint made or any unauthorised development of which an officer is aware.
(2) If additional information is required, serve a planning contravention notice.

(3) Seek to persuade owner to voluntarily remedy the harmful effects of any unauthorised development.
(4) Where appropriate, invite a retrospective planning application.
(5) Consider availability of alternative site and where available, suggest relocation

Preparatory

(1) Identify the breach of planning control.
    (a) has development taken place?
    (b) was planning permission required?
    (c) does the development benefit from permitted development rights?
(2) Check if listed building or conservation area affected.
(3) Assess steps required and period for compliance.
(4) Obtain authority for issuing enforcement notice by committee resolution or delegation
(5) Prepare authorised document containing:
    (a) matters which constitute the breach of planning control alleged;
    (b) para of s 171A(1) within which the breach falls;
    (c) required steps;
    (d) effective date;
    (e) period for compliance;
    (f) area of land to which notice relates;
    (g) statement of reasons for notice;
    (h) explanatory note on right of appeal.
(6) Draw up a plan and prepare a brief description identifying the land to which the notice relates.
(7) Identify the parties to be served.

Taking of enforcement action

(1) Issue enforcement notice.
(2) Enter details of enforcement notice in the planning enforcement register as soon as is practical.
(3) Serve on all parties:
    (a) enforcement notice;
    (b) plan of land to which enforcement notice relates;
    (c) booklet 'Enforcement Notice Appeals—a guide to procedure'; and
    (d) two copies of official appeal form.

Chapter 7

Stop Notices

1 Introduction

There may be circumstances where the LPA consider that a breach of planning control creates such an unacceptable situation that they cannot allow it to continue. An enforcement notice must state a period for compliance with the requirements of the notice, which shall not be less than a period of 28 days before the date specified in it as the date on which it is to take effect (*see* Chapter 6, p 70). Therefore, when an enforcement notice is served, the breach may continue, without sanction, for the period of compliance specified in the enforcement notice.

In recognition of the fact that the breach of planning control may be so severe, the legislation gives the LPA power to serve a stop notice requiring the activity resulting in the breach to cease. Certain safeguards have developed through case law and are contained in the legislation to protect against the inappropriate use of stop notices. However, the power to serve a stop notice is a valuable device for LPAs to control blatant and unacceptable breaches of planning control and offers the best means of urgent action where it is justified.

2 Power to serve a stop notice

Introduction

In certain circumstances, the LPA have power to serve a stop notice when they serve a copy of an enforcement notice, or any time thereafter. Section 183 leaves the exercise of this power to their discretion. It provides that where the LPA consider it expedient that any relevant activity should cease before the expiry of the period for compliance with the requirements of an enforcement notice, they may serve a stop notice prohibiting the carrying out of that activity on the land to which the enforcement notice relates, or any part of that land as specified in the stop notice. A stop notice is parasitic upon an enforcement notice. It will operate to prohibit the carrying out of any relevant activity on the land to which the enforcement notice relates and the exercise of the power to serve a stop notice is dependent upon the existence of the enforcement notice.

What constitutes a relevant activity for the purposes of the exercise of the power is defined in s 183(2) as 'any activity specified in the enforcement notice as an activity which the LPA require to cease and any activity carried out as part of that activity or associated with that activity'.

Expediency

The LPA must consider the question of expediency in determining whether or not to issue a stop notice. It is a separate consideration from that required in relation to the enforcement notice (see Chapter 4, p 38). By its very nature, a stop notice should be served as soon as possible, otherwise any justification for its service is diminished. However, the LPA should assess the situation with care, particularly given the liability to compensation that can attach to the issue of a stop notice.

In the case of *R v Westminster City Council, ex parte Willowcell Ltd* [1994] JPL B38 a stop notice was served in relation to premises used as a peep show. The notice was served one year after the use had first come to the notice of the council. An application was made to the court for the notice to be set aside on the basis that the council were in breach of the requirement to act with expedition and the delay was inconsistent with the lawful service of the stop notice.

The court held that the council had good reason for delay due to lack of manpower and decisions on other actions that they were taking. In the absence of evidence of lack of good faith by the council and the fact that the council considered the stop notice specifically in terms of town planning matters, and recognised the need to consider as a separate question the expediency of issuing a stop notice, the application was dismissed.

Policy advice

Guidance on the use of the power to serve a stop notice is contained in Annex 3 to Circular 21/91. As the effect of serving a stop notice will usually be to halt the breach of planning control or the specified activity almost immediately, LPAs should ensure that a quick but thorough assessment of the likely consequences of serving a stop notice is available to the committee, by means of the officer's report, or to the officer authorising service of the notice.

Each individual case will differ according to its circumstances. Factors to be considered include:

    (a) the type of activity;

    (b) its unacceptability in the light of surrounding land uses;

    (c) previous planning history ie, whether any planning applications have been considered in the past or whether a use that may not have been so unacceptable in planning terms has intensified to such an extent that it is now unacceptable;

    (d) the extent of local objection; and

    (e) the cost in financial terms, both to the operator of the site, or landowner and to the LPA in terms of compensation liability.

An assessment of the consequences of serving a stop notice should examine the foreseeable costs and benefits likely to result from a stop notice. Policy advice on carrying out a cost benefit assessment for stop notices is given in paras 20 to 24 of Annex 3 to Circular 21/91.

(1) The costs

The prohibition of a particular activity could have cost ramifications to a firm in terms of job losses, failure to meet orders and comply with contracts, or even bankruptcy. These effects should always be carefully, but quickly, examined by the LPA. In addition LPAs are advised to approach the person responsible and discuss whether or not the unacceptability of the activity could be overcome, although the need for any delay to be minimised is emphasised.

Paragraph 22 of Annex 3 to Circular 21/91 refers to overcoming objections to a particular operation, activity or use of land in an environmentally acceptable way. This can be interpreted as requiring a consideration of both environmental and planning objections. The LPA should invite a planning application if an acceptable alternative use of the site can be found, for example, a reduction in the amount of raw material stored on site, or a change to hours of working.

(2) The benefits

The benefits to be assessed relate to the improvement in amenity in the relevant neighbourhood and the effect on the locals and surrounding land uses. In assessing the benefit to be derived, LPAs should bear in mind that a stop notice is served in addition to an enforcement notice. They should assume that a valid enforcement notice will eventually take effect thus removing the objectionable activity on expiry of the period of compliance specified in the enforcement notice. For this reason a stop notice may not be justified.

An officer's report to committee should seek to address these issues, so that the LPA are seen to have exercised their discretion in balancing the costs and benefits, and determining whether to authorise service of an enforcement notice or not. The LPA need to consider the expediency of issuing a stop notice as a separate question, as in the *Willowcell* case detailed on p 77.

3 Procedural arrangements

Introduction

The exercise of the power to serve a stop notice involves the consideration of a number of factors. The committee of the LPA usually takes the decision whether or not to authorise the service of a stop notice (although, occasionally, the power can be delegated to a single officer such as the Chief Executive). This should involve a specific consideration of the report prepared for the committee, which should include a cost benefit analysis of the type described above, together with the advice contained in Annex 3 of Circular 21/91.

Where such information has been examined by committee and this has been seen to be done, it would be difficult for a third party to argue that the decision taken by committee to serve a stop notice was perverse or irrational (*R v Rochester-upon-Medway City Council, ex parte Hobday* [1989] 2 JPL 17).

Administrative procedures

Advice is given about the respective responsibilities of the planning department and legal department of the LPA when issuing a stop notice in para 16 of Annex 3 to Circular 21/91. Reference is made to the need to implement the decision to serve a stop notice 'speedily and effectively'. The four elements of the procedure referred to are the:

(1) Necessary preparatory work; eg, obtain the relevant information, ensure the recommendation of the committee is recorded, identify the parties upon whom the stop notice is to be served.

(2) Formulation of the terms of the stop notice; this should be prepared by the legal department in consultation with, or on the basis of information supplied by the planning department.

(3) Arrangements for serving it so that service is in compliance with s 329 (*see* below).

(4) Assessment of its practical effect, including the need to prosecute if necessary; if this is dealt with when the decision is taken to serve a stop notice, the legal department will have the authority to take the necessary action should there be non-compliance with the stop notice.

Authority to exercise the power

The wording of the TCPA 1990 makes it clear that where the LPA exercise their discretion to take enforcement action, the decision to issue an enforcement notice comes first. Only then, if it is justifiable, should the committee authorise the service of a stop notice. In *R v Pettigrove and Roberts* (1990) P & CR 355 Glidewell LJ stated 'that the council must have resolved to serve an enforcement notice before it goes on to serve a stop notice is clear'.

Separate consideration should be given to whether or not a stop notice is necessary (*R v Westminster City Council, ex parte Willowcell* [1994] JPL B38). The resolution to issue an enforcement notice and the resolution to serve a stop notice can be made at the same committee meeting. The minutes of the meeting and the resolutions of the committee ought to make it clear that a two-stage procedure, dealing with the exercise of each power separately, has been carried out.

If it becomes expedient for a stop notice to be issued after the enforcement notice has been served, and the LPA has not authorised such action at the same committee meeting, they may have to convene an emergency meeting in accordance with their standing orders to obtain the necessary authority and ensure service of the stop notice before the enforcement notice takes effect.

4 Service of a stop notice

The LPA may now serve the enforcement notice and the stop notice at the same time (s 183(1)). This follows the decision of the Court of Appeal in the *Pettigrove* case, and removes the requirement that the enforcement notice should be served separately from and before the service of the stop notice. This does not affect the need to consider the exercise of the powers in relation to each notice separately. The stop notice must refer to the enforcement notice to which it relates and have a copy of that notice annexed to it (s 184(1)).

A stop notice can be served at a later date than the enforcement notice, but must be served before the enforcement notice takes effect (before the period for compliance specified in the enforcement notice expires, or before the final determination or withdrawal of an appeal against an enforcement notice). The LPA may serve a stop notice on any person who appears to have an interest in the land or to be engaged in any activity prohibited by the notice (s 183(6)). This includes contractors, as in the *Pettigrove* case. A contractor will not have been served with an enforcement notice where he does not have an interest in the land, and this justifies the requirement that an enforcement notice should be attached to a stop notice. In these circumstances the LPA should try trace the owner or occupier of the land and arrange for the stop notice to be served on them as well.

The procedure and mechanisms for the service of a stop notice is governed by the provisions of s 329 and is the same as that for service of an enforcement notice (*see* Chapter 6). It should always be clear to the recipient of a stop notice that it is an important communication. Paragraph 18 of Annex 3 to Circular 21/91 advises that 'If the notice is served by postal delivery, the envelope containing it should clearly state that it is an urgent and important communication; and it should be sent by recorded delivery service'.

There is also power set out in s 184(6) to display a site notice stating:

      (a)   that a stop notice has been served;
      (b)   that any person contravening it may be prosecuted;
      (c)   giving the date when the stop notice takes effect; and
      (d)   indicating its requirements.

Where a site notice is displayed, the effect of the stop notice is extended to any person contravening it.

There is a residual power granted to the Secretary of State to serve a stop notice where it appears to him to be expedient (s 185). An enforcement notice must have been issued, either by the LPA, or by the Secretary of State under his reserve powers in s 182. Before serving a stop notice, the Secretary of State must consult with the relevant LPA as any liability to pay compensation rests with them.

5 Contents and effect

Mandatory requirements

A stop notice is dependent upon the existence of an enforcement notice. It must refer to the enforcement notice to which it relates and have a copy annexed to it (s 184(1)). It must also specify the date upon which it is to take effect which must not be later than 28 days from the date when the notice is first served (s 184(3)(*b*)).

This date must not be earlier than three days after the date when the notice is served. However, the LPA has the power to serve a stop notice having immediate effect, where they consider that there are special reasons for specifying an earlier date. This would apply where the LPA is of the view that the three day delay is too long in the circumstances, eg, tipping cases. Where the notice has immediate effect, the LPA must serve a statement of the special reasons that apply with the stop notice (s 184(3)(*a*)). The example given in para 29 of Annex 3 to Circular 21/91 is that, 'it may be considered essential to protect an area of special landscape value, or a conservation area, from operational development (such as buildings, roadways or other hard surfaces) which, if it continued, would be especially harmful'.

Additional information

There are no other statutory requirements for the content of a stop notice. However, it should be clear what activities are prohibited and to which area of land it relates. A model form of stop notice is appended to Annex 3 to Circular 21/91 and is reproduced in Appendix 4. Schedule 1 to the model stop notice provides for the area of land to which the notice relates to be described in words and by reference to a plan. Schedule 2 to the model stop notice provides for the relevant activity to be specified.

The model notice contains a statement that the council consider it expedient to prohibit a relevant activity required by the enforcement notice. In the absence of any evidence to the contrary, a prosecution based upon a stop notice which asserts on its face that the council considered it expedient to prevent the activity is well-founded. The presumption is that everything required for the notice to be valid has been done. In the *Pettigrove* case, the Chief Executive of the council had been given delegated power to issue a stop notice as appropriate, but there was no evidence that he considered if it was expedient to prohibit the carrying out of the relevant activity. The court held that the statement contained in the stop notice (that the council considered it expedient to stop the activity) was sufficient.

Scope of the prohibition

The scope of a prohibition in a stop notice is given in para 6 of Annex 3 to Circular 21/91. It may prohibit any, or all, of the activities which comprise the alleged breach of planning control in the related enforcement notice. This includes:

    (a) an ancillary or incidental use to the main use of the land specified in the enforcement notice as a breach of planning control, eg, loading and unloading of commercial vehicles; or

(b) an activity taking place only on part of the land, eg, an activity that would impact on residents living adjacent to one boundary of a large site otherwise surrounded by open land; or

(c) a seasonal or intermittent activity on the land, eg, a market or fair operating on land beyond permitted development rights, or a summer activity, which causes considerable damage to local amenity.

The prohibition in a stop notice should be carefully drafted. Circular 21/91 advises that a stop notice should 'prohibit only what is essential to safeguard amenity or public safety in the neighbourhood; or to prevent serious or irreversible harm to the environment in the surrounding area'. In this context, the local knowledge of the planning or enforcement officer and the detail set out in his report to committee is significant.

Relevant activity

As the *relevant activity* to which a stop notice may be directed can be any activity specified in the enforcement notice or any part of an activity, or an associated activity (s 183(2)), the scope of the prohibition in a stop notice may go further than the terms of the enforcement notice.

The activity specified in the stop notice need only be *associated* with the activity prohibited by the enforcement notice and need not necessarily be a prohibited activity in itself (*R v Dahr* (1993) *The Times*, 22 March). If, therefore, the activity which is unacceptable to the LPA, which would justify the service of a stop notice, is an activity which is merely associated with the activity prohibited by the enforcement notice (eg, the loading and unloading of commercial vehicles associated with the use of land for a commercial activity, prohibited by the enforcement notice), then a stop notice may validly be served under s 183 to prohibit such loading and unloading.

However, where the activity prohibited by the stop notice is clearly outside the breach of planning control alleged by the enforcement notice, it will be invalid. In *Clwyd County Council v Secretary of State for Wales and Welsh Aggregates Ltd* [1982] JPL 696, a stop notice that required mining operations to cease when the actual breach alleged in the enforcement notice was a failure to fence, was held to be invalid.

Limitations

A stop notice can only prohibit a particular activity. To that extent it is a relatively inflexible tool. It cannot impose limitations upon an activity to keep it within reasonable bounds pending an enforcement appeal. Therefore, if a complete cessation of activity is too draconian a measure, the power is of no use in mitigating the effects of an unauthorised use which may continue pending the final determination or withdrawal of an enforcement appeal.

A stop notice cannot operate in advance of a threatened breach of planning control, although a developer can obtain an order of *certiorari* which prevents an LPA from serving an enforcement notice (*Scott Markets Ltd v London*

Borough of Waltham Forest [1979] JPL 392). A stop notice cannot be used to require positive action (*Welsh Aggregates* case). Where development is carried out without compliance with conditions which require positive action, the only remedy is the service of a breach of condition notice or an enforcement notice which cannot be followed up by a stop notice.

Validity

A stop notice that inadequately specifies the activities prohibited will not be invalid for that reason alone. Where a stop notice incorporates the terms of the enforcement notice, then a deficiency of particularity in the stop notice might be validated and cured by the fact that the terms of the enforcement notice can be relied upon (*Bristol Stadium v Brown* [1980] JPL 107). This is supported by the fact that the relevant enforcement notice must be attached to the stop notice.

A stop notice will not necessarily be invalid where the prohibition contained in it is unclear. In *Runnymede Borough Council, ex parte Sarvan Singh Seehra* [1986] JPL 283 an enforcement notice alleged a breach of planning control by an unauthorised change from residential to a mixed use for residential purposes and religious meetings. The relevant stop notice required that the land cease to be used for purposes other than those incidental to a dwellinghouse use. Although the wording used incorporated matters of fact and degree, the court held that such wording was admissible in both enforcement notices and in stop notices

6 Exclusions

Certain activities may not be the subject of a stop notice. It shall not prohibit:
   (1) The use of any building as a dwellinghouse (s 183(4)). This exclusion ties in with the four-year period of immunity conferred on a change of use of any building to use as a single dwellinghouse (s 171B(2), *see* Chapter 5).
   (2) Any activity which commenced more than four years before the service of the stop notice. It does not matter if the activity was continuous or not. When in calculating the four year period, no account is to be taken of any period during which the activity was authorised by a planning permission (s 183(5)). The rationale behind this exclusion is that, where the activity has continued for a four-year period, there can be little basis for a claim of expediency in seeking to prohibit that activity. The provision in s 183(5) only confers immunity on changes of use occurring more than four years prior to the notice. It does not extend to activities involved in operational development, or the deposit of refuse or waste materials (s 183(5A)).

There is no longer any exclusion preventing the use of land for a residential caravan occupied as a sole or main residence. This exclusion previously provided protection even for residential caravans used on land in full knowledge of a stop notice prohibiting such use (*Runnymede Borough Council v Smith and Others* [1986] JPL 592). In planning terms the use of land for residential caravans can cause serious detriment to amenity and in such cases, the stop notice procedure should be available. This is recognised in the draft circular on Gypsy Sites and Caravans, which advises that LPAs should regard gypsies in the same manner as other small businesses and self-employed people when considering possible enforcement action. However, the breach of planning control would need to be serious enough to justify the use of the stop notice procedure.

There is no jurisdiction for the LPA to serve a stop notice prohibiting any of the statutorily-excluded activities. If they seek to do so, eg serving a stop notice which relates to activities which commenced more than four years previously, the court can consider the correct facts in relation to a defence against a prosecution (*R v Jenner* [1983] 2 All ER 46, which applied to the 12-month immunity period under previous rules).

7 Cessation of effect

There are four circumstances in which a stop notice will no longer have effect:
- (1) Where the enforcement notice to which the stop notice relates is withdrawn or quashed on appeal, it will cease to have effect (s 184(4)(*a*)). This means that, where the supporting enforcement notice fails on a technicality, the stop notice also cease to have an effect, whether the use or operation it relates to was lawful or not. There will be no opportunity for that question to be tested, unless the LPA subsequently serve a technically correct enforcement notice and stop notice. On any claim for compensation under s 186, the Lands Tribunal may find that no compensation is to be awarded for any activity prohibited by the stop notice which constitutes or contributes to a breach of planning control when the notice is in force (see p 88).
- (2) Where the period for compliance with the enforcement notice expires, the stop notice will cease to have effect (s 184(4)(*b*)). At that point, it will become an offence not to comply with the requirements specified in the enforcement notice (*see* Chapter 12).
- (3) The LPA can serve a notice to withdraw the stop notice (*see* p 86 below). The stop notice will cease to have effect when this notice to withdraw is first served (s 184(4)(*c*)).
- (4) When an enforcement notice is varied, for example on appeal to the Secretary of State, a stop notice shall cease to have effect if, or to the extent that, the activities prohibited by it cease to come within the alleged breach of planning control (s 184(5)).

8 Challenge to validity

There is no right of appeal to the Secretary of State against the prohibition in a stop notice. As it is dependent upon the existence of an enforcement notice, a challenge to the validity of the matters specified in such notice as constituting a breach of planning control is dealt with by appeal against the enforcement notice under s 174. Section 285 does not extend to stop notices. There are only three methods of challenge available to a person aggrieved by a stop notice.

(1) *Defence to a prosecution*   A person upon whom a stop notice is served can continue the prohibited activity and then challenge the validity of the stop notice when prosecuted. The court does have the power to consider the jurisdiction of the LPA to serve the stop notice and to determine whether or not a defendant was subject to its prohibitions, eg, whether the prohibited activity is within one of the exclusions set out above (*R v Jenner* [1983] 2 All ER 46). In effect, the court will be indirectly ruling on the validity of the stop notice, but ought not to deal directly with questions of fact, which are subject to a framework of civil proceedings under the TCPA 1990.

(2) *Judicial review*   As the service of a stop notice is a discretionary administrative action by the LPA, it is subject to judicial review. A challenge by way of judicial review will relate to an issue of legality or *vires* rather than fact (*Runnymede Borough Council, ex parte Sarvan Singh Seehra* [1986] JPL 283). Paragraph 13 of Annex 3 to Circular 21/91 provides that, 'The validity of a stop notice, and the propriety of the LPA's decision to issue a notice, may be challenged by seeking leave of the High Court to apply for judicial review'. An application for judicial review has been successful in preventing a LPA from serving a stop notice (*Scott Markets Ltd v Waltham Forest London Borough Council* [1979] JPL 392).

(3) *Claim compensation*   This is not a direct challenge to a stop notice, but enables compensation to be obtained in certain circumstances where a stop notice ceases to have effect (*see* p 87).

The validity of a stop notice cannot be challenged on the ground that it has not been served on someone who should have been served, as a person prosecuted for contravention of a stop notice can plead in his defence that the stop notice was not served on him and that he did not know, and could not reasonably have been expected to know, of its existence (s 187(3)). As with an enforcement notice, an entry in the planning enforcement register relating to the stop notice is sufficient evidence that the person was put on notice (*see* below). However, the LPA should try to serve the notice on all affected persons.

A stop notice is not invalid if the related enforcement notice is not properly served. However, the LPA must show that they took all such steps as were reasonably practicable to effect proper service (s 184(8)).

9 Registration

The LPA is required to enter details of the date of service of a stop notice in the planning enforcement register maintained under s 188. The entry should also include a statement or summary of the activity prohibited by the notice. In the event that a stop notice is withdrawn details of the date of withdrawal shall be entered on the register, which is available for inspection by the public at all reasonable hours.

The publicity requirements for a stop notice relate to the display of a site notice as set out above at p 80. However, this is not a mandatory requirement.

10 Withdrawal of the notice

The LPA may withdraw a stop notice. The notification of withdrawal must be served on everyone who was served with the stop notice (s 193(9)). This may take place before the stop notice comes into effect, as on the first service of the notification of withdrawal it ceases to come into effect (s 184(4)(c)).

This provision is without prejudice to the LPA's power to serve another stop notice and is a useful tool to use where a threat to transgressors would serve a purpose and would persuade them to make a planning application. However, if such a tactic is to be used, the LPA may be liable for compensation. If a site notice has been displayed, which the LPA subsequently withdraw, the withdrawal notice must be displayed in its place (s 184(8)).

11 Contravention of a stop notice

Failure to comply with the prohibition contained in a stop notice gives rise to criminal liability. However, liability for contravention of the notice does not arise until the date upon which it comes into effect (s 184(2)).

Any person contravening a stop notice after a site notice has been displayed, or a stop notice has been served on him, is guilty of a criminal offence (s 187(1)). The maximum penalty on summary conviction in the magistrates' court is a fine of £20,000, and on conviction on indictment, there is an unlimited fine. When determining the level of any fine, the court will consider any financial benefit which has accrued, or is likely to accrue as a result of the offence and where possible, the prosecuting authority should provide details about the proceeds resulting from the offence. The offence may be charged by reference to a day or a longer period and a person may be convicted of a second or subsequent offence. In addition, the offence extends to persons who cause or permit the contravention of a stop notice, eg a landlord instructing his tenants to continue a prohibited activity.

It is a defence to proceedings under s 187 that the stop notice was not served on the defendant and that he did not know of its existence (s187(3)). This will be difficult to sustain where the LPA have displayed a site notice and where details of the stop notice have been entered in the planning enforcement register.

12 The use of injunctions

The courts have held that LPAs can use an injunction to enforce against the breach of planning control (*Westminster City Council v Jones* [1981] JPL 750). This case involved the development and use of an amusement arcade. It was opened before an application for planning permission had been considered by the LPA who first served an enforcement notice and then a stop notice. An appeal was lodged against the enforcement notice solely on the ground that planning permission ought to be granted. The operator did not find out what the attitude of the LPA would be prior to the opening of the arcade. He ignored the stop notice and it was clear that he intended to challenge every decision against him while continuing to operate and profit from the development. The LPA therefore sought civil relief to enforce the provisions of the stop notice.

A local authority has wide powers to take legal proceedings under the Local Government Act 1972, s 222, restricted only by the requirement that they must act for the promotion or protection of the interests of the inhabitants in their area. In the *Jones* case the crucial factor to justify the taking of such action by a local authority was held to be 'a deliberate and flagrant flouting of the law and a plain breach of the law'. However, the use of an injunction should be exceptional and should not interrupt the normal operation of the statutory remedies. Section 187B now provides LPAs with express statutory power to serve an injunction in support of their enforcement functions (*see* Chapter 12).

13 Compensation for loss

Entitlement to compensation

LPAs are well informed about the entitlement to compensation for loss or damage due to the use of the stop notice procedure. This liability has resulted in the cautious use of stop notices. Section 186(1) provides for the entitlement for compensation in respect of a prohibition contained in a stop notice in circumstances where the:

    (a) enforcement notice to which the stop notice relates is quashed;

    (b) enforcement notice is varied so that the activity prohibited by the stop notice ceases to be a relevant activity specified in the enforcement notice;

    (c) enforcement notice is withdrawn by the LPA; or

    (d) stop notice is withdrawn by the LPA.

However, there is no entitlement to compensation where any of the circumstances in (a), (b) or (c) arise as a result of the grant of planning permission for the development to which the enforcement notice relates. Compensation is not due where the enforcement notice or stop notice is subsequently found to be a nullity, as such notice is of no effect and is therefore incapable of being quashed, varied or withdrawn.

Person entitled

The entitlement to compensation lies with a person who, when the stop notice is served, has an interest in or occupies the land to which the notice relates (s 186(2)). This would not include a person, such as a contractor, carrying out any activities on the land which are prohibited by the stop notice. However, compensation paid for breach of contract would cover the losses of such a person (s 186(4)).

Assessment of compensation

Compensation is payable for any loss or damage directly attributable to the prohibition contained in the stop notice and is not tied solely to any deprecia-tion in the value of the claimant's interest in the land.

There are a number of principles that apply to the assessment of compensa-tion:

(1) Loss or damage shall include any sum payable for a breach of contract caused by the taking of action necessary to comply with the prohibition (s 186(4)).

(2) Compensation is not payable for any activity prohibited by the stop notice which, at any time when the notice is in force, constitutes or contributes to a breach of planning control (s 186(5)(*a*)).

(3) Compensation is not payable where a claimant fails to respond to a planning contravention notice served under s 171C or any other statu-tory notice requiring information for any loss or damage which could have been avoided if this information had been provided or co-opera-tion given to the LPA when responding to the notice (s186(5)(*b*)).

(4) There is no requirement for the loss or damage to be reasonably fore-seeable (*Sample (Warkworth) v Alnwick District Council* [1984] JPL 670).

(5) Interest is payable on compensation awarded from the date of service of the stop notice (Planning and Compensation Act 1991, s 80 and Sched 18).

(6) Continuing interest on expenditure incurred on the development which has been stopped by the notice is recoverable (*Graysmark v South Hams District Council* [1989] 03 EG 75).

(7) The deferment of the profit which would have been made on the devel-opment is recoverable (*Graysmark*).

(8) Loss arising by reason of impecuniosity or difficulty in raising finance for commercial adventure is not recoverable (*Graysmark*).

(9) Damages which are remote, for example loss of credibility with bank-ers, embarrassment, and worry are not recoverable (*Graysmark*).

(10) The costs of pursuing an enforcement appeal are not recoverable as compensation, as these costs can be recovered through the appeal pro-cedure (*Sample*).

The LPA should seek to agree sums for compensation with the claimant. Disputed claims shall be referred to the Lands Tribunal (s 186(6)), and the provisions of the Lands Compensation Act 1961, ss 2 and 4 shall apply.

Making a claim

Claims for compensation under s 186 are to be made to and paid by the LPA. Regulation 12 of the Town and Country Planning (General) Regulations 1992 (SI No 1492) provides that these must be made in writing within 12 months from the date of the decision in respect of which the claim is made. They must be served on the LPA by delivery at their offices, or by pre-paid post.

The entitlement to compensation arises when the decision is made to quash, vary or withdraw the notice. The Secretary of State has the power to extend the period allowed for the claim to be made, even in circumstances where the 12 month period has already lapsed.

The claim does not need to be detailed, ie it need not be in any particular form or state the sum claimed. All that is required is that the document should be unequivocal and make it clear that a claim is being made and not merely state that a claim would be made (*Texas Homecare Ltd v Lewes DC*)

14 LPAs checklist for serving stop notice

Preliminary

(1) Obtain all relevant information on breach of planning control.
(2) Make a full assessment of the likely consequences of serving a stop notice, including:
    (a) type of activity;
    (b) surrounding land uses affected;
    (c) previous planning history;
    (d) extent of local objection;
    (e) compensation liability;
    (f) effect of prosecution.
(3) Carry out a cost benefit assessment.
(4) Ensure decision already taken to issue enforcement notice.

Preparatory

(1) Obtain authority for issuing stop notice by committee resolution or through delegation.
(2) Prepare authorised document containing:
    (a) reference to enforcement notice to which it relates;
    (b) effective date;
    (c) prohibited activities;
    (d) area of land to which it relates; and
    (e) statement that the council consider it expedient to prohibit the activity.
(3) Draw up a plan and prepare a brief written description of the land to which the notice relates.
(4) Prepare site notice (not mandatory).
(5) Identify parties to be served.

Service of stop notice

(1) Serve on all parties to be served:
    (a) stop notice;

    (b) copy of enforcement notice to which it relates;

    (c) plan of land to which it relates.

(2) Display site notice (not mandatory).

(3) Enter details of stop notice in the planning enforcement register as soon as practicable after service.

Chapter 8

Breach of Condition Notices

1 Introduction

Section 2 of the Planning and Compensation Act 1991 gave LPAs a radical new power to enforce planning conditions by means of a new breach of condition notice. This power gives LPAs some flexibility in enforcing planning control, particularly where a planning condition has clearly been breached but the situation does not merit enforcement action which would be unduly onerous. The statutory provisions follow a recommendation in the Carnwarth Report 'that provision be made for a new procedure for summary enforcement of breach of condition'. This was first proposed by the National Development Control Forum in 1985, who identified a gap in enforcement powers relating to the enforcement of conditions. The power to serve a breach of condition notice is intended to provide an alternative to an enforcement notice for remedying a breach of control arising from failure to comply with any condition or limitation attached to a planning permission.

Annex 2 to Circular 17/92 provides guidance on the use of breach of condition notices, indicating that it not only provides an alternative remedy to the use of an enforcement notice, but may be used in addition to any other planning enforcement powers, including reinforcing the effect of an enforcement notice. It is also intended to give LPAs a simpler, less expensive way of controlling breaches of planning control, particularly where other methods would be too draconian or unjustified.

The content of this chapter is based on the statutory provisions relating to breach of condition notices and the guidance contained in Annex 2 to Circular 17/92. As the use of breach of condition notices becomes more prolific (as recent statistics indicate that it will) problems will emerge and difficulties will be identified which may require clarification by the courts

2 Power to serve breach of condition notices

The power to serve a breach of condition notice is set out in s 187A(2). It applies where planning permission for carrying out any development of land has been granted subject to conditions which have not been complied with. Section 171A provides that failure to comply with any condition or limitation subject to which planning permission has been granted, constitutes a breach of planning control and the service of a breach of condition notice constitutes taking enforcement action.

As failure to comply with the requirements of a breach of condition notice constitutes a criminal offence under s 187A(9), a potential criminal liability attaches to conditions. The drafting of conditions therefore assumes a significance that should not be overlooked, as conditions may be open to critical examination. If a condition is ambiguous or imprecise, there may be difficulties for the LPA in enforcing it, and uncertainty for developers in ensuring compliance.

When drafting conditions, the six tests for conditions contained in Circular 1/85 should be borne in mind. These state that conditions should only be imposed where:

(a) they are necessary;
(b) relevant to planning;
(c) relevant to the development to be permitted;
(d) enforceable;
(e) precise; and
(f) reasonable in all other respects.

Article 25 of the 1988 GDO requires that the LPA give full reasons for any condition imposed on the grant of planning permission. Circular 1/85 gives guidance on the adequacy of reasons. Judicious use of reasons as well as the wording of conditions themselves will not only enable developers to understand the need for conditions and to comply with them, but may assist in making it clear when a breach has occurred.

The exercise of the power to serve a breach of condition notice is entirely at the discretion of the LPA. Due to the number of uncertainties which are set out above, it may be worthwhile for LPAs to consider carrying out a cost/benefit analysis before serving a breach of condition notice, similar to the assessment recommended in para 19 of Annex 3 to Circular 21/91 in relation to stop notices (*see* Chapter 7, p 78).

For the statutory provisions to apply, the grant of planning permission must be subject to conditions. Section 187A(13)(*a*) makes it clear that 'conditions' include 'limitations' and there is a distinction between these terms.

Conditions

When determining planning applications, s 70(1)(*a*) empowers LPAs to grant planning permission, either unconditionally, or subject to such conditions as they think fit. This power is supplemented by s 72(1) which permits the imposition of conditions regulating the development or use of any land under the control of the applicant, whether the subject land of the planning application or not, or requiring the carrying out of works on any such land, or granting planning permission for a limited period. A condition can therefore be imposed upon an express grant of planning permission.

LPAs have a wide discretion to impose such conditions as they think fit, subject to the powers of the courts. This was considered in *Pyx Granite Company Ltd v Minister of Housing and Local Government* [1958] 1 QB 554 and subsequently in *Newbury District Council v Secretary of State for the Environment* [1981] AC 578. There are three limitations on the exercise of the discretionary power to impose conditions, which were identified by the House of Lords in the *Newbury* case:

(a) a condition must be imposed only for a 'planning' purpose and not for any ulterior purpose;

(b) a condition must fairly and reasonably relate to the development permitted by the planning permission; and

(c) a condition should not be so unreasonable that no reasonable LPA could have imposed it.

A condition can also be imposed on a planning permission granted by a development order. This power is given to the Secretary of State by the provisions of s 60(1). The most familiar are perhaps those conditions imposed on the permitted development rights granted under Sched 2, art 3 to the 1988 GDO. For example, an agricultural building erected on agricultural land pursuant to permitted development rights granted under Sched 2, Part 6 to the 1988 GDO is subject to the condition that a developer must obtain a determination from the LPA as to whether the prior approval of the authority will be required to the siting, design and external appearance of the building.

Whether a condition is imposed on an express grant of planning permission, or on a planning permission granted by a development order, it is usually clear what constitutes a condition. What constitutes a limitation is not so clear cut.

Limitations

A planning permission may be restricted otherwise than by express condition and will authorise that use or development as qualified by the words of limitation. Section 75(2) contains statutory authority for restricting planning permission by words of limitation. It provides that, 'where planning permission is granted for the erection of a building, the grantor's permission may specify the purposes for which the building may be used'.

Limiting words specified in the grant of planning permission itself are of functional significance, eg an *agricultural* dwelling which restrict the occupier of the dwelling to a person connected with agriculture. However, in these circumstances a change in occupier to a person not connected with agriculture, will not necessarily constitute a breach of planning control unless it amounts to a material change of use or operational development. If the restriction on occupation was imposed by condition, non-compliance with that condition would amount to a breach of planning control and a breach of condition notice could be served.

In *Peacock Homes Ltd v Secretary of State for the Environment and Epsom and Ewell Borough Council* [1984] JPL 729, the Court of Appeal held that 'the word "limitations" did not carry any technical meaning under the Act (of 1971), and would seem to be surplusage in that any limitation on a planning permission would have to be imposed by way of condition'. This appears to support the argument that a breach of a limitation in the wording of the permission itself only constitutes an unauthorised development if it amounts to a material change of use or operational development, it is not a mere breach of condition.

This view is supported by the guidance given in para 5 of Annex 2 to Circular 17/92 which states that 'the reference to conditions includes reference to "limitations" which are statutorily imposed by certain of the provisions for "permitted development" rights in Schedule 2 to the Town and Country Planning General Development Order 1988'. A limitation imposed by words of restriction on a planning permission is not statutorily imposed by the provisions for permitted development rights in the GDO. Therefore, following the guidance in Circular 17/92, they are not limitations to which the provisions of s 187A refer.

Statutory power is given in s 60(1) to impose limitations on planning permissions granted by a development order and s 60(4) makes it clear that permission granted by the 1988 GDO for the use of land for any purpose on a limited number of days in a specified period is a permission granted subject to a limitation. Schedule 2, Part 4 to the 1988 GDO permits the use of any land subject to the restriction that it is used for not more than 28 days in total in any calendar year and, for certain specified purposes, for not more than 14 days in total. A breach of this restriction would be a breach of planning control that could properly be enforced by a breach of condition notice.

Other words of limitation contained in the descriptions of permitted development in the 1988 GDO are not expressly stated as limitations in the TCPA 1990. Whether or not they are still considered as *statutorily imposed* in accordance with the guidance in Annex 2 of Circular 17/92 is open to doubt. A breach of such limitation may be regarded as a material change of use or operational development, rather than a mere breach of condition, as it is a breach of the development permitted as a whole. The view of the Court of Appeal in the *Peacock Homes* case would support this

A limitation may also take the form of a restriction to permitted development in the 1988 GDO, Sched 2 which is set out under the side heading of 'Development not Permitted', eg, a restriction on the size of a satellite antenna on a dwelling house under para 1(a) of Class H of Part 1 of Sched 2 to the 1988 GDO. In these circumstances, it is arguable that a breach of a limitation is a breach of the permitted development and therefore the whole development is in breach of planning control. In such instances, the correct form of enforcement action would be the service of an enforcement notice rather than a breach of condition notice.

The words of clarification in s 187A(13)(*a*) avoid the need to make a clear distinction between what constitutes a condition and what constitutes a limitation. However, to ensure the correct use of a breach of condition notice, it is important to recognise that the breach of planning control must relate to a specific restriction on the planning permission and not the development as a whole where the unauthorised development would amount to a material change of use or operational development.

Appropriate use of breach of condition notice

The following situations are those where enforcement by a breach of condition notice might be appropriate:
- (a) condition attached to an express grant of planning permission;
- (b) condition imposed on a class of permitted development under Sched 2 to the 1988 GDO and defined as such by the use of the word 'condition' in the side headings;
- (c) time limitation under the 1988 GDO as provided for in s 60(4).

Inappropriate use of breach of condition notice

Enforcement by serving a breach of condition notice may not always be appropriate. In the following cases, service of an enforcement notice would be preferable:
- (a) non-compliance with a limitation set out in the wording of the permission itself, rather than in the conditions attached to it;
- (b) non-compliance with words of limitation contained in the description of permitted development in the GDO.

The recurring theme of the guidance contained in Circular 17/92 is that the breach of condition notice should only be used where the issues are clear cut. In any case of doubt, 'it is suggested that the issue of an enforcement notice may be more appropriate than the use of the new breach of condition notice procedure'.

3 Criteria

Planning permission granted subject to conditions

A breach of condition notice can only be served where planning permission has been granted for the carrying out of any development of land subject to conditions imposed on the permission.

Planning permission can be granted by the LPA, the Secretary of State or a planning inspector on appeal. The Secretary of State can also grant planning permission in a development order such as the 1988 GDO. The power to serve a breach of condition notice applies to any development and therefore relates to a material change of use as well as operational development.

Non-compliance with the terms of a condition

It is necessary for a breach of condition to occur before the power to issue a breach of condition notice can be exercised. The provisions for the enforcement of conditions is on the basis that a breach of condition will be clear cut. Section 187A(2) states that the LPA may serve a breach of condition notice 'if any of the conditions [subject to which planning permission has been granted] is not complied with'. However, to prosecute successfully a breach of the requirements of a breach of condition notice, the burden of proof lies with the LPA to show non-compliance with the specified condition (*see* below p 104).

Valid and enforceable conditions

For a breach of condition to occur, the condition must be valid and enforceable. Circular 1/85 contains guidance in relation to the ability to enforce. It points out that, 'precision in the wording of conditions may be vital when it comes to enforcement'. The potential criminal liability that attaches to a breach of condition makes it important that a condition is drafted in such a manner as to enable a breach of its requirements to be proved. The example given in para 23 of Circular 1/85 illustrates the potential difficulties:

> A condition imposed for traffic reasons restricting the number of persons resident at any one time in a block of flats would be impracticable to monitor, and pose severe difficulties in proving an infringement. However, where a condition is intended to prevent harm to the amenities of an area which is clearly likely to result from the development (for example, a condition requiring an amusement centre to close at a certain time in the evening), it will not usually be difficult to monitor, as those affected by the contravention of its requirements are likely to be able to provide clear evidence of any breaches.

A condition must also be capable of being reasonably enforced. Where the requirements of a condition can only be enforced by taking action against a third party, for example, where works are to be carried out on land in which the person with the benefit of the planning permission has no interest, it would be unreasonable to take action against a third party who had derived no benefit from the development.

Implementation of the planning permission

A condition will only take effect when the planning permission to which it is attached is implemented. Section 56 gives some statutory guidance as to when development shall be taken to have begun. This provides assistance in determining when a planning permission is implemented. Works that are *de minimis* are unlikely to be sufficient to constitute the implementation of a planning permission. In *Malvern Hills District Council v Secretary of State for the Environment* [1982] JPL 439, the court held that, for a planning permission to be implemented, works must 'genuinely be done for the purpose of carrying out the development'.

Application of immunity periods

The power to enforce against a breach of planning control can only be exercised properly where the breach is not immune from enforcement. Section 171B(3) specifies that enforcement action cannot be taken against (among other cases) a breach of planning control 'after the end of the period of ten years beginning with the date of the breach'. The ten-year immunity period applies to all breaches of planning condition except breach of a condition relating to use as a single dwellinghouse, where s 171B(2) provides that the period of immunity is four years, and breach of condition attached to a planning permission for mining operations (*see* Chapter 15). These provisions were introduced by the Planning and Compensation Act 1991 and are dealt with in more detail in Chapter 5.

The effect of s 171B(3) is that all breaches of planning condition are immune from enforcement after ten years. There is one important exception to this set out in s 171B(4)(*b*). Where enforcement action has already been taken within the ten-year period, the LPA may issue a further breach of condition notice within four years. Such provision applies where, for example, a breach of condition notice served within the ten-year period was found to be defective, and in the meantime the ten-year period had expired. Section 171B(4)(*b*) gives the LPA a second chance to serve a further enforcement notice within four years of the date when enforcement action was first taken. It should be remembered that s 171A(2)(*b*) provides that it is the service of the breach of condition notice that constitutes the taking of enforcement action, regardless of the validity or efficacy of that notice.

4 Service of a breach of condition notice

The requirements for serving a breach of condition notice are specified in s 187A(2). What constitutes proper service is dealt with in Chapter 6. In relation to the breach of any condition, whether that condition regulates the development or use of any land, or requires the carrying out of works on any land, the breach of condition notice may be served on any person who is carrying out or has carried out the development to which the conditional planning permission relates. By virtue of s 187A(13)(*b*) such person includes any person causing or permitting another to carry out the development. This provision protects persons such as third party contractors carrying out development as an agent of the owner. In these circumstances, the person to be served would be the owner.

Alternatively, a breach of condition notice may be served on any person having control of the land. However, under s 187A(4) such a person can only be served where the contravened condition regulates the use of the land. The effect of this provision is that a person having control of the land is protected against enforcement action of this nature, where he had no part in carrying out the development, and the contravened condition regulates the development rather than the use of the land.

In providing guidance on the service of a breach of condition notice, para 12 of Annex 2 to Circular 17/92 gives the example of enforcing compliance with a condition imposed on a planning permission for residential development which requires the completion of a landscaping scheme. In circumstances where such a condition is contravened, a breach of condition notice cannot be used against the owners of the individual dwellinghouses, who were not involved in the construction of the houses. As a landscaping condition does not regulate the use of the land, but regulates the development, a breach of condition notice relating to such a condition can only be used against the developer. It is important to note that the Circular goes on to state that provided the breach has not gained immunity from enforcement action, an enforcement notice may be issued in order to remedy the alleged breach.

The LPA must ensure that a breach of condition notice is served on the correct person. Section 187A(3) defines any person on whom the LPA serve a breach of condition notice as 'the person responsible'. In the event that any condition specified in a breach of condition notice is not complied with after the expiration of the compliance period, it will be 'the person responsible', ie the recipient of the notice, who will be guilty of an offence and liable to prosecution. For these reasons, it is essential for the LPA to consider and decide at the outset of each case who is to be regarded as *the person responsible* for an alleged breach of a planning condition. In this regard, the issue of a planning contravention notice under s 171C can be valuable in ascertaining the correct person to be served. This is dealt with in Chapter 3.

Unlike the service of an enforcement notice, a breach of condition notice should have only one recipient. It would not be correct to serve everyone who had an interest in the land concerned, regardless of the extent of that interest. It should be remembered that the breach of condition notice requires compliance with a specified condition or conditions and in almost all cases only one person will be *the person responsible* and be in a position to ensure compliance with the specified condition.

5 Contents of a breach of condition notice

Introduction

As with an enforcement notice, the criminal liability that attaches to non-compliance with the requirements of a breach of condition notice makes it critical that the wording of the notice tells the person on whom it is served 'fairly what he has done wrong and what he must do to remedy it', per Upjohn LJ in *Miller-Mead v Minister of Housing and Local Government* [1963] 2 QB 196. The statutory requirement to specify certain details in the breach of condition notice imposes an obligation on LPAs to be precise and accurate with regard to those elements of the notice.

Section 187A provides that the breach of condition notice shall:

    (a) specify the conditions that are not complied with (s 187A(2));
    (b) require the person on whom the notice is served to secure compliance with the specified conditions (s 187A(2));
    (c) specify the steps which the authority consider ought to be taken, or the activities which the authority consider ought to cease, to secure compliance with the specified conditions (s 187A(7));
    (d) specify the period allowed for compliance with the condition to which the notice relates (s 187A(7)).

Annex 2 to Circular 17/92 contains guidance on drafting a breach of condition notice. One notice may be directed at the contravention of two or more planning conditions. However, as non-compliance with the requirements of any breach of condition notice after the end of the compliance period specified in the notice is a criminal offence, para 9 of Annex 2 to the Circular suggests that:

> Where one notice is to be directed at the contravention of two or more planning conditions and this would involve specifying more than one compliance period in the same notice, it may be more satisfactory to serve a breach of condition notice for each contravention, so that there is no doubt about which compliance period is applicable to each case.

A model form of breach of condition notice is attached to Circular 17/92 and this is reproduced in Appendix 5.

Required steps

In terms of steps which the authority consider ought to be taken or the activities that ought to cease, para 10 of Annex 2 to Circular 17/92 advises that a notice may be drafted in terms of positive steps, giving the example of a requirement to carry out and complete a landscaping scheme in accordance with the terms of a landscaping condition imposed on a grant of planning permission, or in terms of a prohibition, giving the example of requiring a restaurant, or take-away food shop, to stop opening to customers after the specified closing time in a planning condition.

Section 187A(5) gives the LPA discretion in terms of the steps to be taken or the activities to be stopped. It is intended that a breach of condition notice will apply to clear cut cases of breach and in those instances it should be clear what steps would be reasonable. It should be borne in mind that it is a statutory defence to a prosecution for the defendant to show that he took all 'reasonable measures' to secure compliance with the notice. If the steps required are excessive, the statutory defence may be made out (*see* p 105 below).

Compliance period

The compliance period specified in the breach of condition notice is critical as it triggers the offence under s 187A(9). A breach of the notice will occur unless the specified condition is complied with in an allowed period. If the person responsible is in breach of the notice, he shall be guilty of an offence (*see* p 104 below). As a result, LPAs should give careful consideration to specifying a realistic period for compliance.

The period allowed for compliance with the notice is a period not less than 28 days beginning with the date of service of the notice, or that period as extended by further notice served by the LPA (s 187A(7)). Any such extended period should be reasonable in relation to the condition specified in the notice. Were the LPA to specify a compliance period that was clearly unreasonable, the person on whom the notice has been served may successfully defend a subsequent prosecution for non-compliance (*see* p 105 below).

Additional information

The model breach of condition notice contains a warning statement that there is no right of appeal against the notice. It also states that it is an offence to contravene the compliance requirements specified in the notice after the end of the compliance period. However, it does not contain any information about the defences available, stating only that the validity of the notice may be contested by an application to the High Court for judicial review. There are certain defences to a prosecution for non-compliance, including statutory defences contained in s 187A(11). These are dealt with below. It may prevent unnecessary concern to the recipient of the notice if the availability of certain defences was referred to in the statement at the end of the breach of condition notice.

6 Effect of a breach of condition notice

A breach of condition notice identifies what the recipient must do to secure compliance with the notice and within what time scale. Non-compliance with the requirements of the notice results in a breach of the notice which constitutes a criminal offence. Care should be taken when drafting the notice, both in specifying the condition or conditions that are to be complied with and, more particularly, specifying accurately the steps that are to be taken or the activities that are to cease. Failure to do so can lead to unnecessary concern on the part of the recipient of the notice and the possibility of protracted litigation while the courts resolve the issues

7 Challenging a breach of condition notice

Introduction

There is no right of appeal to the Secretary of State against a breach of condition notice. Nor can the Secretary of State vary the terms of a breach of condition notice. The merits of the condition are not in issue and an opportunity already exists for conditions to be challenged. An application can be made to the LPA for planning permission for the development of land without complying with conditions subject to which a previous planning permission was granted (s 73).

The Carnwath Report considered that a right of appeal is inappropriate for a breach of condition, as the issues are likely to be clear cut, there is likely to be a need for an urgent remedy, and by implementing the permission, the developer has by implication accepted the condition. The Government has followed this recommendation.

However, in order to provide some means of challenging the validity of a breach of condition notice, a challenge can be made by way of an application to the High Court or by defence submission to the magistrates' court in the event of the prosecution of an offence. There is no provision in the TCPA 1990 to provide protection from a challenge in the High Court as there is under s 285 in relation to the validity of an enforcement notice. There are four matters

that can be the subject of a challenge:
    (a) the decision to serve a breach of condition notice;
    (b) the validity of the specified condition;
    (c) the validity of the notice itself; and
    (d) the validity of the decision to prosecute.

The decision to serve a breach of condition notice

This involves the exercise of an administrative power by the LPA and is open to challenge by way of judicial review, eg, where the LPA go beyond their powers (ie act *ultra vires*) or fail to exercise their powers reasonably in accordance with *Wednesbury* principles (*Associated Provincial Picture Houses Ltd v Wednesbury Corporation* [1948] 1 KB 223).

Notwithstanding the fact that the decision to serve a breach of condition notice can be challenged in public law, it can also be raised as a substantive defence to an action brought by the LPA (*Wandsworth London Borough Council v Winder* [1984] 3 All ER 976). Therefore, the defendant can challenge the decision to serve a breach of condition notice as a defence to the substantive action brought against him. If the validity of the decision of the LPA is an essential element in the proof of the crime alleged, then it can be challenged in the courts (*R v Crown Court at Reading, ex parte Hutchinson and Another* [1988] 1 All ER 333).

The validity of the specified condition

The specified condition must be legally valid and enforceable and must satisfy the criteria for the imposition of conditions contained in Circular 1/85 (*see* p 96 above). If the condition is not sufficiently precise for a person to be able to ascertain what he must do to comply with it, or it is unreasonable in accordance with *Wednesbury* principles, it can be challenged by judicial review.

It can also be challenged as a defence to proceedings in the magistrates' court. In the *R v Crown Court at Reading* case, the court was considering the validity of the Royal Air Force Greenham Common Byelaws 1985. It held that magistrates have always had jurisdiction to inquire into the validity of a byelaw, and they are not only entitled but bound to do so when the defendant relies on the validity of the byelaw as a defence. It was also held that it is not necessary or appropriate for proceedings to be adjourned so that the validity of the byelaw or decision can be determined by judicial review.

A condition will only be valid if the permission on which it is imposed has been implemented (*see* p 96 above).

The validity of a breach of condition notice

Where it is not clear on the available evidence that a condition has not been complied with and therefore that the alleged breach has actually occurred, the breach of condition notice may be invalid. It can be challenged by an application for judicial review in accordance with the usual principles. It can also be raised as a defence to proceedings in the magistrates' court in accordance with the decision in the *R v Crown Court at Reading* case.

The validity of the decision to prosecute

It appears that the validity of the decision to prosecute cannot be raised as a defence to proceedings in the magistrates court, it can only be challenged by way of judicial review. In *Waverley Borough Council v Hilden and Others* [1988] 1 All ER 807, the court held that the proper method for a defendant to challenge the decision of the LPA was by way of judicial review, not a substantive defence. To challenge such a decision was to assert that the action was commenced and is being prosecuted without proper authority and therefore could only be the subject of an application for judicial review.

A person may be prosecuted for an offence under s 187A(9) and raise any of the above defences. At the same time, an application can be made to the LPA, under s 73 'for the development of land without complying with conditions subject to which a previous planning permission was granted'. Such an application could be made on the ground that the relevant condition is invalid. In such circumstances, both the magistrates' court and the LPA would be exercising jurisdiction over the same matter at the same time.

It has been suggested that the magistrates may stay proceedings, or at least sentencing, until the outcome of the planning application is known. However, in *R v Beaconsfield Magistrates, ex parte South Buckinghamshire District Council* [1993] JPL B53, an application was made for judicial review of a decision of magistrates to adjourn two cases. Enforcement notices required the removal of caravans from land and the LPA prosecuted for breach of these notices. The defendants were awaiting the outcome of applications for planning permission. The High Court held that, as a general rule, the magistrates must deal with the matter forthwith, unless the outcome of the planning application will be known shortly. In this particular case, the application failed because of unusual circumstances, including a very substantial period of inaction by the LPA.

If the magistrates were unable to deal with the matter until the planning application was determined, the unauthorised use could continue throughout protracted litigation, as in *R v Kuxhaus* [1988] QB 631 (*see* Chapter 9, p 109). There is no provision relating to the effect of a breach of condition notice similar to that in s 289(4A) which allows the High Court or Court of Appeal to order that an enforcement notice shall have effect pending the final determination of proceedings challenging a decision to refuse planning permission (*see* Chapter 11, p 157).

These challenges to the validity of a breach of condition notice 'may result in protracted litigation which will negate the primary purpose of this new procedure to provide a swift and simple means of ensuring that planning permissions and limitations are complied with' (para 20 of Annex 2 to Circular 17/92). In cases where a breach of condition is not clear cut, and there may be scope for argument, Circular 17/92 suggests that the issue of an enforcement notice may be more appropriate than the use of a breach of condition notice.

8 Effect of the grant of planning permission

The grant of planning permission under s 73 for the development of land without compliance with a condition would render a breach of condition notice ineffective, to the extent that the requirements of the notice are inconsistent with the terms of the planning permission (s 180(1)). This also applies if any of the conditions are discharged. However, the grant of a planning permission shall not affect the liability of any person for an offence for failure to comply with the breach of condition notice prior to the date when planning permission is granted (s 180(3)).

Where magistrates convict for an offence under s 187A(9) and impose a daily fine, if planning permission for the development of land without complying with a condition was subsequently granted, the fine would be payable up to the day such permission was granted.

9 Registration

LPAs are under a statutory duty pursuant to s 188(1) to keep a register containing prescribed information about a breach of condition notice (together with information about enforcement and stop notices). Each register is to be available for inspection by the public at all reasonable hours. This operates in parallel to the requirement for LPAs to maintain a planning register containing a record of all planning applications and decisions. The planning register and the register of enforcement and stop notices are separate, but are maintained by the same authority which is the local planning register authority. This is defined in art 27 of the 1988 GDO as the local planning authority in the London Boroughs and metropolitan counties, the county planning authority for land in a National Park and the district planning authority in the shire counties (*see* Chapter 4).

The information required to be kept in the register is prescribed by art 28 of the 1988 GDO. For every breach of condition notice served the register must contain:

    (a) the address of the land to which the notice relates, or a plan by reference to which its situation can be ascertained;

    (b) the name of the serving authority;

    (c) the date of service of the notice;

    (d) details of the relevant planning permission sufficient to enable it to be identified; and

    (e) a statement or summary of the condition which has not been complied with and the requirements of the notice, including the period allowed for compliance.

All entries relating to a breach of condition notice shall be removed from the register if the notice is quashed by a court.

Article 28 of the 1988 GDO makes it a requirement that where a county planning authority serve a breach of condition notice they must supply the prescribed information about the notice to the LPA in whose area the land to which the notice relates is situated and to inform that authority if the breach of condition notice is withdrawn or quashed.

10 Withdrawal of the notice

The LPA may, by notice served on the person responsible, withdraw a breach of condition notice (s 187A(6)). This does not affect their power to serve a further notice for the conditions specified in the earlier notice or any other conditions. However, for a further breach of condition notice to be served, the criteria set out above must still be met and, in particular, the breach must not be immune from enforcement action as a result of the passage of time between the occurrence of the breach and the service of the further enforcement notice.

Paragraph 15 of Annex 2 to Circular 17/92 makes it clear that withdrawal can take place at any time, including after expiry of the compliance period. If the breach of condition notice is withdrawn, the information in the register of enforcement and stop notices relating to the breach of condition notice must be removed (art 28 of the 1988 GDO).

11 Contravention and prosecution

Introduction

If, at any time after the expiry of the compliance period specified in the breach of condition notice, any of the conditions specified in the notice are not complied with and the steps specified in the notice have not been taken or, the activities specified in the notice have not ceased, the person responsible is in breach of the notice (s 187A(8)). Both elements of non-compliance with the condition and failure to take the steps specified or to cease the activities specified are required for a breach to have occurred. Therefore, if the person responsible complies with the condition specified by taking steps other than those specified in the notice, no breach will have occurred. This approach means that the LPA do not need to be exhaustive in specifying the steps to be taken to ensure compliance with the specified condition.

The offence

Where the person responsible is in breach of the notice, he is guilty of an offence (s 187A(9)). Once an offence has occurred, the LPA can take proceedings against the person responsible in the magistrates' court. The maximum penalty on summary conviction is a fine not exceeding 'level 3' on the standard scale (currently £1,000).

Paragraph 17 of Annex 2 to Circular 17/92 advises that an information should be laid as soon as possible for summary proceedings relating to a breach of condition notice, as the six-month limitation period contained in the Magistrates' Courts Act 1980, s 127(1) applies. This period runs on a continuing basis, and only so much of the offence as falls within the six-month period can be charged. For example, if the breach of the notice continued for three months and an information was laid four months after the last date on which that breach occurred, only the last two months of the breach will fall within the limitation period and thus be chargeable.

An offence may be charged by reference to any day or longer period of time and a person may be convicted of a second or subsequent offence (s 187A(10)). Therefore, where the person responsible has already been convicted and fined, but persistently fails to comply with the notice, a further prosecution can be brought by the LPA.

The offence under s 187A(9) is a criminal offence and therefore the criminal standard of proof applies. The prosecution must prove its case *beyond reasonable doubt*. This burden of proof applies to showing that the defendant is the person responsible, and that he is in breach of the requirements of the notice. It must be shown that the defendant is the person on whom the notice was served and that he is the correct person to be served, ie, he is carrying out or has carried out the development, or has caused or permitted another to do so, or he is the person in control of the land to which the notice relates (*see* p 97 above).

To show that the defendant is in breach of the requirements of the notice, both elements of non-compliance with the condition and failure to take the required steps, as set out in s 187A(8) must be proved beyond reasonable doubt. When this is so proved, the provisions of s 187A(9) will be satisfied. It is not necessary for the prosecution to prove beyond reasonable doubt that the specified condition, or the notice itself is valid (*DPP v Bugg* (1987) *The Independent*, 14 January). However, the defendant may raise the question of validity in his defence.

Statutory defences

There are two statutory defences for a person charged with an offence under s 187A(9). If the defendant can prove that he took all reasonable measures to secure compliance with the conditions specified in the notice; or, where the notice was served on him as the person having control of the land, he can prove that he no longer had control of the land, then he will be acquitted (s 187A(11)).

The first defence requires the defendant to prove that he took all reasonable measures to secure compliance with the conditions specified in the notice. This is a wide ranging defence and envisages a situation where a person took steps other than those specified in the notice, and that these were sufficient to secure compliance with the specified conditions. This defence is also available to a defendant who has no power to take the steps specified in the notice, and he can show that it would require more than reasonable measures to require him to do so.

The second statutory defence applies in a situation where a defendant can prove that he no longer had control of the land at the date when the offence is alleged to have taken place. If the defendant did have control of the land at one time, and subsequently sold it, but the breach occurred before the sale was completed, then he could be convicted for the period during which he controlled the land and the breach occurred, but not for the period after he sold the land, even if the breach continued. In those circumstances, the LPA would only be able to prosecute the subsequent owner for breach of condition as he would then be the person able to secure compliance with the condition as required by the breach of condition notice, and would be the person responsible for the purposes of the offence under s 187A(9). In such circumstances, the subsequent owner must have been served with a breach of condition notice relating to the relevant period.

The effectiveness of summary proceedings will depend upon the attitude of the courts. LPAs may discover that they successfully prosecute for a breach of the requirements of a breach of condition notice, only to find that the court imposes a derisory fine. However, as suggested in para 6 of Annex 2 to Circular 17/92, the salutary experience of summary prosecution itself (or the threat of prosecution) may provide sufficient remedy to ensure compliance with a condition.

12 LPAs checklist for serving breach of condition notice

Preliminary

(1) Investigate any complaint made or any breach of condition of which an officer is aware.
(2) If additional information is required, serve a planning contravention notice.
(3) Consider whether:
  (a) planning permission granted subject to condition;
  (b) there has been non-compliance with the condition;
  (c) the condition is valid and enforceable;
  (d) the planning permission has been implemented;
  (e) any immunity period applies.

Preparatory

(1) Identify the condition that has not been complied with.
(2) Assess the steps required and the period for compliance.
(3) Obtain authority for issuing a breach of condition notice by committee resolution or through delegation.
(4) Prepare authorised document containing:
  (a) the condition that is not complied with;
  (b) the planning permission to which it relates;
  (c) the required steps;

    (d) period for compliance;

    (e) area of land to which the notice relates; and

    (f) warning statement that there is no right of appeal.

(4) Draw up a plan and prepare brief written description of the land to which the notice relates.

(5) Identify the parties to be served.

Taking enforcement action

(1) Serve on all parties to be served:

    (a) breach of condition notice; and

    (b) plan of land to which it relates.

(2) Enter details in the planning enforcement register as soon as practicable after issue.

Chapter 9

Appeal to the Secretary of State

1 Introduction

It is an established tenet of the enforcement of planning control that the validity of an enforcement notice can only be challenged by way of an appeal to the Secretary of State on prescribed grounds. It shall not otherwise be questioned in any legal proceedings whatsoever, except in certain limited circumstances (s 285). What these circumstances are, and how such a challenge may be made, is dealt with in more detail in Chapter 11. This chapter deals with the means of challenging the validity of an enforcement notice by way of an appeal to the Secretary of State under the TCPA 1990, Part VII.

2 The right of appeal

Introduction

The right of appeal against an enforcement notice is a statutory right. A person having an interest in the land to which an enforcement notice relates, or a relevant occupier may appeal to the Secretary of State against the notice. It does not matter if a copy of the notice has not been served on him, as long as he has an interest in the land or is a relevant occupier (s 174(1)). Circular 21/91 indicates that the owner, tenant, lessee or mortgagee of the land to which the enforcement notice relates, all of whom hold a legal or equitable interest in the land, would have the right to appeal against the validity of the enforcement notice.

Person having an interest in the land

Whether a person has an interest in the land or not is usually a matter of fact for the Secretary of State to determine on deciding whether or not he has jurisdiction to accept the appeal. In the case of *R v Secretary of State for the Environment and another, ex parte Davis* [1989] 3 PLR 73, it was held that one year's adverse possession of land was not sufficient to create a legal or equitable interest for the purposes of the right to appeal. In other words, a trespasser has no right of appeal. However, the LPA have the power to serve an enforcement notice on the occupier of land. This would include a trespasser. It follows that the LPA could then prosecute such a person for breach of the enforcement notice. Although, if that person had no right to be there in the first place, a prosecution may well be justifiable.

In the *Davis* case the court pointed out that it is always open to a trespasser, such as a gypsy, to seek judicial review by arguing that it was unreasonable on the part of a local authority to have issued an enforcement notice in such circumstances (*Wednesbury* case). Such a person could always make an application for planning permission for the alleged breach, and in the event that such permission were refused, appeal to the Secretary of State. If planning permission was subsequently granted for the matters to which the enforcement notice related, the requirements of the enforcement notice would cease to have effect (s 180) and the LPA would be unable to prosecute for breach.

Relevant occupier

The 'relevant occupier' for the purposes of the right to appeal is defined in s 174(6). The term means any person who occupies the land to which the enforcement notice relates on the date on which the notice is issued, by virtue of any licence, either written or oral, and continues to occupy the land when the appeal is brought. This means any person who occupies the land to which the notice relates with the owner's written or oral consent, and therefore encompasses all types of licensee. It does not however include a trespasser (*see* the *Davis* case above).

3 The effect of an appeal

Final determination or withdrawal

Where an appeal is made to the Secretary of State against an enforcement notice, s 175(4) provides that the notice shall have no effect pending the final determination or the withdrawal of the appeal. The period stated in the enforcement notice for compliance with the requirements of the notice does not run if an appeal is made. Therefore, the alleged breach of planning control can continue until the final determination or the withdrawal of the appeal.

What constitutes the final determination of the enforcement appeal process was considered by the court in *R v Kuxhaus et al* [1988] JPL 545. As explained in Chapter 11, there is a right of appeal to the courts against the Secretary of State's decision on an appeal against an enforcement notice (s 289). Where this is exercised, it may remain undetermined for a considerable length of time (in the case of *Kuxhaus*, it approached six years).

It is likely that this situation will be avoided in the future as s 289(4A) now provides that the High Court, or as the case may be, the Court of Appeal may, on such terms as the court thinks fit, order that the enforcement notice shall have effect, or have effect to such extent as may be specified in the order, pending the final determination of the appeal process (*see* Chapter 11). This can effectively negate any benefit derived in terms of 'buying time' by appealing to the High Court. A court order may include terms requiring the LPA to give an undertaking as to damages or any other matter, to protect the appellant in the event that an appeal is ultimately successful.

Another means of preventing appeals without any merit from being brought merely to suspend the effect of the enforcement notice, was introduced by the Planning and Compensation Act 1991. Under s 289(6), leave of the court is required for proceedings to be brought against the Secretary of State's decision on an appeal against an enforcement notice (*see* Chapter 11). At that stage the court may decide to grant leave, but make an order under s 289(4A) that the enforcement notice shall still have effect.

It appears that the 'final determination of an appeal' occurs in the following circumstances:

(1) The date of the Secretary of State's decision on an enforcement appeal, plus 28 days, if no appeal is made to the High Court. An application for leave to appeal to the High Court must be made within 28 days of the decision (RSC Ord 94, r 12, *see* Chapter 11).

(2) Where an appeal is made to the High Court, and the enforcement notice is remitted to the Secretary of State for redetermination, the date of the Secretary of State's decision on the redetermination of the appeal, plus 28 days, if no fresh appeal is made to the High Court.

(3) Where an appeal is made to the High Court, the appeal is dismissed, and then no appeal is made to the Court of Appeal within four weeks (RSC Ord 59, r 4) or such longer time as the court may allow (RSC Ord 3, r 5), the date of the dismissal, plus four weeks.

(4) If a further appeal is made to the Court of Appeal or the House of Lords, the same as in (2) and (3) above, with reference to the relevant higher court.

(5) By virtue of s 289(4A) the court may give the enforcement notice interim effect by making an order on that basis as detailed above.

The compliance period

When an appeal is made to the Secretary of State, the compliance period specified in the enforcement notice will not take effect. However, if the enforcement notice is ultimately upheld, the compliance period will commence from the date of such decision. It was held in the *Kuxhaus* case that the compliance period specified in the enforcement notice would run concurrently with the time allowed to make an appeal to the courts, subject to the effect of the notice being suspended if such an appeal was made, or leave to appeal was obtained.

4 Making an appeal

Notice of appeal

Any person with a right to appeal may do so to the Secretary of State. Section

174(3) specifies that an appeal shall be made, either by giving written notice of the appeal to the Secretary of State before the date specified in the enforcement notice as the date on which it is to take effect; or by sending such notice to him in a properly addressed and pre-paid letter posted to him at such time that, in the ordinary course of the post, it would be delivered to him before that date.

An appeal must be made in writing. There is no specified form to be completed, but the DoE have issued a standard form of appeal which is recommended and can be obtained from any of the regional offices of the DoE (Ref No DoE 14069 (Revised 07/93)). It will be accompanied by an explanatory booklet 'Enforcement Notice Appeals—A guide to procedure', which gives advice about making an appeal.

Information provided by appellant

The DoE form requires information about:
 (a) the appellant;
 (b) any agent or professional representative;
 (c) the date of the enforcement notice;
 (d) the name of the issuing authority; and
 (e) a description of the land to which the enforcement notice relates.

A copy of the relevant enforcement notice should be attached to the form. The form provides for the appellant to specify which of the grounds in s 174(2) he is pleading, and to provide a statement of facts in support of each ground of appeal.

The statutory grounds of appeal are set out in s 174(2) and are dealt with in detail below. Although the appellant is required to specify which of the grounds of appeal he is pleading, an appeal can validly be made without any grounds being lodged. The Town and Country Planning (Enforcement Notices and Appeals) Regulations 1991 (SI No 2804), reg 5 gives the Secretary of State power to send a notice to the appellant requiring him to deliver a statement in writing specifying the grounds on which he is appealing against the notice, and stating briefly the facts upon which he proposes to rely in support of each of those grounds. Such a statement must be delivered to the Secretary of State not later than 14 days from the date of the notice sent by the Secretary of State.

The appellant's statement in support of the grounds of appeal must be submitted to the Secretary of State, either when giving the notice of appeal, or within the period required by the Secretary of State under reg 5 (s 174(4)). The Secretary of State may summarily dismiss an appeal if such a statement is not made within the prescribed time (s 176(3)), without giving either the appellant or the LPA an opportunity of being heard, unless the appellant can show genuine extenuating circumstances which prevent him from providing the required information.

When preparing the statement of facts in support of each ground of appeal, the appellant should seek to express the facts accurately and concisely as they will form the basis of the appeal, and can be developed at a later stage. Each ground of appeal should be dealt with separately. To make the statement of facts clear, the appellant should express the ground of appeal (ground (a), ground (c), etc) as a sub-heading and detail the facts relevant to that particular ground in paragraphs below that sub-heading.

The supporting facts must be made in relation to each ground of appeal. The Secretary of State has power to determine an appeal on the grounds pleaded, which are supported by fact, without considering any ground in relation to which the appellant has failed to give a statement of fact in support, either when giving the notice of appeal, or within the period of time prescribed by the Secretary of State (s 174(5)). A note on the DoE form brings these matters to the attention of the appellant by advising that failure to provide facts in support of each ground of appeal may result in the dismissal of the appeal or the refusal to consider a ground of appeal with supporting facts.

As an appeal against an enforcement notice constitutes a deemed application for planning permission (see p 115 below), the appellant should include any points he wishes the Secretary of State to take into account concerning the planning merits of the appeal. These should include details of any previous relevant application for planning permission affecting the site concerned and any correspondence relating to the matter at issue. As the Secretary of State can determine any purpose for which the land may lawfully be used (s 177(1)(c)), if the appellant wishes to have such a determination made, he should make it clear when presenting his case on appeal, and provide any relevant information.

Circular 21/91 advises that intending appellants should consider the LPA's statement of reasons for issuing the enforcement notice and address their arguments to that statement and the alleged breach of planning control. The minutes of the relevant committee meeting are a public document, as is the planning or enforcement officer's report to committee. These should be obtained by the appellant, and the rationale behind the actions of the LPA examined and, where possible, addressed by the appellant in the statement of facts. It should be borne in mind that the statement given in the appeal form is a statement of *fact* not opinion. Matters of opinion can be expressed at a later date for consideration by the Secretary of State.

In circumstances where it becomes apparent that the LPA are prepared to grant conditional planning permission for the alleged breach of planning control, Circular 21/91 advises that an appellant should consider whether, instead of appealing, it would be preferable to make the appropriate planning application, and that this should be discussed urgently with the LPA, who may then be prepared to withdraw the enforcement notice.

The DoE will acknowledge receipt of the appeal and inform the appellant who is the case officer dealing with the appeal and how to contact that person. All further dealings on the appeal should then be through the case officer, not the local authority concerned. The DoE will correspond with the local authority and supply them with all relevant correspondence. However, it is courteous for the appellant to provide the relevant local authority with a copy of the appeal to the Secretary of State so that they are aware that there is an appeal against the enforcement notice they issued for the land.

Timing of the appeal

An appeal must be lodged before the date specified in the enforcement notice as the date on which it is to take effect. Whereas the requirement to specify the grounds of appeal and to state the facts upon which the appellant is relying in support of those grounds is directory, the requirements for the notice of appeal to be in writing and to be delivered within a specified time limit are mandatory (*Howard v Secretary of State for the Environment* [1973] 1 QB 235). The time limit for making an appeal is absolute. The Secretary of State has no discretion to vary it.

The explanatory booklet emphasises the strict time limits and advises the appellant not to wait until the end of the appeal period before submitting an appeal. The appeal form issued by the DoE contains the warning that:

> The appeal must arrive (*or be posted in time to arrive in the normal course of post*) in the Department not later than the day before the date, stated by the Council, for the enforcement notice to take effect. If the notice takes effect on a Saturday, this will be the preceding Friday or the preceding Thursday if the Friday is a Public Holiday. If the notice takes effect on a Sunday, Monday or Public Holiday, this will be the last working day before the Holiday or the last day on which post is delivered before the Sunday or Holiday.

If an appeal is lodged after the date on which the enforcement notice is to take effect, the Secretary of State will not have jurisdiction to hear it and the right to appeal will be lost. This was clearly demonstrated in the case of *R v Secretary of State for the Environment and Bromley LBC, ex parte Jackson* [1987] JPL 790. In that case the appeal documents were duly posted, but never arrived and were presumed lost in the post. The court held that an appeal was made only when the Secretary of State received the notice of appeal and not when it was posted. The appellant was out of time for her appeal and the enforcement notice remained effective.

In addition, documents must arrive *before* the enforcement notice becomes effective. Where appeal documents arrive on the same day as the notice becomes effective, the appeal will be invalid (*R v Secretary of State for the Environment, ex parte JBI Financial Consultants* [1989] JPL 365).

Means of lodging an appeal

Section 174(3)(*b*) provides that an appeal correctly addressed, stamped and posted would be presumed to be delivered within the ordinary course of post. To ensure that there is no risk of the appeal documents failing to be delivered within the specified time period, the appellant should use registered letter post or recorded delivery. This will provide added certainty and proof of delivery. Under the Interpretation Act 1978, s 7 delivery is deemed to be effected at the time at which the letter would be delivered in the ordinary course of the post, although it does not specifically require the posting to be registered by recorded delivery.

Interestingly, in the *JBI Financial Consultants* case, the court held that the presence of a letter box at the DoE was a holding out that documents put through the letter box would be treated as having been received inside, and therefore delivery in a letter box on a Sunday would be effective, as long as it was within the specified period. However, the use of a fax to lodge an appeal would not work, because the fax machine is not presented as being there to receive appeals. Although in the subsequent case of *Barraclough v Secretary of State for the Environment and Leeds City Council* [1989] JPL 911, the LPA's statement of submission, which they proposed to put forward on the appeal, was served by fax. The court accepted that this constituted proper service, although in that case, the statement was served one day late.

Information provided by LPA

Once the LPA are notified by the DoE that an appeal has been lodged, the Secretary of State may require the LPA to send to him within 14 days a copy of the enforcement notice and a list of the names and addresses of the persons on whom a copy of the notice was served (Town and Country Planning (Enforcement Notices and Appeals) Regulations 1991 (SI No 2804), reg 6).

The Secretary of State may also ask the LPA to send a copy of the statement of reasons why they considered it expedient to issue the notice. Where a plan was attached to the enforcement notice, a true copy of the plan, endorsed to that effect and coloured, if the original plan was coloured, should also be sent to the Secretary of State if requested.

The LPA may receive a questionnaire from the DoE seeking further details on the matters to which the enforcement notice relates. A separate questionnaire should be completed for each enforcement notice appealed against and copies sent to the appellant. The details required may include:

(a) whether the LPA wish to appear before and be heard by an inspector;
(b) the site area, where the notice relates to building, engineering or mining operations, and the floor space created by the development;
(c) any planning permission previously granted and any relevant plans and correspondence;
(d) whether any building to which the enforcement notice relates is used for agricultural purposes;
(e) whether the enforcement notice relates to a single private dwelling;
(f) whether the appeal site is within 67 metres of a trunk road, or is Crown land, or is situated within a conservation area;
(g) whether there are currently any related appeals under s 78, either in relation to the site, or the application of policy;
(h) any relevant direction made by the LPA.

The LPA must serve on both the Secretary of State and the appellant a statement of the submissions which they propose to put forward on the appeal, including a summary of the authority's response to each ground of appeal and a statement as to whether the authority would be prepared to grant planning permission for the matters alleged in the enforcement notice to constitute the breach of planning control and, if so, particulars of any conditions which they would wish to impose on such permission (Enforcement Notices and Appeals Regulations, reg 7(1)).

There are specified time limits for the service of the LPA's statement which are detailed below. If the LPA fail to comply with the requirements of reg 7, the Secretary of State has the discretion to allow the appeal and to quash the enforcement notice (s 176(3)(b)). Paragraph 32 of Annex 2 to Circular 21/91 states that 'It should be exceptional to quash a enforcement notice in these circumstances because the time limits provide ample opportunity for an LPA's statement to be served'. Where an enforcement notice is quashed in such circumstances, this has no effect on the LPA's powers to issue another notice.

The LPA must serve on the appellant a list of documents upon which they may rely and make them available for inspection. Where they propose to rely on a view or opinion of a government department or other local authority, a statement to that effect with a copy of that view or opinion must also be served.

5 Grounds of appeal

Introduction

An appeal to the Secretary of State against an enforcement notice can only be brought on certain specific grounds (s 174(2)). An appeal can be made on any of the seven grounds of appeal specified. The burden of proof in appeals against enforcement notices rests on the appellant.

Whether or not the appellant seeks planning permission for the alleged breach of planning control under ground (a) (*see* below), an enforcement notice appeal is deemed to include an application for planning permission for those matters stated in the enforcement notice as constituting a breach of planning control (s 177(5)). A fee must be paid for the deemed application for planning permission (*see* p126 below). Subject to that requirement, the Secretary of State will, in determining the appeal, consider the planning merits of those matters which constitute the breach of planning control alleged.

Other than the deemed application for planning permission, the Secretary of State's jurisdiction on the appeal is restricted to the grounds made. However, it is possible to add or delete grounds of appeal as the procedure progresses, as the true facts may not emerge until the appeal is being determined (*Howard v Secretary of State for the Environment* [1973] 1 QB 235).

The seven grounds of appeal set out in s 174(2) are set out below:

Ground (a)

that, in respect of any breach of planning control which may be constituted by the matters stated in the notice, planning permission ought to be granted or, as the case may be, the condition or limitation concerned ought to be discharged.

The matters stated in the notice are those which appear to the LPA to constitute the breach of planning control. They could relate to operational development, a material change of use, or breach of a condition or limitation subject to which planning permission was granted.

Where there is a deemed application for planning permission under s 177(5), or where the appellant has expressly brought the appeal on ground (a), the Secretary of State will consider the planning merits of the matters stated in the enforcement notice as constituting the breach of planning control, and will determine whether planning permission for those matters should be granted. To that extent, the determination of the Secretary of State is limited to the description of the breach of planning control given in the enforcement notice (*Richmond-upon-Thames London Borough Council v Secretary of State for the Environment* (1972) 224 EG 1555). This may cause difficulties where the description given in the enforcement notice is wrong. However, the Secretary of State has the power to correct such defects on appeal (s 176, *see* p 122) and any such correction would change the terms of the deemed planning application. It was also suggested in the case of *Brent LBC v Secretary of State for the Environment and Jain* [1994] JPL 154, that the imposition of conditions or limitations on the grant of a planning permission would achieve the same result.

In exercising jurisdiction under s 177(5), the Secretary of State shall determine the matter in accordance with the development plan, unless material considerations indicate otherwise (s 54A) and in accordance with the guidance contained in PPG 1—'General Policy and Principles', and other relevant Planning Policy Guidance Notes.

The determination of this ground of appeal or the deemed application for planning permission will proceed on the basis that the Secretary of State is determining an ordinary planning appeal, and s 177(2) provides that the Secretary of State shall have regard to the provisions of the development plan, so far as it is material to the subject matter of the enforcement notice and to any other material considerations.

Where there are multiple enforcement notices relating to the same area of land the Secretary of State is under a duty to consider whether or not planning permission should be granted for those matters to which each notice relates. In *Reed v Secretary of State for the Environment and Tandridge District Council* [1993] JPL 249, ten enforcement notices were served, one related to the whole site, the remaining nine to individual units within the whole. The court held that each individual unit should be considered on its own planning merits and permission could not be refused for a unit by virtue of uses on other units. In addition, where the LPA has not divided up a site and served separate notices, regard should be had to whether there is in fact more than one planning unit, and if so, separate consideration should be given to each unit.

Where planning permission is granted on an enforcement appeal for operational development or a material change of use, or a condition or limitation is discharged, the enforcement notice shall cease to have effect, so far as it is inconsistent with that decision (s 180). Therefore, if the appeal on ground (a) is wholly or partly successful, the Secretary of State will quash the enforcement notice to the extent that the matters stated in the enforcement notice are now permitted.

Ground (b)

> that those matters have not occurred

Again this refers to those matters stated in the enforcement notice, which appear to the LPA to constitute the breach of planning control. It is a question of fact as to whether or not those matters have actually occurred. The Secretary of State will be asked to consider evidence as to the factual situation and if those matters have not occurred, will have no choice but to quash the enforcement notice. The onus on proving the factual situation lies with the appellant.

Ground (c)

> that those matters (if they occurred) do not constitute a breach of planning control

An appeal brought under ground (c) relates to whether or not the matters alleged to constitute the breach of planning control required planning permission. If, for example, the appellant can rely upon permitted development rights under the GDO, or changes of use within the same use class, or in accordance with the provisions of the GDO, then he may be able to show that the matters do not constitute a breach of planning control.

Such a situation may arise, for example, where a swimming pool is erected within the curtilage of a dwellinghouse, and the appellant can show that it is required for a purpose incidental to the enjoyment of the dwellinghouse, and not for any commercial purpose (Sched 2, Part 1, Class E of the 1988 GDO). Alternatively, the appellant may be able to show that matters alleged to constitute the breach of planning control comprise a general industrial use of the land within Class B2 of the Use Classes Order and falls within the same use class as a previous lawful use.

This ground of appeal can also be pleaded if an enforcement notice alleges a breach of planning control as a result of non-compliance with an invalid planning condition. There is no requirement for such a condition to be declared invalid by the Secretary of State, or a court, before the appellant can raise this ground of appeal (*Elmbridge Borough Council v Secretary of State for the Environment and Hill Samuel & Co Ltd and Case Poclain Corporation Ltd.* [1989] JPL 277). If an appeal made under ground (c) is successful, the Secretary of State will quash the enforcement notice.

Ground (d)

> that, at the date when the notice was issued, no enforcement action could be taken in respect of any breach of planning control which may be constituted by those matters.

This ground of appeal requires the appellant to show that the enforcement action taken by the LPA was out of time and that the matters alleged to constitute the breach of planning control were immune from enforcement by virtue of the time limits imposed by s 171B (*see* Chapter 5). Again the Secretary of State has no choice but to quash the enforcement notice if this ground is successfully made out.

Ground (e)

> that copies of the enforcement notice were not served as required by section 172.

Improper service of the enforcement notice is a limited ground of appeal. Although a person has not been served with an enforcement notice, he has a right to appeal if he has an interest in the land to which the notice relates or is a relevant occupier of the land (s 174(1)). Neither he nor any other person can in any other proceedings complain of the failure to serve the appellant (s 175(5)).

Ground (f)

> that the steps required by the notice to be taken, or the activities required by the notice to cease, exceed what is necessary to remedy any breach of planning control which may be constituted by those matters or, as the case may be, to remedy any injury to amenity which has been caused by any such breach.

An enforcement notice must specify the steps which the authority require to be taken, or the activities which the authority require to cease (s 173(3)). This ground of appeal provides the appellant with a form of challenge to the requirements specified by the authority in the enforcement notice. It is not a challenge that goes to the validity of the notice. It is a question of whether the steps required to remedy the situation go beyond what is reasonable to rectify the planning consequences of the breach of planning control.

Where this ground of appeal is used, the Secretary of State must make a judgment based on the circumstances of the particular case. It should be borne in mind that the Secretary of State has power to vary the terms of the enforcement notice (s 176(1)(*b*), *see* p 122) and may deal with excessive or unreasonable requirements in such a manner (eg, planning appeal decision [1993] JPL 484 at 489). This is often pleaded as a makeweight to more substantive grounds of appeal.

Ground (g)

> that any period specified in the notice in accordance with section 173(9) falls short of what should reasonably be allowed.

This ground of appeal is similar to that in ground (f) in that it does not go to the validity of the notice. Again it is a question of judgment for the Secretary of State whether any time period specified in the notice is unreasonable, given the breach of planning control alleged, the planning consequences of the breach and the circumstances of the case (eg, Planning Appeal Decisions at [1993]

JPL 175 at 182 and 182 at 186). For example, in the case of small businesses, particular guidance is given to LPAs in PPG 18 on how to handle unauthorised development. It may be necessary to consider the constraints imposed upon such an organisation when determining the period for compliance, eg, the financial burden in relocation, in retracting the size of the business, and the effect upon employees. Again the Secretary of State has power to vary the enforcement notice in this respect to make the compliance period more reasonable (s 176(1)(*b*)) and, as a result, an appeal on this ground is of limited value, except possibly as a makeweight ground to other more substantive grounds of appeal.

6 Methods of appeal

Introduction

An enforcement notice appeal can be dealt with, either on the basis of written representations by the parties and an inspection of the site by an officer of the DoE, by an informal hearing, or by public local inquiry. The procedure for a public local inquiry is detailed in the following chapter.

The appellant may elect to have the appeal dealt with on the basis of written representations, and Form DoE 14069 provides for such election to be made. However, such an election may be amended by the DoE at the request of the LPA, or on their own initiative. The circumstances of the case and the extent of local controversy about the impact of the alleged development may lead the DoE to consider that the appeal ought to be heard in the public domain. Conversely, where the appellant or the LPA request a local inquiry, the DoE may suggest that the appeal is dealt with by the written representations procedure, or informal hearing, where they consider that the appeal is a suitable case. However, it is open to either party to insist upon being heard at a public local inquiry.

Other than appeals by statutory undertakers involving their operational land, all appeals made under s 174 have been prescribed for decision by an inspector under the Town and Country Planning (Determination of Appeals by Appointed Persons) (Prescribed Classes) Regulations 1981 (SI No 804). However, it is open to the Secretary of State to recover jurisdiction on an appeal at any stage, and the inspector can also ask him to do so.

Written representations

Where an appeal proceeds by way of written representations, the LPA must give notice of the appeal to occupiers of properties in the locality of the land to which the enforcement notice relates and to any other persons who, in the opinion of the LPA, are affected by the breach of planning control alleged in the enforcement notice (Town and Country Planning (Enforcement Notices and Appeals) Regulations 1991 (SI No 2804), reg 8). Failure to do so may lead to a judicial review of the decision on the appeal. The notice must include:

(a) a description of the alleged breach of control;
(b) a statement of reasons why the LPA considered it expedient to issue the enforcement notice;
(c) the grounds on which the appeal has been made; and
(d) a statement inviting interested persons to submit written representations to the LPA within a specified time limit.

Both the appellant and the LPA will have an opportunity to see and comment upon any such written representations submitted by a third party. These will not be taken into account on the determination of the appeal, unless both the appellant and the LPA have had an opportunity to comment on them.

The LPA are required to serve a statement of submissions which they propose to put forward on the appeal, together with a list of documents, as detailed above at p 115. The appellant will be given an opportunity to comment on this statement within a time period specified by the DoE (usually 14 days). The LPA will be provided with a copy of the appellant's comments and given time to respond further (again, usually 14 days).

For an appeal being dealt with by the written representations procedure, the statement must be served on both the Secretary of State and the appellant not later than 28 days from the date on which the Secretary of State sends the LPA a notice requesting it (Enforcement Notices and Appeals Regulations 1991, reg 7(2)). If the LPA fail to do so, the Secretary of State may allow the appeal and quash the enforcement notice (s 176(3)(b)).

The appeal is then determined on the basis of a consideration of all written statements made by the appellant, the LPA, and any interested third party, together with a site inspection. Such visits can be carried out by the planning inspector alone. Where it is necessary for the planning inspector to enter the site, he is usually accompanied by a representative of the appellant and the LPA, although, he cannot discuss the merits of the case or listen to arguments from any of the parties.

The formal written representation procedure contained in the Town and Country Planning (Appeals) (Written Representations Procedure) Regulations 1987 (SI No 701) does not apply to enforcement notice appeals, only to appeals under s 78.

Informal hearing

Both parties to an enforcement notice appeal have a right to appear before, and be heard by a person appointed by the Secretary of State. Whether or not an informal hearing is an appropriate way of dealing with an enforcement notice appeal will again depend upon the circumstances of the case and the extent of local controversy. Paragraph 25 of Annex 2 to Circular 21/91 suggests that 'Where the dispute is solely about the planning merits of the notice and the appeal, or the requirements of the notice or the period for compliance, and there has been a request to be heard, it may be appropriate to proceed by way of an informal hearing rather than a public inquiry'. It goes on to advise that where there is a dispute on evidential facts, or on one of the legal grounds of appeal, eg, under grounds (d) or (e) of s 174(2), then an informal hearing would be inappropriate.

As with an appeal proceeding by way of written representations, where there is an informal hearing, the LPA must give notice of the appeal to occupiers of properties in the locality of the land to which the enforcement notice relates, and to any other persons affected. The content of the notice is the same as that detailed on p 120.

As the name suggests, an informal hearing allows the inspector to lead a general discussion about the matters raised by the enforcement notice and the appeal. Both the appellant and the LPA must agree to an informal hearing. When agreement has been reached, the DoE will send out a letter to the parties to confirm that a hearing will be held. The date of this letter will be the 'relevant date' for the purposes of the procedure relating to an informal hearing.

The DoE have published a Code of Practice for hearings for enforcement appeals, dated March 1993. There is no statutory procedure for informal hearings, but both parties to an appeal will be expected to comply with the 'spirit' of the Town and Country Planning (Enforcement) (Inquiries Procedure) Rules 1992 (SI No 1903) (see Chapter 10), although, there is no right to cross-examine witnesses at an informal hearing. To reflect the 1992 Rules, the LPA must serve their statement not later than eight weeks after the 'relevant date', and the appellant must make a statement of the case that he intends to present at the hearing, not later than ten weeks after the 'relevant date'.

Other points that arise from the Code of Practice are as follows:

(1) The importance of observing the requirements relating to the exchange of statements is critical, as the inspector must be fully aware of the issues involved and the arguments likely to be made at the hearing, to be able to lead the discussion.

(2) If the inspector cannot be provided with the necessary information in sufficient time before the hearing, it may be necessary to delay or defer it, or to revert to the formal public inquiry procedure.

(3) The inspector will conduct the hearing. He will outline what he considers to be the main issues and indicate those matters on which further information is required. The parties may also refer to other aspects which they consider to be relevant. The appellant will start the discussion. The parties will be encouraged to ask questions informally throughout the proceedings, subject only to the discussion being conducted in an orderly manner. The appellant will be given the opportunity to make any final comments.

(4) If at any time during the hearing it becomes apparent that the informal procedure is inappropriate and cannot satisfactorily be continued, the inspector will close the proceedings and a formal local inquiry will be arranged in the normal way.

The inspector is entitled to adjourn the hearing to the site, if it appears to him that certain matters could more easily be resolved there. The Code of Practice states that such discretion would only be exercised where the inspector is satisfied that:

(a) the discussion could proceed satisfactorily and that no one involved would be at a disadvantage;

(b) all parties involved in the hearing had the opportunity to attend; and

(c) nobody participating in the hearing objected to discussion being continued on the site.

An appellant will often appear in person, or be represented by an agent or planning consultant, rather than having legal representation. This results in a more relaxed and less formal atmosphere than a public local inquiry. Informal hearings also have the benefit of being cheaper than a public local inquiry and a decision can often be achieved more quickly, in some cases at the close of the hearing itself. The Code of Practice indicates that, in general, decision letters are issued within seven weeks of the date of the hearing.

Public inquiry

Recent statistics show that the number of public local inquiries being held to determine enforcement notice appeals is a rising proportion of all public local inquiries dealing with planning matters. This is a reflection, not only of more active enforcement action by LPAs, but also of the extent of public interest in such matters. It is also a side effect of a reducing number of appeals against the refusal of planning permission, which reflects the recent economic environment in property development.

It is usual that, where either of the parties elect to have the matter heard, evidence will be taken and submissions on the appeal heard at a public local inquiry. Paragraph 25 of Annex 2 to Circular 21/91 advises that an inquiry is usually essential where the grounds of appeal raise issues involving disputes about relevant facts between the LPA and the appellant, eg, under grounds (c) and (d) of s 174(2). In these circumstances, the Town and Country Planning (Enforcement) (Inquiries Procedure) Rules 1992 (SI No 1903) will apply. The procedures relating to an enforcement notice appeal proceeding by way of public inquiry are detailed in Chapter 10.

7 Powers of the Secretary of State on Appeal

Power to vary or correct the enforcement notice

The Secretary of State is given specific powers under s 176 to correct any defect, error or misdescription in the enforcement notice, or to vary the terms of the notice, if he is satisfied that the correction or variation will not cause injustice to the appellant or to the LPA.

The power vested in the Secretary of State to correct or vary an enforcement notice means that it is not fatal if the LPA make an error in drafting or law when preparing enforcement notices. The Secretary of State's power to amend extends into a wide range of matters, but LPAs should be wary of making an error which results in the notice becoming a nullity, as the Secretary of

State's powers to amend do not extend to notices that have no legal effect (*see* Chapter 6, p 71).

It is open to the Secretary of State, on appeal, to invite representations from the parties as to an appropriate correction or variation, particularly where it transpires during the appeal procedure that the enforcement notice contains a defect, error or misdescription. For example, where the alleged breach of planning control does effectively draw the attention of the recipient of the notice to the unauthorised development on the site, notwithstanding the fact that it contains a defect, then it is not incurable (planning appeals decision at [1994] JPL 290).

(1) Distinction between correction and variation

The wording of s 176(1) indicates that a defect, error or misdescription can be corrected, whereas the terms of an enforcement notice can be varied. It is often considered that, because of the wording of s 176, the power to correct enforcement notices is to be used where the LPA have made mistakes in drafting the notice, eg, where the body of the notice alleges a material change of use, while the schedule alleges a breach of condition (*Epping Forest DC v Matthews* [1987] JPL 132) and the power of variation relates to differences between the LPA and the Secretary of State on policy or in the judgment of what constitutes a breach of planning control.

However, the distinction is not critical. There is no need to determine whether the enforcement notice requires a correction or a variation, as the qualifying criteria for injustice is the same for both. In practice, as long as there will be no injustice to the appellant or to the LPA, the Secretary of State can exercise his powers under s 176, regardless of any distinction. However, the most fundamental alteration is a variation, which is a wider term than correction (*Harrogate Borough Council v Secretary of State for the Environment and Procter* [1987] JPL 288).

(2) Description of the breach of planning control

The power to vary or correct the notice is particularly useful where the description of the breach of planning control alleged in the enforcement notice is wrong. The Secretary of State's power to grant planning permission for the matters which constitute the breach, either under ground (a) of s 174(2), or by the deemed planning application under s 177(5), is limited to the description contained in the enforcement notice (*see* p 116 above). In circumstances where there is a misdescription in the notice, he can correct it and then consider whether planning permission should be granted for the corrected description of development.

(3) Injustice caused by the variation or correction

The Secretary of State must determine how the respective interests of the parties will be affected and if the suggested variation or correction will cause injustice to the appellant or to the LPA. Factors that he is likely to consider include the:

    (a) different time limits for enforcement action that apply to operational development, material changes of use, breach of condition and other breaches of planning control (*see* Chapter 5);

    (b) reasons given by the LPA in the enforcement notice for taking enforcement action, as these may not apply to the proposed amended terms of the notice; and

    (c) guidance in PPG 18 on the general approach to enforcement, which may indicate that an amendment would cause an injustice.

The variation or correction of an enforcement notice may be made in favour of the LPA to ensure that the alleged breach of planning control, or the requirements specified in the notice, are expressed properly. The notice (corrected and varied to reflect the true situation) may then be upheld and any appeal against it dismissed. However, if this would cause injustice to the appellant, such correction or variation cannot be made (s 176(1)) and the notice will be void.

Where the LPA allege a breach of planning control which involves a material change of use and it subsequently becomes clear that the breach is one of operational development, the courts have held that an amendment is usually likely to cause an injustice to the appellant, as the issues which arise in each case can be quite different and the time limits for taking enforcement action relating to each type of development are different (*Wealden District Council v Secretary of State for the Environment and Innocent* [1983] JPL 234).

The variation or correction of an enforcement notice may be made in favour of the appellant eg, the deletion of a requirement contained in an enforcement notice to remove works which converted a dwellinghouse into bedsit and flat units (*Hereford City Council v Secretary of State for the Environment and Davies* [1993] JPL B71, where that part of the enforcement notice relating to the change of use of a dwellinghouse was upheld). Where such a variation or correction in favour of the appellant would cause injustice to the LPA eg, rendering the enforcement action taken out of time, the notice cannot be so varied or corrected and will be void.

(4) Limitations on the power

Although the Secretary of State has wide powers to correct or vary an enforcement notice, the exercise of such powers is not unlimited.

(a) Fundamental alteration

The Secretary of State cannot amend something that 'goes to the substance of the matter', ie an amendment that involves a fundamental alteration of the enforcement notice. (*Miller-Mead v Minister of Housing and Local Government* [1963] 2 QB 196). In those circumstances, he must quash the enforcement notice.

Whether or not the defect, error or misdescription in the enforcement notice is fundamental is a question of judgment for the Secretary of State or the courts. Recently, the courts have begun to state that even fundamental errors could be saved by rewriting the notice (*R v Tower Hamlets London Borough Council, ex parte PF Ahern (London) Ltd* [1989] JPL 757). However, in *Alistair Graham v Secretary of State and East Hampshire District Council* [1993] JPL 353, the court retained the concept of an error which was so fundamental that the notice could not be saved, even where no injustice would be caused.

(b) Enforcement notice with no legal effect

The Secretary of State cannot correct or vary a notice which is a nullity and therefore without legal effect (*see* Chapter 6). However, where the notice can be amended without injustice, 'it should be amended rather than that the notice should be quashed or declared a nullity' (*Miller-Mead* case). There is also the limitation contained in s 176(1) that an enforcement notice cannot be amended if it will cause injustice to the appellant or to the LPA.

(c) The 'Mansi' principle

The Secretary of State's power to vary the terms of the enforcement notice is restricted by a principle established by the Divisional Court in the case of *Mansi v Elstree Rural District Council* (1964) 16 P & CR 153. The Secretary of State must ensure that the appellant's rights so far as the extent to which the land has previously been used are safeguarded. The terms of the enforcement notice must not go beyond what is necessary to remedy the breach of control alleged.

The principle is most often used to protect existing use rights, ie, development of land that is immune from enforcement action by virtue of the passage of time (*see* Chapter 5), as in *Trevors Warehouses Ltd v Secretary of State for the Environment* (1972) 33 P & CR 215. However, it has also been used to protect rights conferred by the Use Classes Order, as in *Day and Mid-Warwickshire Motors Ltd v Secretary of State for the Environment* [1979] JPL 538. The principle also applies to extant lawful uses, legitimate ancillary rights (*Cord v Secretary of State for the Environment* [1981] JPL 40), and rights conferred by the 1988 GDO.

The Mansi principle constitutes a material consideration. In the case of *Kennelly v Secretary of State for the Environment and Another* (1994) EGCS 6, an enforcement notice was served which alleged the use of land for scrap vehicle dismantling and storage of scrap. An appeal was made to the Secretary of State and although the inspector found that an area of the land had been used for storage since the 1950s, and that there had been some industrial use rights on other areas of the site since before 1964, he dismissed the appeal. The appellant appealed to the High Court and it was held that, in the absence of abandonment, substantive discontinuance or a planning permission inconsistent with the established use rights, the inspector was obliged to consider what part of the sites enjoyed such established use rights. He thus failed to give effect to the evidence as to the existence of such rights and therefore failed to have regard to a material consideration.

The principle will now apply to development and uses protected by the new immunity periods. In *South Ribble Borough Council v Secretary of State for the Environment* (1991) 1 PLR 29, the Court of Appeal held that the Mansi principle could be reconciled with the statute and with recent case law.

A number of limits to the Mansi principle have developed over the years. These are as follows:

(1) It may not be possible to vary the terms of an enforcement notice in such precise terms as to ensure that an established use can be protected (the *Trevors Warehouses* case).

(2) It is not necessary for obvious rights to be given special protection (*Cord v Secretary of State for the Environment* [1981] JPL 40, recently endorsed by *Stevens and Others v Secretary of State for the Environment and Penwith District Council* [1993] JPL B48).

(3) The power of variation may be used to specify a different means of remedying the breach of planning control (*Murfitt v Secretary of State for the Environment* (1980) 40 P & CR 254).

Other powers

The Secretary of State also has power to do any of the following:

(1) To grant planning permission for any of the matters specified in the enforcement notice in whole or in part, or in relation to the whole or part of the land to which the enforcement notice relates (ss 177(1)(*a*) and s 177(3)).

(2) To discharge any condition or limitation subject to which planning permission was granted (s 177(1)(*b*)) and substitute another condition for it (s 177(4)).

(3) If he is satisfied that the grounds of appeal are made out, to allow the appeal and quash the enforcement notice (s 176(2)).

(4) To give any directions necessary to give effect to his determination on the appeal (s 176(2A)).

(5) To issue a certificate of lawful use or development under s 191 (*see* Chapter 13) where he is satisfied that, on the date on which the appeal was made, any matters alleged to constitute the breach of planning control were lawful (s 177(1)(*c*)).

(6) To grant temporary planning permission if the appellant raises the point on the appeal (*Frances Joseph Tierney v Secretary of State for the Environment and Spelthorne Borough Council* [1983] JPL 799).

The Secretary of State's decision on the appeal will be notified to the appellant and the LPA by letter. The 28-day period for application to the High Court for leave to appeal runs from the date of that letter (*see* Chapter 11).

8 Fees on appeal

Payment of fees

An appeal to the Secretary of State against an enforcement notice constitutes a deemed application for planning permission, whether or not the appellant pleads ground (a) (s 177(5)). A fee is payable for that application. The Secretary of

State will give notice in writing to the appellant specifying the period within which the fee must be paid. If it is not paid within that period, any appeal on ground (a) and the deemed application for planning permission will lapse (s 177(5A)).The fee is payable in duplicate. One is paid to the LPA and the other to the Secretary of State within whatever time limit he may specify. A separate written request for the fee will be made by the LPA. The Secretary of State has a discretion to extend the time for payment where a challenge is made against his assessment of the amount due, or a reasonable requirement for more time to pay is made within the initial time limits.

Assessment of the fee

The fee structure is set out in the Town and Country Planning (Fees for Applications and Deemed Applications) Regulations 1989 (SI No 193) (as amended). The fee is calculated on the category of development in accordance with Sched I, Part II to the 1989 Regulations as amended. It is proposed that local authorities will set their own fees for planning applications, although legislation is unlikely to come into effect until 1996.

   Where an appellant has made an application for planning permission for the development to which an enforcement notice relates, and paid the appropriate fee, reg 10 provides that, where this has been made before the date when the notice was issued, or when it takes effect, no further fee is payable on the deemed planning application that arises on an enforcement notice appeal.

Refund of the fee

If the appeal is withdrawn by the appellant, or the enforcement notice is withdrawn by the LPA before the date of the public inquiry or the site inspection if the written representation appeal procedure is being used, a refund is due. This is also due where an enforcement:

   (a)   appeal succeeds on any of the grounds (b) to (e), unless the appeal involves stationing a residential caravan on land;
   (b)   appeal is rejected as invalid, or it is summarily dismissed for lack of facts in support of the grounds of appeal under s 176(3);
   (c)   notice is quashed and the appeal allowed, because the LPA have failed to submit information within a prescribed period; or
   (d)   notice is found to be invalid, or to contain a defect which the Secretary of State cannot correct on appeal.

These circumstances are detailed in para 53 of Annex 2 to Circular 21/91 and reflect the fact that the fee relates to the consideration of a deemed planning application.

9 Withdrawal of an appeal

The appellant may withdraw an enforcement appeal at any time. The appeal will then have no effect (s 175(4)) and the enforcement notice will come into effect from date of withdrawal of the appeal.

The Secretary of State has no power to reinstate an appeal once it has been withdrawn (*R v Secretary of State for the Environment, ex parte Monica Theresa Crossley* [1985] JPL 632). In that case, the appellant withdrew the appeal where the county council had advised the LPA to withdraw the enforcement notice and had informed the appellant that if she withdrew her appeal, the LPA would have grounds to withdraw the enforcement notice. She did so, but the enforcement notice was not withdrawn and the LPA prosecuted for breach. The court held that once an appeal was withdrawn, the enforcement notice came into effect and once the time for appealing against it had passed, the Secretary of State had no power over the matter at all.

The LPA are entitled to withdraw an enforcement notice issued by them at any time, whether or not it has taken effect (s 173A). In the event of the withdrawal of an enforcement notice, the appellant is entitled to a refund of any fee paid for a deemed planning application (*see* p 127 above).

Where an enforcement notice is served on several parties, eg, the owner and a tenant or occupier, an appeal by one party will put the enforcement notice into abeyance against all other parties (s 175(4)). If that appellant then withdraws the enforcement notice for whatever reason, the notice will again be effective against all the parties and it is no defence that any one of the other parties were unaware that the notice had been withdrawn (*South Cambridge District Council v LFW Stokes* [1981] JPL 594). In that case, a tenant had appealed against a notice and then withdrawn the appeal. The owner had taken no steps at all to find out about the progress of the appeal. The court held that he could easily have asked the LPA what the current position was and was therefore successfully prosecuted for failing to comply with the notice.

10 Costs on appeal

The Secretary of State has the power to award costs on an enforcement appeal, both where a public local inquiry or an informal hearing is held (s 320), in appeal proceedings where an inquiry or hearing has been arranged, but does not take place (s 322A) and where the appeal is dealt with by written representations.

The power to award costs is derived from the Local Government Act 1972, s 250. Section 250(5) provides that the Secretary of State 'may make orders as to the costs of the parties at the inquiry, and as to the parties by whom such costs are to be paid, and any such order may be made a rule of the High Court on the application of either party named in the order'. In the event of non-payment, the advantage of the order being made a rule of the High Court is that interest becomes payable. The criteria to be considered on determining an application for costs is contained in Circular 8/93. Decisions to award costs are based on substantially the same principles as for planning appeals.

The power to award costs where an appeal is dealt with by written representations does not apply across the board to planning appeals. However, by virtue of the Planning (Consequential Provisions) Act 1990, Sched 4, costs may be awarded where an enforcement appeal:

(a) does not proceed by an inquiry or hearing, but is determined by written representations and a site inspection;

(b) is proceeding by written representations and a site inspection, but is not determined because of withdrawal by one of the principal parties at any stage during the proceedings; and

(c) is proceeding by an inquiry or hearing, but one of the principal parties withdraws before arrangements have been formally notified by the DoE.

In the particular circumstances where an enforcement appeal is withdrawn, para 17 of Annex 2 of Circular 8/93 describes the circumstances in which an award of costs may be made, both where an enforcement appeal is withdrawn *at any stage* of such an appeal which is proceeding by written representations, or *before* an inquiry or hearing date has been formally notified by the DoE in such a case where the parties are being 'heard'.

Where the LPA was put to unreasonable expense by withdrawal of the enforcement appeal or any ground of appeal by the appellant, unless there has been a material change in the LPA's case, or any other material change in circumstances relevant to the planning issues arising on appeal, an award of costs may be made against the appellant. It should be noted that the power to award costs applies equally to the withdrawal of any ground of appeal.

Similarly, where the appellant was put to unreasonable expense by withdrawal of the enforcement notice at any time after an appeal is made, an award of costs may be made against the LPA. In the case of *Hammersmith and Fulham London Borough Council v Secretary of State for the Environment and Shorr* [1993] JPL B33, the court recognised the financial constraints of local authorities, but upheld a costs order made against the authority for unreasonable delay in withdrawing an enforcement notice and unreasonable conduct by the LPA in their part of the appeal.

An application for costs may be successful where an appeal is pursued, so long as the enforcement notice remains in existence, notwithstanding the grant of planning permission for the matters constituting the breach of alleged planning control. In *R v Secretary of State for the Environment, ex parte Three Rivers District Council* [1983] JPL 730, the LPA issued an enforcement notice, but then granted planning permission for the development which was alleged to constitute the breach of planning control. Although the requirements in the enforcement notice ceased to have effect, the court held that the actual notice remained in effect and the appeal outstanding, until withdrawn by the LPA. The appellant pursued the appeal and the LPA failed to withdraw the enforcement notice until a few days before the inquiry. The appellant then sought and was awarded costs against the LPA.

Chapter 10

Public Inquiries

1 Right to an inquiry

The right of appeal to the Secretary of State is dealt with in detail in Chapter 9. As explained on p 120 of that chapter, both the appellant and the LPA have a right to be heard by a person appointed by the Secretary of State for the purpose (s 175(3)). This right is exercisable through a public local inquiry, should either party desire it.

The procedure for a public inquiry is dealt with by regulations, statute, and circular advice. The relevant regulations for public inquiries relating to enforcement notice appeals are the Town and Country Planning (Enforcement) (Inquiries Procedure) Rules 1992 (SI No 1903) (referred to in the remainder of this chapter as the 'Inquiries Procedure Rules') . The statutory provisions are found in the Local Government Act 1972, s 250(2)–(5), applied to public inquiries concerning enforcement notice appeals by s 320. Circular advice is contained in Annex 2 of Circular 21/91. Guidance on good practice at planning inquiries is given in the Annex to Circular 24/92 and much of this can be applied to enforcement appeal inquiries.

2 The Inquiries Procedure Rules

The Inquiries Procedure Rules set out the procedure to be followed in connection with local inquiries held for the purposes of appeals against enforcement notices made under s 174. The Rules came into force on 1 September 1992, and update the enforcement inquiries procedure so as to correspond more closely to the rules governing the procedure pertaining to planning inquiries. They apply to both 'non-transferred appeals' (defined in the rules as an appeal which falls to be determined by the Secretary of State), and to 'transferred appeals' (defined in the Rules as an appeal which falls to be determined by a person appointed by the Secretary of State). There are no separate inquiries procedure rules for each type of appeal as there are with planning appeal inquiries.

Provision is made in the Rules for the appointment of an assessor (rule 10), however, it is unlikely that a technical assessor will often be required for the purposes of an enforcement appeal inquiry.

Non-compliance with the procedural rules in relation to enforcement notice appeals can result in a case being dismissed (*R v Wychavon District Council and Secretary of State for the Environment, ex parte Saunders* [1992] JPL 753). Under s 176(3), the Secretary of State may dismiss an appeal if the appellant fails to provide a statement in writing specifying the grounds on which he is appealing and giving such further information as may be prescribed, or allow an appeal and quash the enforcement notice if the LPA fail to comply with the requirements of the procedural rules relating to the provision of information. Although both sides may be penalised, the consequences for each are very different. The appellant loses for ever the chance of appealing against the notice which automatically takes effect when an appeal is dismissed. His only remedy is to seek planning permission. However, the LPA can serve another enforcement notice provided that the time for taking enforcement action has not expired. The stronger position of the LPA is justified as being in the public interest.

3 Preparation for the inquiry

It is important for each party to an enforcement notice appeal to prepare properly. The Inquiries Procedure Rules are intended to provide for proper preparation to improve the efficiency and effectiveness of the local inquiry process. Annex 3 to Circular 17/92 states that the aim of the new rules

> is to make the best possible use of the period before the inquiry opens, to exchange information so that as much as possible of each party's case can be properly considered by the other participants in advance of the inquiry's opening.

The guidance on good practice in Circular 24/92 points out that the task of the inspector at the inquiry is to obtain the material necessary to make an informed and reasoned decision or recommendation. The inspector is also responsible for ensuring that the inquiry is run efficiently and that inquiry time is not wasted, but used to the best advantage of all concerned. Proper preparation for the inquiry by the parties will assist the inspector in this task.

A public inquiry on an enforcement notice appeal should be tackled by both parties as a campaign. Proper preparation is essential to ensure that the case is put over as fully, as clearly and as concisely as possible. The fact that an appeal against an enforcement notice constitutes an application for planning permission (s 177(5)), whether or not the appeal has been made on ground (a) under s 174(2) (*see* Chapter 9), means that both the appellant, and the LPA, need to prepare a case on the planning merits of the development alleged to constitute the breach of planning control. This will be in addition to presenting evidence on any other grounds of appeal.

Assembling a team

Before lodging an appeal against an enforcement notice, a developer should consider assembling a team of experts to present his case. It is critical to remember that an appeal must be lodged before the enforcement notice comes into effect, after which the right to appeal is lost (*see* Chapter 9). Therefore in assembling a team, the appellant must act quickly.

On making an appeal, the appellant should specify the grounds of appeal and state the facts on which he is relying in support of those grounds. Although these requirements are directory, not mandatory, the appellant ought to have a fair idea of the basis for his appeal and the facts surrounding it before lodging the appeal documentation. For that reason, there is some urgency in assembling a team of relevant experts to advise on the approach to be taken on the appeal.

The type of expert involved will depend on the basis of the appeal. In terms of the deemed planning application, the approach to be adopted will be similar to that required for a planning appeal. The particular issues that the appeal raises will dictate the expertise required. Likely experts to be instructed include a planning consultant, a highways or traffic consultant, a noise consultant, or other specialist. An appellant will commonly instruct a solicitor to co-ordinate the team and where the development concerned justifies it, an appellant may also instruct specialist counsel to advise on the matter. Care should be taken to ensure that, so far as possible, each witness addresses a discrete topic. Overlap should be avoided to prevent confusion.

Other grounds of appeal may require evidence to be presented by persons with particular knowledge of the site and development concerned. This may include the chairman of a local representative body, a land agent, surveyor, or it may involve a particular individual with expertise on the difficulties associated with compliance with the requirements of the enforcement notice, where an appeal has been made on grounds (f) or (g) of s 174(2), or with knowledge of the history of the site, where an appeal has been made on ground (d) of s 174(2).

The relevant team should be identified, assembled as soon as possible and instructed accordingly, as once the appeal is lodged the case will need to be developed, and statements of case, proofs of evidence and any summary prepared and produced within a prescribed timetable.

The LPA will also need to assemble a team of relevant experts and should start to consider this as soon as they become aware that an appeal is to be lodged. This may not become known until the DoE write to the LPA on receipt of an appeal, although it is good practice for an appellant to inform the relevant LPA when an appeal is lodged. The LPA may wish to call officers or in-house consultants, or third party representatives, eg, Council for the Protection of Rural England, National Rivers Authority, Nature Conservancy Council, to give evidence on behalf of the authority at the inquiry, particularly where the LPA seek to rely upon the views or opinions of such bodies.

Assembling relevant documentation

An essential part of an appeal will be the evidence in support of the grounds of appeal. This may take the form of oral evidence presented to the inquiry by someone with personal knowledge of the relevant facts, eg, that the development has, or has not, existed for four years in the case of operational development, or ten years in the case of a material change of use (except change of use to a single dwelling house, for which the period of immunity is four years). Factual evidence will usually be presented in the form of a proof of evidence (*see* below).

Documentary evidence may also be presented to the inquiry. This will usually include plans, photographs and diagrams. Such evidence will need to be collated and possibly scheduled so as to be given to the inquiry in a readily understandable form, and the relevance of the document explained in evidence or submissions to the inquiry.

The guidance on good practice in Circular 24/92 states that the purpose of documentary evidence is to set out in a readily identifiable and assimilable form the factual material and technical data upon which evidence is based. Detailed requirements relating to the presentation of documents is given in the Circular. Such requirements include the use of:

(a) identifiable reference numbers for each document;
(b) documents of A4 size if possible, or folded to A4 size;
(c) any plans, maps, diagrams; and
(d) extracts from published material (which should indicate their precise context with full titles, chapter headings and dates).

The guidance also suggests that core documents, such as policy statements and development plan extracts should be compiled and indexed by LPAs and submitted with statements of case. Co-operation between parties should ensure that the extracts contain all the material to be referred to. There may be relevant photographic evidence that will need to be retrieved, collated and possibly scheduled. Photographs should be mounted on a series of A4 cards, individually numbered and their viewpoints shown on a separate OS extract.

The type of evidence required will depend on the grounds on which the appeal is lodged. The team of experts should be able to advise on this, as well as obtaining relevant documentation themselves. As such an exercise can be very time consuming, the earlier it is embarked upon, the better the case can be presented.

4 Lead up to the inquiry

The procedure leading up to the inquiry is governed primarily by the Inquiries Procedure Rules. These establish a timetable for the lead up to a public inquiry. On receipt of the appeal, the Secretary of State will serve written notice on the appellant and the LPA of his intention to cause an inquiry to be held. This is defined in the Rules as the 'relevant notice' and the date of the relevant notice is defined as the 'relevant date'. These provide a base reference for a number of procedures set out in the Rules.

On receipt of a relevant notice, the LPA shall inform the appellant in writing of the name and address of any person on whom a copy of the enforcement notice has been served (rule 4). This enables an appellant to be aware of who else is involved and of their possible interest and participation in an appeal. For example, a tenant may be pursuing an appeal while being unaware of the landowner's knowledge of the situation, and could find that the landowner intends to undermine the tenant's position to achieve his own ends. It also informs the appellant who is entitled to receive a copy of his statement of case in accordance with rule 8 (*see* below).

The Secretary of State is required to notify the name of the inspector to every person entitled to appear at the inquiry (rule 5). If a substitute is appointed, and the Secretary of State is unable to notify the new appointment before the inquiry is held, the substitute inspector shall introduce himself at the commencement of the inquiry.

To aid the efficiency of the inquiry, rule 7 enables the Secretary of State, or the inspector, to serve on the LPA, the appellant, any person required to serve a statement of case (*see* below), and any other person on whom a copy of the enforcement notice has been served, a statement of the matters about which he particularly wishes to be informed for the purposes of his consideration of the appeal. This enables the parties to prepare their case on the basis of addressing these matters. However, it does not preclude any party to the appeal from raising any other matters that they wish the Secretary of State or the inspector to address.

5 Pre-inquiry meeting

In the case of enforcement appeals that are particularly complex or are likely to be lengthy, an inspector may hold a pre-inquiry meeting if he thinks it desirable (rule 6), although this will not often be required at enforcement appeal inquiries. The purpose of such a meeting is to consider what may be done to ensure that so far as possible the inquiry is conducted efficiently and expeditiously. The pre-inquiry meeting can be used to:
- (a) identify the issues to be raised by each of the parties entitled to be heard;
- (b) identify the number of witnesses that each party intends to call;
- (c) estimate the length of time each party will take to present its case and on this basis arrange a time-table for the proceedings;
- (d) specify a date when proofs of evidence and summaries shall be sent;
- (e) arrange for any public meetings that may be required;
- (f) arrange a time for the site visit to take place.

Where a pre-inquiry meeting is to be held, the inspector shall give at least two weeks' written notice of the meeting to the LPA, the appellant, and any other person entitled to appear at the inquiry (rule 6(2)).

6 Statements of case

A statement of case is defined in the Rules as 'a written statement which contains full particulars of the case which a person proposes to put forward at an inquiry, and a list of any documents which that person intends to refer to or put in evidence'. This is in addition to any statement of facts in support of the grounds of appeal which may have already been lodged by the appellant with the appeal. Circular 17/92 provides that the full particulars of the case 'should include any point of law to be argued, or any allegation of defect or nullity in the notice'. A statement of case is sometimes referred to as a pre-inquiry statement.

Service of statements of case

Rule 8 governs the service of statements of case, for which there is a prescribed timetable. This is based on the 'relevant date' as defined above. Starting with the relevant date the timetable is as follows. *Twelve weeks* after the relevant date, the LPA shall serve a statement of case on the Secretary of State, the appellant, and any person on whom a copy of the enforcement notice has been served. *Fifteen weeks* after the relevant date, the appellant shall serve a statement of case on the Secretary of State, the LPA, and any person on whom a copy of the enforcement notice has been served (it is for this purpose that the LPA are required to inform the appellant of the name and address of any person on whom a copy of the enforcement notice has been served).

In circumstances where the date fixed for the holding of the inquiry is less than 18 weeks after the relevant date, the LPA must serve their statement of case at least *six weeks* before that date, and the appellant must serve its statement of case at least *three weeks* before that date.

In both cases, the LPA must serve their statement of case first. The appellant will have already provided a statement of facts in support of the grounds of appeal and the LPA will be able to consider and address these when preparing their statement of case (*see* Chapter 9). The appellant will then have a period of three weeks after service of the LPA's statement of case to examine the issues raised by it and to address these accordingly.

In addition to the statements of case served by the LPA and the appellant, the Secretary of State may in writing require any other person who has notified him in writing of an intention or a wish to appear at the inquiry, to serve a statement of case, within a specified period, on him, the LPA, the appellant and any other party on whom a copy of the enforcement notice has been served (rule 8(4)). In such a case the Secretary of State shall provide a copy of the LPA's and the appellant's statement of case and shall inform that person of the names and addresses of everyone on whom his statement of case should be served.

Following service of the parties' statements of case, it may become clear that one or more of the parties will be relying on technical evidence. The guidance on good practice in Circular 24/92 suggests that in such a case, there are advantages in the parties contacting each other at an early stage to discuss procedural matters, define issues in dispute and agree basic factual information. This will assist in the efficient use of inquiry time.

Although the Rules prescribe a timetable for the service of statements of case, there is no sanction where the statement is served out of time. To that extent, the requirements are without teeth. In the case of *Barraclough v*

Secretary of State for the Environment and Leeds City Council [1989] JPL 911, it was indicated that a breach of the timetable in the Town and Country Planning (Enforcement Notices and Appeals) Regulations 1991 (reg 7 of which provides for the service of a statement by the LPA on an enforcement notice appeal), can be remedied by an adjournment of the inquiry, and that breaches of one or two days are unlikely to lead to the enforcement notice being quashed.

However, there may be a liability for costs if any other party is put to extra expense as a result of a breach of the rules (*see* below). In addition, see *R v Wychavon District Council and Secretary of State for the Environment, ex parte Saunders* [1992] JPL 753. The Secretary of State or the inspector may not look favourably upon a party who failed to comply with the requirements, but he would have no justification for penalising a party for late service, as there is no statutory basis for so doing.

List of documents

The list of documents attached to each party's statement of case should identify those documents on which the LPA, the appellant or any other person who has prepared such a list intends to rely in support of his case. The importance of assembling the relevant documentation is referred to above. The need to list the documents in the statement of case emphasises the need to identify the relevant documents as soon as possible in the preparation of the case. Agreed statements dealing with uncontested factual matters may be included in the list of documents and then merely referred to in proofs of evidence.

The LPA and the appellant may require the other party to provide a copy of any document, or the relevant part of any document, referred to in the list of documents comprised in the statement of case (rule 8(3)). This will assist both parties in the preparation of their proofs of evidence. The LPA then has an obligation to give any person who requests a reasonable opportunity to inspect and, where practicable, take copies of the LPA's statement of case and any document, or the relevant part of any document referred to in the list comprised in that statement and any other statement of case or other document which has been served on the LPA (rule 8(8)). The time and place for affording such an opportunity must be specified in the LPA's statement of case.

If a person other than the appellant serves a statement of case on the LPA, and refers to a document in the list of documents attached to the statement that is not already available, that person shall provide the LPA with a copy of that document or any relevant part of that document (rule 8(7)). The LPA will then be in a position to make that document available for inspection, together with that person's statement of case, in accordance with rule 8(8).

Further information

Once a statement of case has been served, the Secretary of State or an inspector may require a person who has served a statement of case to provide further information about any matters contained in the statement. That information must be provided in writing and copies sent to any other person on whom the statement of case has been served (rule 8(6)).

7 Date and notification of inquiry

Timing

The Inquiries Procedure Rules impose a requirement on the Secretary of State to fix a date for the holding of an inquiry not later than 24 weeks after the relevant date, unless he considers such a date impracticable (rule 11(1)), in which case the date fixed for the inquiry shall be the earliest date thereafter. There is, however, a residual power for the Secretary of State to vary the date fixed for the holding of an inquiry (rule 11(4)). The requirement in rule 11(1) is intended to speed up the whole procedure relating to the determination of enforcement appeals.

Notice period

The Secretary of State is required to give not less than four weeks' written notice of the date, time and place fixed by him for the holding of an inquiry to every person entitled to appear at the inquiry. However, he may agree a lesser period of notice with the appellant and the LPA (rule 11(3)). Annex 3 to Circular 17/92 provides that each principal party to an appeal will generally be permitted only one refusal of a date offered for the inquiry before the DoE will proceed to fix a date. A period of one month will normally be allowed for negotiating a date. The DoE reserves a residual right to impose a date on the parties.

The Secretary of State has the power to vary the time or place for the holding of an inquiry. Where he does so, he shall give such notice as appears to him to be reasonable (rule 11(5)). The LPA usually provides a venue (normally the council offices) for a public inquiry which are convenient to the land to which the enforcement notice relates. Another venue may be required, eg if the LPA underestimate the interest in a particular appeal or other council business involves the use of the building. The provisions of rule 11(5) enable an alternative venue to be allocated.

Method of notification

General notification of an inquiry is usually devolved on the LPA by the Secretary of State under rule 11(6). Notification may involve one or more of the following steps, as required by the Secretary of State:

(1) Publishing a notice of the inquiry in one or more newspapers circulating in the locality in which the relevant land is situated, not less than two weeks before the date fixed for the holding of the inquiry.
(2) Serving notice of the inquiry on such persons and within such period as the Secretary of State may specify.

(3) Posting a notice of the inquiry in a conspicuous place near to the land, within such period as the Secretary of State may specify.

The Secretary of State may require the appellant to fix a notice of the inquiry firmly to the land or to some object on or near the land, in such a manner as to be readily visible to and legible by members of the public, for such period as he may specify (rule 11(7)). This will usually be the case where the land is under the control of the appellant and the LPA do not have access. This requirement will be in addition to the requirements imposed on the LPA as detailed above.

Failure of the LPA or the appellant to comply with requirements for publicity of the inquiry will not invalidate the proceedings. However, the inspector may adjourn the inquiry, if he considers it necessary, to ensure that the public are aware that the inquiry is taking place. There may be a costs liability associated with such an adjournment on the party who failed to publicise the inquiry, if another party was put to extra expense as a result (*see* p 147 below).

Contents of the notice

Rule 11(8) prescribes the contents of a notice published, served or posted pursuant to the rules. It must contain a:

(a) clear statement of the date, time and place of the inquiry and of the powers enabling the Secretary of State or inspector to determine the appeal in question;

(b) written description of the land sufficient to identify approximately its location; and

(c) brief description of the subject matter of the appeal.

The whole basis of the enforcement notice appeal process dealt with by public inquiry, is that it is dealt with in the public domain. The requirements as to notice are therefore critical, and compliance will ensure that the public are fully involved and are aware of the proceedings, and able to take part where appropriate.

8 Appearances

The nature of a public inquiry is such that any interested party should be able to take part if he should so wish. Rule 12 of the Inquiries Procedure Rules prescribe the persons *entitled* to appear at an inquiry. These are:

(a) the appellant;

(b) the LPA;

(c) any of the following if the land is situated in their area and they are not the LPA;

(i)   a county or district council;

(ii) a National Park Committee;

(iii) a joint planning board;

(iv) an urban development corporation;

(v) an enterprise zone authority;

(vi) the Broads Authority;

(vii) a housing action trust;

(d) where the land is in an area designated as a new town, the development corporation for the new town or the Commission for the New Towns, as appropriate;

(e) any person on whom a copy of the enforcement notice has been served;

(f) any other person who has served a statement of case.

The inspector, is also entitled to permit any other person to appear and such permission shall not be unreasonably withheld (rule 12(2)).

Any person entitled or permitted to appear at an inquiry may do so on his own behalf, or be represented by counsel, solicitor or any other person. Commonly parties will instruct specialists to present their case at an inquiry (*see* p 131 above) and such persons have a right to appear at the inquiry by virtue of rule 12(3).

The LPA may refer to a view or opinion of a government department in support of their case. Where this is expressed in writing to the LPA and referred to in their statement of case, the appellant is entitled to make a request in writing that a representative of the department concerned attend the inquiry (rule 13). Such a request must be made not later than two weeks before the date of the inquiry. A representative attending the inquiry will be expected to state the reasons for the expressed view and give evidence and be cross-examined to the same extent as any other witness. To this end, a representative may serve a statement in writing on the appellant before the inquiry, or the Secretary of State could require that such a statement be served. Rule 13(4) provides that such a representative is not required to address the merits of government policy.

9 Proofs of evidence

Proofs of evidence may be prepared for the purposes of presenting evidence to the inquiry in a clear and concise manner. They should contain the facts and expert opinions deriving from witnesses' own professional or local knowledge. A person entitled to appear at an enforcement appeal inquiry may give evidence or call another person to give evidence to the inquiry by reading a proof of evidence.

In general, proofs of evidence should contain all the submissions that the parties wish to put before the inquiry. Such matters should not be left to be drawn out in cross-examination or re-examination. In *K G Diecasting (Weston) Ltd v Secretary of State for the Environment and Woodspring District Council* [1993] JPL 925, an enforcement notice was issued relating to the use of a building in breach of planning control. On application for leave to appeal against the decision of the inspector on an appeal against the enforcement notice, the applicant alleged that the inspector's decision was reached without regard to material evidence concerning the proposed use of the building. At a late stage in the appeal against the enforcement notice, the applicant had introduced evidence that the building concerned was used for mushroom growing. This evidence was not contained in the applicant's written proof of evidence given at the inquiry. Potts J held that, had the evidence been regarded by the applicant as a serious issue, the applicant should have stated that fact and have emphasised it. As the evidence was introduced at a late stage and was not in the written proof of evidence of the applicant, the inspector was entitled to conclude that mushroom growing was not a serious alternative use. Therefore, it could not be argued that he had failed to have regard to material evidence.

Timetable

The Inquiries Procedure Rules set out a timetable for the preparation of and submission of proofs of evidence with summaries, prior to the commencement of the inquiry. This brings the procedure relating to proofs of evidence in line with the procedure on a planning inquiry. Adherence to the timetable will enable the parties to the inquiry to absorb the other parties cases, and the inquiry can then concentrate on the key issues.

Rule 14 provides for a timetable for sending proofs of evidence to the other parties, and for the preparation of summaries. It applies to proofs of evidence that relate, in whole or in part, to the deemed application for planning permission that arises on an enforcement notice appeal by virtue of s 177(5). Proofs of evidence may be prepared for aspects of the enforcement appeal other than the planning merits of the development. Rule 14 does not expressly apply to these aspects. However, where proofs of evidence relating to them are to be read at the inquiry, it is good practice for the proofs and any summaries to be circulated beforehand.

Rule 14(3)(*a*) requires that the proof of evidence shall be sent to the inspector not later than *three weeks* before the date fixed for the holding of an inquiry, unless the inspector has arranged, at a pre-inquiry meeting, an alternative date for proofs to be made available. At the same time, a copy of the proof of evidence shall be served on the other parties entitled to appear (rule 14(4)). Copies of a proof shall be accompanied by the whole or the relevant part, of any documents referred to in it, unless a copy of that document is already available for inspection in accordance with rule 8(8) (*see* p 136 above).

Summaries

Where a proof of evidence which contains more than 1,500 words is to be read at the inquiry, rule 14(1) requires that a written summary of the proof be sent to the inspector, together with the proof of evidence itself, in accordance with the timetable set out above, and copies provided to the other parties. Both the proof of evidence and any summary should be submitted together to avoid the possibility of the summary containing new evidence not actually included in the proof and to avoid a dispute arising at the inquiry. However, where a summary does contain new evidence, the inspector has a discretion to allow such evidence (*see* p 143).

Where a summary is provided, it will be read at the inquiry, rather than the proof of evidence, unless the inspector permits or requires otherwise (rule 14(5)). This is to enable efficient use to be made of inquiry time, and mirrors the requirements for a planning appeal inquiry.

It is open to any of the other parties appearing at the inquiry to make a request to the inspector that part of or the whole proof of evidence is read instead of, or as well as the summary. For example, if there is a discrepancy between the content of the proof and the summary, then this may need to be clarified at the inquiry. However, this is at the discretion of the inspector, as clarification can be dealt with by cross-examination.

The guidance on good practice in Circular 24/92 suggests that summaries should not exceed 1,500 words or ten per cent of the length of the proof of evidence, whichever is the greater. This criteria can be applied to summaries prepared in relation to an enforcement appeal. However, where the inspector holds a pre-inquiry meeting, he may specify an alternative requirement for the length of summaries. To assist the inspector, the parties should ensure that these requirements are met as far as possible, although there is no statutory sanction if they are not met.

It is not always an easy task to condense a proof of evidence into a document that is approximately ten per cent of its length. However, it should not be forgotten that all the parties will have seen the actual proof of evidence itself, and it is this document that the inspector will consider in detail when determining the deemed application for planning permission, or other aspects of the appeal for which proofs of evidence and summaries have been provided. In addition, the full proof will still be treated as tendered in evidence and cross-examination takes place on the proof in its entirety (rule 15(5)). The exception to this is where the person reading the summary notifies the inspector that he now wishes to rely on the contents of that summary only.

Availability of proofs of evidence

The LPA are required to afford to any person who so requests a reasonable opportunity to inspect and, where practicable, take copies of any proof of evidence, summary or other document sent to them in accordance with rule 14. Usually the place for inspection will be at the same place as the statements of case and relevant documents are kept for inspection (*see* p 136 above).

Supplementary proofs

Where proofs of evidence are exchanged in accordance with the timetable set out in the Inquiries Procedure Rules, one party may wish to rebut points raised in another party's evidence. In these circumstances, supplementary proofs may be submitted. This should be done at the earliest opportunity and made available by the opening of the inquiry. No distinction is made in the Inquiries Procedure Rules between main and supplementary proofs. The guide to good practice advises that revised proofs should be avoided as they lead to confusion.

10 Procedure at the inquiry

The usual procedure to be followed at the inquiry is prescribed by rule 15 of the Inquiries Procedure Rules. However, as the procedure at the inquiry is at the discretion of the inspector he has the right to determine an alternative procedure if he should require it, or consider it to be appropriate. Rules of evidence prevailing in the courts of law do not apply to public inquiries. The evidence that may be admitted is at the discretion of the inspector.

Presentation of evidence

The Inquiries Procedure Rules provide that the appellant shall begin and shall have the right of final reply, and the other persons entitled or permitted to appear shall be heard in such order as the inspector may determine. This may be varied by the inspector with the consent of the appellant (rule 15(2)).

It is usual for the evidence to be heard at an inquiry in the following order:
(1) Opening statements shall be given by the appellant, then by any other party appearing in support of the appellant's case.
(2) Opening statements shall then be given by the LPA, followed by any other interested party, eg, the county council or the Commission for New Towns, and third party objectors.
(3) The appellant will then present his case, giving evidence of the substantive proposition before giving evidence in support.
(4) Each of the appellant's witnesses will be cross-examined by the LPA and, if the inspector allows, by the other parties appearing at the inquiry usually in the order in which the other parties will subsequently appear.
(5) The appellant's witnesses will be re-examined, if necessary, to clarify any points that arose in cross-examination (at this point, the appellant cannot introduce any new evidence, or if he does so, the other parties can ask the inspector to allow them to cross-examine further, but only in relation to any such new evidence).
(6) Any party appearing in support of the appellant will then present its case.
(7) That party's witnesses will then be cross-examined and re-examined as detailed above.
(8) The LPA will then present their case and their witnesses will be cross-examined and re-examined as above.
(9) Any third party will then be heard and will be cross-examined and re-examined as above (this is subject to the availability of such third parties, particularly interested members of the public who may not be able to attend the inquiry through to this stage in the proceedings, in which event, the inspector may exercise his discretion to allow a third party to be heard at an earlier stage).
(10) Each party will then give its closing submissions, usually in reverse order, with the appellant having the right of final reply.

The above procedure may be varied by the inspector at the inquiry eg, a witness may need to be recalled. At the commencement of the inquiry, the inspector will outline the procedure that he intends to follow. If any party advises the inspector that he will have difficulty in attending the inquiry at the time intimated for him to present his evidence, the inspector will usually endeavour to accommodate such a party and ensure that he is not prejudiced in any way.

Onus of proof

An enforcement inquiry appeal may raise legal issues. In such a case, the onus of proof is on the appellant. The test of evidence is 'the balance of probability'— there is no requirement that the appellant should prove his case beyond all reasonable doubt (*F W Gabbitas v Secretary of State for the Environment and Newham Borough Council* [1985] JPL 630). The appellant's own evidence does not need to be corroborated by independent evidence in order to be accepted.

Inspector's powers

The inspector is given a number of powers by the Inquiries Procedure Rules in relation to the procedure at an inquiry. He may:

(a) use his discretion on the calling of evidence and the cross-examination of persons giving evidence, subject to the fact that persons entitled to appear at an inquiry in accordance with the rules are entitled to call evidence and cross-examine persons giving evidence (rule 15(3));

(b) refuse to permit the giving of evidence which he considers to be irrelevant or repetitious, but where he refuses to hear this the person may submit the evidence in writing before the close of the inquiry (rule 15(4));

(c) direct that copying facilities for documentary evidence open to public inspection shall be made available (rule 15(6));

(d) require a person who is behaving in a disruptive manner to leave the inquiry, and may refuse re-entry. This person may submit evidence in writing to the inspector before the close of the inquiry (rule 15(7));

(e) the inspector may allow any person to alter or add to a statement of case served under rule 8, but shall give the other parties an adequate opportunity of considering any fresh matter or document (rule 15(8)). This may involve an adjournment (a party put to additional expense as a result of this may make an application for costs);

(f) proceed with an inquiry in the absence of any person entitled to appear at it (rule 15(9));

(g) take into account any written representation or evidence or any other document received by him before or during the inquiry, provided that he discloses it at the inquiry (rule 15(10)). However, he is likely to attach less weight to it than if the evidence had been given on oath and the person giving the evidence cross-examined;

(h) adjourn the inquiry from time to time (rule 15(11)).

Good practice

The guidance on good practice in Circular 24/92 provides a guide for the procedure at enforcement appeal inquiries which are now based on very similar rules to those governing planning appeal inquiries. The main points that come out of the guidance are as follows:

(1) Opening statements should be concise. They should outline the case to be presented, and explain how far agreement has been reached between the parties due to pre-inquiry co-operation. The appellant's opening statement should state the grounds of appeal on which he relies, and indicate the nature of the evidence that he will call in support of them.

(2) Where a summary of a proof of evidence is provided, witnesses will normally read only that summary.

(3) Cross-examination may take place on any point in the full proof of evidence and any summary, and on any relevant matter within the knowledge of the witness. The LPA and the appellant are entitled to cross-examine each others witnesses, but any other party may only cross-examine to the extent allowed by the inspector. On cross-examination, the witness should have the case of the party carrying out the cross-examination put to him, cross-examination on his proof alone is insufficient. It is not permissible for those representing third parties to cross-examine those appearing on the same side, ie, local action groups cannot cross-examine the LPA where both parties appear against the appellant.

(4) The parties to the inquiry should produce 'best evidence'. Documentary or oral evidence which is hearsay may be challenged if better evidence is available.

(5) The inspector has the power to obtain a summons to require a witness to attend at the inquiry (LGA 1972, s 250(2)). Representatives of government departments may be unable to attend and give evidence at a public inquiry without a summons, eg, police, fire brigade.

(6) The inspector may require evidence to be given under oath, particularly where, as is common in enforcement appeal inquiries, the appellant is relying on statements of fact in support of a ground of appeal.

(7) Inspectors may themselves ask relevant questions.

(8) Re-examination must not deal with matters not covered in cross-examination, and leading questions should not be put in re-examination.

(9) Participation by interested persons and groups is encouraged. Groups and individuals with similar cases may co-operate by nominating a spokesperson.

(10) Closing submissions should summarise the case presented and should

draw attention to detail where it is crucial to the case, but not otherwise. Full written copies of closing submissions are often useful to inspectors in long and complex inquiries, but their provision is not obligatory.

11 Site inspections

As with a planning appeals inquiry, the inspector will usually carry out a site inspection to familiarise himself with the land that is the subject of the enforcement notice. This may be made unaccompanied, *before* or *during* an inquiry without notice to the persons entitled to appear at the inquiry (rule 16(1)).

Alternatively, the inspector may inspect the land in the company of the LPA, the appellant, and any person on whom a copy of the enforcement notice was served, either *during* an inquiry, or *after* its close. In such a case, the inspector shall announce during the inquiry the date and time at which he proposes to make the site visit (rule 16(3)). Rule 16(2) provides that the inspector shall make this inspection if so required by the LPA or the appellant before or during an inquiry.

Where the inspector makes an accompanied site visit, he will usually try to limit the numbers attending, and it is usually only one or two representatives of the LPA and the appellant who will attend. Other interested parties may attend at the inspector's discretion. If a particular technical issue has arisen in evidence, the appropriate consultant or officer of the LPA will accompany the inspector, eg, a highways or drainage issue. The site visit may be used as an opportunity to point out features of the site that have been discussed, or will be discussed at the inquiry, but the inspector will not allow any party to make representations to him during the site visit.

12 Procedure after inquiry

Non-transferred appeals

On a non-transferred appeal, after the close of the inquiry, the inspector shall make a report in writing to the Secretary of State, which shall include his findings of facts, his conclusions and his recommendations or his reasons for not making any representations (rule 17(2)). Where an assessor has been appointed, he shall make a report in writing to the inspector. The inspector shall append this report to his own , and shall state how far he agrees or disagrees with it and, where he disagrees, his reasons (rule 17(4)).

The Secretary of State may find that he differs from the inspector on a material matter of fact, which led to the conclusion reached by the inspector, or he takes into the consideration new evidence or a new matter of fact (not being a matter of government policy). In such circumstances, the Inquiries Procedure Rules prescribe the action that the Secretary of State must take before coming to a decision on the matter. He

    (a)   must notify the persons entitled to appear at the enquiry who appeared at it of his disagreement and the reasons for it;

    (b)   must afford those persons the opportunity of making written representations to him within three weeks of the date of the notification, or, where he has taken into consideration new evidence or a new matter of fact, of asking for the re-opening of the inquiry;

(c) may as he thinks fit, cause the inquiry to be re-opened, and shall do so if asked by the LPA or the appellant in the circumstances and within the period specified in (b) above;

(d) must, where an inquiry is re-opened, send to the persons who appeared at it, a statement of the matters for which further evidence is invited, and the rules as to the date and notification of an inquiry (rule 11, *see* p134) shall apply to the re-opened inquiry.

The Secretary of State shall notify his decision on the appeal and his reasons for it to all persons entitled to appear at the inquiry and to any other party who appeared and asked to be notified of the decision (rule 19(2)). Where a copy of the inspector's report is not sent with the decision, a statement of the inspector's finding of facts, his conclusions and any recommendations made by him shall be sent. A copy of the report shall be supplied within four weeks of the date of the decision where a person entitled to be notified makes a request in writing for a copy from the Secretary of State (rule 19(3)). A person who has received a copy of the report may apply to the Secretary of State in writing, within six weeks of the date of the decision for an opportunity to inspect any documents appended to the report that were not included with the report (rule 19(4)).

Transferred appeals

In the case of a transferred appeal, the inspector is responsible for the decision without reference to the Secretary of State. In such a case, where an assessor has been appointed, he may make a report in writing to the inspector for him to take into consideration in reaching his decision.

If, after the close of the inquiry, the inspector proposes to take into consideration any new evidence or any new matter of fact (not being a matter of government policy), which was not raised in the inquiry, and which he considers to be material to his decision, the Inquiries Procedure Rules require that he carry out the same procedure of notification and gives to those parties entitled to appear at the inquiry who did appear, the same opportunities as the Secretary of State is required to do under rule 17, detailed above (rule 18).

The inspector shall notify his decision on the appeal, and his reasons for it, in writing to all persons entitled to appear at the inquiry who did appear, and to any other person who appeared at the inquiry and asked to be notified of the decision (rule 20). Any person entitled to be notified of the decision may apply to the Secretary of State in writing, within six weeks of the date of the decision, for an opportunity to inspect any documents listed in the notification and any assessor's report.

13 Costs

Throughout the inquiry procedure, the parties are at risk of an award of costs if they fail to comply with the Inquiries Procedure Rules and another party is put to additional expense as a result of 'unreasonable' behaviour. The inspector is empowered to make orders as to the costs of the parties at the inquiry and as to the parties by whom such costs are to be paid (Local Government Act 1972, s 250(5)). The question of costs is dealt with in more detail in Chapter 9. A party seeking costs must make a specific application for costs before the inquiry closes and must show that unnecessary expense has been incurred as a result of another party's actions.

14 Suggested timetable

As the procedure for a public inquiry is largely governed by rules, it is important to ensure that the procedure is clear at the outset, so that the preparation for and presentation at the inquiry proceeds as smoothly as possible. The information on pp144 and 145 are suggested timetables for use by the appellant, and the LPA. The timetables can be adapted for use by other parties to the appeal.

The Appellant

Receipt of enforcement notice

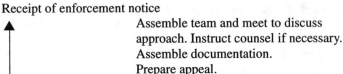

Assemble team and meet to discuss
approach. Instruct counsel if necessary.
Assemble documentation.
Prepare appeal.

LODGE APPEAL

Date before enforcement notice takes effect
Relevant date

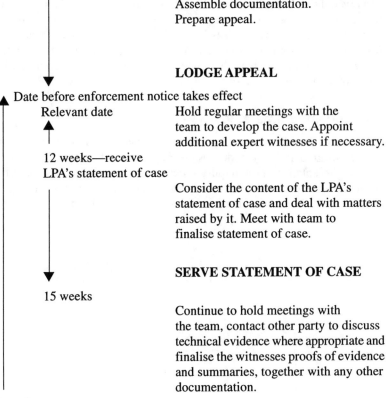

Hold regular meetings with the
team to develop the case. Appoint
additional expert witnesses if necessary.

12 weeks—receive
LPA's statement of case

Consider the content of the LPA's
statement of case and deal with matters
raised by it. Meet with team to
finalise statement of case.

SERVE STATEMENT OF CASE

15 weeks

Continue to hold meetings with
the team, contact other party to discuss
technical evidence where appropriate and
finalise the witnesses proofs of evidence
and summaries, together with any other
documentation.

24 weeks

3 weeks

**SERVE PROOFS OF EVIDENCE
AND SUMMARIES**

Consider the LPA's (and any other
party's proof of evidence). Determine
whether any supplementary proofs
of evidence are required.

INQUIRY DATE

The LPA

Notification of enforcement appeal

Assemble team and meet to discuss approach.
Instruct counsel if necessary.
Consider appellant's statement of case.
Assemble documentation.
(see above)

Relevant date

Inform appellant of parties on
whom enforcement notice served.
Hold regular meetings with the
team to develop the case. Appoint
additional witnesses if necessary. Finalise
statement of case.

12 weeks   **SERVE STATEMENT OF CASE**

15 weeks—receive   Consider the content of the
appellant's   appellant's statement of
statement of case   case and meet with the team
                          to deal with matters raised by it.
                          Contact appellant to discuss
                          technical evidence where appropriate.
                          Finalise the witnesse's proofs of
                          evidence and summaries, together
                          with any other documentation.

24 weeks

3 weeks   **SERVE PROOFS OF EVIDENCE
                           AND SUMMARIES**
                          Consider the appellant's (and any
                          other party's proof of evidence).
                          Determine whether any supplementary
                          proofs of evidence are required.

INQUIRY DATE

Chapter 11

Appeal to the High Court

1 Introduction

There is a statutory right of appeal to the High Court relating to any decision made by the Secretary of State in proceedings on an enforcement notice appeal. This right is contained in s 289 and is exercisable by the appellant, the LPA, or any other person having an interest in the land to which the enforcement notice relates, whether or not a copy of the notice was served on him. It does not extend to any person on whom a copy of the enforcement notice had been served but who has no interest in the land.

Section 289 and the Rules of the Supreme Court govern the exercise of the right of appeal and the application to the court, detailing the procedure for an appeal, and the extent of the court's powers in relation to an appeal. Although s 289 permits a party to require the Secretary of State to state and sign a case for the opinion of the High Court, no applicable rules of the High Court have been made and therefore this procedure is not available.

This chapter deals with the provisions of TCPA 1990, s 289 (hereafter s 289) the exercise of the right of appeal, the circumstances in which a party can resort to the courts, and the procedure for making an appeal to the High Court.

2 Scope of the right

The decision

The right of appeal to the High Court applies to any decision in proceedings on an enforcement appeal given by the Secretary of State. Two elements of this right are specifically dealt with by statute and case law. Section 289(7) provides that 'decision' includes a direction or order, and that references to the giving of a decision shall be construed accordingly. It would therefore encompass an order for costs, or a ruling that the Secretary of State could not entertain an appeal on the basis that no statement of facts was provided by the appellant (*Button v Jenkins* [1975] 3 All ER 585).

However, a decision does not include the reasons given for it. In *Young v Secretary of State for the Environment* [1990] JPL 671, the Court of Appeal held that an appeal could not be brought under s 246 of the TCPA 1971 (now s 289) against a finding that there had in fact been a breach of planning control. In that case, an enforcement notice was served which alleged a change of use of land. The appellant appealed and the inspector directed that the notice should be quashed, as the breach of planning control alleged in the notice was incorrect, and as the defect went to the root of the notice, it could not be amended. The appellant appealed to the High Court on the basis that the inspector had also determined that there had been a breach of planning control and there was a risk of serious injustice to the appellant. The Court of Appeal held that there could be no appeal against a decision which was wholly in favour of the appellant. The right of appeal to the High Court was intended to enable those who would be adversely affected by a decision which was wrong in law to appeal. It was the decision itself, not the reasons for the decision that was subject to the right of appeal.

In proper circumstances, judicial review could be used to challenge the legality of the reasoning of a decision, even if the actual decision was in favour of the applicant. In *Greater London Council v Secretary of State for the Environment and Harrow LBC* [1985] JPL 868, there were special circumstances that made it desirable to test the inspectors approach in relation to the reasoning for his decision. The inspector had refused planning permission on an appeal, but indicated that it should be granted if a s 52 (now s 106) agreement was concluded. It was likely that his objectionable reasoning would be reapplied in the immediate future. The GLC had given a direction to the LPA not to grant planning permission. In these circumstances, were the LPA to refuse permission despite the conclusion of a s 52 agreement as specified by the inspector, the applicant would appeal, based on the inspector's reasoning given in the earlier appeal. The court held that in order to avoid this cumbersome procedure, the GLC could be granted leave to apply for judicial review of the inspector's decision.

Proceedings on an appeal

The right to appeal only applies to any decision given in proceedings on an appeal. Once the Secretary of State has accepted jurisdiction on the appeal, proceedings on an appeal commence. The right would not apply to a decision by the Secretary of State not to entertain an appeal, as that decision is not a decision 'in proceedings on an appeal'. Any challenge to such a decision would be by way of judicial review (*Lenlyn Ltd v Secretary of State for the Environment* [1985] JPL 482).

Where the Secretary of State determines that an enforcement notice is a nullity and therefore no notice at all (*see* Chapter 6, p 71), there can be no proceedings in relation to the notice, and therefore the right to appeal to the High Court under s 289 would not arise. Where the notice is held to be a nullity, the appropriate procedure for a challenge would be by way of judicial review (*Rhymney Valley District Council v Secretary of State for Wales and G Issac* [1985] JPL 27).

Appeal limited to a point of law

Under s 289(1), appeals to the High Court are limited to a point of law. The court will not be concerned with matters that are purely a question of fact for the inspector (*Tyler v Secretary of State for the Environment and Woodspring District Council* [1994] JPL B37). There are a number of cases that deal with the issues that the court can consider when an appeal to the High Court is made.

The consideration of a point of law

An appeal made to the High Court cannot be made against a decision on a point of law when the point raised before the court was neither put to, nor determined by, the Secretary of State (*London Parachuting Ltd v Secretary of State for the Environment and South Cambridgeshire District Council* [1986] JPL 428). This view was supported in *Leslie Gwillim v Secretary of State for the Environment and Ashford Borough Council* [1988] JPL 263, where the court held that points of law cannot be taken at the High Court stage if they have not been previously built up at the appeal stage. A decision maker does not misdirect himself in law by failing to address an issue which had never been put to him.

The treatment of evidence as a point of law

Some guidance on what constitutes a point of law was given by the High Court in *ELS Wholesale (Wolverhampton) Ltd and Crownbrae Ltd v Secretary of State for the Environment and Cheltenham Borough Council* [1987] JPL 844. In that case May LJ stated that:

> If there were no evidence for a particular finding, or if the tribunal had not taken into account at all a relevant consideration then these could well be grounds of appeal raising a question of law. But the contention that a tribunal had failed to give adequate weight to evidence, or adequate or sufficient consideration to a particular circumstance did not.

The relevance of decision letters

In the *ELS Wholesale* case, the court held that decision letters should not be analysed as a statutory instrument or statute, but should be looked at broadly. This was endorsed in *Barnet Meeting Room Trust v Secretary of State for the Environment* [1990] JPL 430, where the court held that it was not appropriate to scrutinise the decision letters as though they were contracts, or subject them to fine legal analysis. It was their substance and conclusions that were important. It would not be appropriate to examine the minutiae of a decision letter in determining whether an appeal to the High Court could be made under s 289. The real sense and the basic content of the decision letter would be what the court was interested in.

Evidence presented to the High Court

Where an appeal is made to the High Court under s 289, the court should not receive evidence relating to the appeal itself, unless it is being argued that the inspector had not properly summarised the evidence, or had disregarded evidence. An appeal under s 289 is an appeal on issues of law and it is not for the court to find that the inspector's findings of fact were absurd or perverse (*Clarke v Secretary of State for the Environment* (1992) *The Times,* 24 June).

Since the appeal is limited to a point of law, the court is not allowed to conduct a re-hearing of the primary facts relating to the enforcement notice (*Green v Minister of Housing and Local Government* [1967] 2 QB 606). However, the court can receive further evidence on questions of fact under the Rules of the Supreme Court, Ord 55, r 7(2).

The right of appeal under s 288

In circumstances where an appeal under s 289 is being contemplated in relation to a refusal to grant planning permission under ground (a) of s 174(2), or a deemed application for planning permission under s 177(5), it may be better to appeal under s 288 as this section is worded in broader terms and is not limited to a point of law.

There is a clear choice as to which section to use when the challenge relates to the grant, or the refusal to grant planning permission. The court have held that a challenge to a grant of planning permission by the Secretary of State on an enforcement appeal can be made under s 289, notwithstanding that an appeal to the High Court under s 288 would be more appropriate (*Gill v Secretary of State for the Environment and North Warwickshire District Council* [1985] JPL 710).

3 Relationship between s 289 and judicial review

Administrative decisions made by public bodies can be examined by the courts by means of judicial review. This applies to decisions given in enforcement appeal proceedings. There is no statutory bar to the challenge of such decisions under the usual rules of judicial review. It is therefore open to any party to apply to the High Court to challenge a decision given in proceedings on an enforcement appeal either by way of judicial review or under s 289.

This was endorsed by the court in the case of *R v Secretary of State for the Environment and Another, ex parte Davidson* (1989) *The Times,* 23 June. In that case an application had been made to the court for judicial review of a decision of the Secretary of State dismissing an enforcement appeal. The court held that, notwithstanding the fact that the matter could have been brought to the court under TCPA 1971, s 246 (now s 289), the court could consider the matter on its merits, where the grounds so justified it, by way of an application for judicial review. The right of an individual to natural justice meant that his recourse to the courts should not be limited by the fact that there was a statutory procedure in place to deal with the circumstances of the case. However, where an application for leave to appeal under s 289 has been refused, there is no residual right to apply for judicial review (*R v Secretary of State for the*

Environment, ex parte KG Diecasting (Weston) Ltd [1993] JPL B129). Even where new points of law arise, the right to apply for judicial review could not be exercised when the legal point could have been taken in the statutory appeal and was not.

Under s 289, the court only has power to remit the matter back to the Secretary of State for determination (*see* p 157), whereas, on an application for judicial review, the court can make an order of *mandamus, prohibition* or *certiorari*, which would dispose of the matter conclusively.

Under s 289, an appeal must be made within 28 days of the decision (*see* p 155), whereas, an application for judicial review must be made promptly and within three months of the decision, unless the applicant can show good reason for delay.

4 Relationship between s 289 and s 285

Section 285 provides that the validity of an enforcement notice shall not, except by way of an appeal to the Secretary of State, be questioned in any legal proceedings whatsoever on any of the grounds on which such an appeal may be brought. There are, however, other grounds on which the validity of an enforcement notice may be challenged, eg, fraud, or the fact that the issue of the enforcement notice is unauthorised.

Once an appeal has been made against an enforcement notice, the decision given by the Secretary of State can be challenged by way of appeal to the High Court under s 289 and by way of judicial review (*see* above). This right of appeal is not limited to challenges to the validity of the notice, although the right to challenge validity is limited by s 285.

5 Obtaining leave to appeal

Introduction

The Carnwath Report identified the difficulties associated with legal delay in the courts. This was well illustrated by the case of *Kuxhaus* (*see* Chapter 9, p 109). To weed out those cases without any merit at an earlier stage and to provide some disincentive for such appeals to the High Court, Carnwath recommended that there should be a requirement for leave for an appeal to the High Court. The Planning and Compensation Act 1991 introduced a new subs (6) to s 289. and it is now a statutory requirement that the leave of the court must be obtained before proceedings can be brought under s 289. Proceedings in the High Court require the leave of that court and any further appeal requires the leave of the Court of Appeal or of the High Court.

Procedure

The procedure for an application for leave is set out in the Rules of the Supreme Court Ord 94, rr 12 and 13. An application for leave to appeal to the

High Court under s 289 shall be made within *28 days* after the date on which notice of the decision against which the challenge is being made was given to the applicant (rule 12(1)). No fee is payable on an application for leave, but a fee of £15 is payable on the entry of the notice of motion (*see* below). An application shall be made in writing setting out the reasons why leave should be granted, and if the time for applying has expired, shall include an application to extend the time for applying, and the reasons why the application was not made within that time (rule 12(2)(*a*), (*b*)).

The court has the power under the Rules of the Supreme Court, Ord 3, r 5 to extend the period of time allowed for an application for leave to appeal. However, this rule does not provide an easy escape route for those who do not conduct their clients' cases with reasonable expedition. In *Smith v Secretary of State for the Environment* (1987) *The Times*, 6 July it was held that merely setting out the chronology of events which had resulted in delay without giving any reasons which would tend to excuse it, did not constitute a sufficient explanation.

An extension of time will not be granted on the ground that the applicant was pursuing an alternative remedy, as this may prejudice the LPA where they have started criminal proceedings and incurred costs *(Bailey and Bailey v Secretary of State for the Environment and Sedgemoor District Council* [1994] JPL B52).

A copy of the application shall be served together with the draft originating notice of motion and a copy of the affidavit to be filed with the application (rule 12(2)(*d*)), on:

(a) the Secretary of State;
(b) where the appeal is brought by the appellant or applicant in the proceedings in which the decision being appealed against was given, the LPA who served the enforcement notice or gave the decision;
(c) where the appeal is brought by the LPA, the appellant or applicant in the proceedings in which the decision being appealed against was given; and
(d) any other person having an interest in the land.

(rule 13(5)).

An application shall be made by filing it in the Crown Office together with the decision that is the subject of the challenge, a draft originating notice of motion, and an affidavit verifying the facts relied on (rule 12 (2)(*c*)). The application shall be accompanied by an affidavit giving the names and addresses of, and the places and dates of service on all persons who have been served with the application and, if any person who ought to be served has not been served, the affidavit must state that fact and the reason for it (rule 12(2)(*e*)). If on the hearing of an application for leave, the court is of the opinion that any person who ought to have been served has not been served, the court may adjourn the hearing to allow such a person to be served (rule 12(4)).

Any respondent who intends to use an affidavit at the hearing shall file it in the Crown Office and serve a copy on the applicant as soon as practicable, and in any event, unless the court otherwise allows, at least two days before the hearing. The court may then allow the applicant to use a further affidavit (rule 12(6)).

It is essential that those advising applicants in relation to an appeal to the High Court are aware of the 28-day time limit. In *Ynes Mon Borough Council v Secretary of State for Wales* [1992] 3 PLR 1, the authority's solicitor, wrongly believing the time allowed for an appeal to the High Court to be six weeks rather than 28 days, did not lodge a notice of motion until one day after the expiry of the 28-day period. The court refused an application for an extension of time and held that legal advisors should know or find out the law and a misunderstanding about time limits was not a reason for time to be extended.

The hearing

An application for leave to appeal shall be heard by a single judge sitting in open court, and unless the court otherwise orders, shall be heard not less than 21 days after the application was filed at the Crown Office (rule 12(3)).

As a result of the time limits associated with an application for leave to appeal, an applicant must develop his case for leave to appeal as soon as possible after notice of the decision being challenged has been given. Sufficient evidence must be available to the judge to determine whether or not there is a case on a point of law on which to base an appeal under s 289. This evidence is presented to the court by affidavits filed by the appellant and in answer by the respondent. The LPA will usually have the conduct of an appeal, rather than the Secretary of State, particularly where the issues raised concern a public inquiry and relate to what was said or occurred at the inquiry. However, in such cases the Secretary of State will lend his support.

The standard to be applied by the court in deciding whether to grant leave under s 289(6) was considered by the court in *R v Secretary of State for the Environment and Gojkovic, ex parte Kensington and Chelsea RLBC* [1993] JPL 139. Here, the court applied the same standards as those applied when deciding whether to grant leave to apply for judicial review, ie, whether there was a *prima facie* arguable case.

If the court grants leave, it may impose any terms as to costs as it thinks fit. The general rule is that the costs of the application should follow the event, and an unsuccessful applicant should pay the respondent's costs. However, it may be inappropriate to order an unsuccessful applicant to bear more than one set of costs eg, where the Secretary of State and the LPA both appeared and advanced duplicated arguments (*R v Secretary of State for Wales, Dyfed County Council and National Parks Department, ex parte Rozhon and Rozhon* [1994] JPL B53).

The court may also give directions (rule 12(5)(a) and (b)), including directions as to the exercise of the power to serve and institute proceedings (including criminal proceedings) concerning a stop notice and a breach of condition notice (rule 13(9)).

Once leave is granted, the originating notice of motion by which the appeal is to be brought (and which was served in draft with the application for leave) shall be served and entered within seven days of the grant (rule 12(5)(*c*)). A fee of £15 is payable on the entry of the notice of motion.

6 Effect of an appeal on the enforcement notice

A second recommendation contained in the Carnwath Report was that, where the court allows an appeal to be brought under s 289 it should have the power to give directions as to the operation of the enforcement notice in the period prior to any further decision of the Secretary of State. A provision to this effect was inserted into s 289 by the Planning and Compensation Act 1991.

Under s 175(4) an enforcement notice shall be of no effect pending the 'final determination' of an appeal against the notice (*see* Chapter 9). This includes an appeal to the High Court. However, there is now provision made in s 289(4A) for the court to order that the enforcement notice shall have effect, or have effect to such extent as may be specified in the order, pending the final determination of the proceedings and any re-hearing and determination by the Secretary of State. The order may be made on such terms if any as the court thinks fit, and this may include terms requiring the LPA to give an undertaking as to damages or any other matter. Should the notice eventually be quashed, an undertaking as to damages would protect the respondent to the application (often the appellant in relation to the original enforcement notice) against any losses. The court may make an order under s 289(4A) when granting leave to appeal or at any other stage in the proceedings brought under s 289.

7 The substantive appeal

Power to remit the matter to the Secretary of State

On the substantive appeal, the powers of the court are limited to remitting the matter to the Secretary of State. Rule 13(7) of the Rules of the Supreme Court provides that:

> Where the Court is of opinion that the decision appealed against was erroneous in point of law, it shall not set aside or vary that decision but shall remit the matter to the Secretary of State with the opinion of the Court for re-hearing and determination by him.

The court has no power to quash a decision or to set aside an enforcement notice. The Secretary of State should be allowed to correct any error, provided that the enforcement notice itself is not invalid. If the court find that there has been an error in law, the matter should be remitted to the Secretary of State. The appellant does not have to prove that he has been substantially prejudiced by the error of law (*LTSS Print and Supply Services v Hackney London Borough Council* [1975] 1 WLR 138 at 142).

In exceptional or rare cases, the court may decline to remit the matter to the Secretary of State for re-hearing and determination, notwithstanding that there has been an error in law. The court has a discretion not to remit where there is no chance that the error of law affected the outcome. For example, where the error did not relate to the merits or substance of the application, but related to the time in which remedial work should be completed in order to comply with the requirements of an enforcement notice, it was appropriate to exercise the discretion so as not to remit (*Botton v Secretary of State for the Environment and London Borough of Bromley* [1992] JPL 941).

Even at the preliminary stage of obtaining leave, where the court is satisfied that no substantial wrong or miscarriage of justice has been occasioned by any misdirection, then it need not grant leave (*PG Vallance Ltd v Secretary of State for the Environment and Mole Valley District Council* [1994] JPL 50). This proposition was based on Ord 55 r 7(7) which states that

> the court shall not be bound to allow the appeal on the ground merely of misdirection, or of the improper admission or rejection of evidence, unless in the opinion of the court substantial wrong or miscarriage has been thereby occasioned

Power to institute stop notice proceedings

In determining the substantive application (and the application for leave to appeal) under s 289, the court may give directions as to the exercise, until an appeal is finally concluded and any re-hearing and determination by the Secretary of State has taken place, of the power to serve and institute proceedings (including criminal proceedings) concerning a stop notice (*see* Chapter 7) and a breach of condition notice (*see* Chapter 8) (rule 13(9)). In this way, the public interest can be protected.

This ties in with the new power contained in s 289(4A) for the court to give directions as to the operation of the enforcement notice in the period prior to any further decision of the Secretary of State (*see* p 187 above). Where such a direction is made, the court may require an undertaking as to damages, and in any event, the compensation provisions associated with the service of a stop notice would apply.

8 Redetermination by the Secretary of State

Where a matter is remitted to the Secretary of State by the court for redetermination, it is his policy to redetermine the enforcement appeal remitted to himself and therefore to recover jurisdiction from the inspector by issuing a direction under TCPA 1990, Sched 6, para 3(1) (Planning Appeal Decision [1987] JPL 529).

On remission of the matter to the Secretary of State for re-hearing and determination, he is entitled to consider the enforcement notice appeal afresh. He is not restricted to simply correcting the error of law on the face of the document. He may conclude that as a result of the court's judgment, other alterations to his decision are necessary. However, if the Secretary of State went further than the view of the court called for, without reference to compelling new material, then his decision could be challenged (*Newbury District*

Council v Secretary of State for the Environment and George Rawlings [1988] JPL 185).

In the case of *Kingswood District Council v Secretary of State for the Environment* [1988] JPL 248, the court held that where a decision on a planning appeal is quashed, the Secretary of State must start afresh and reconsider all the issues raised by the appeal. This would apply to an enforcement notice appeal concerned with the grant of planning permission, either under ground (a) of s 174(2), or by virtue of the deemed application for planning permission under s 177(5). An appeal to the High Court potentially re-opens the whole matter, including any grant of planning permission and the court held that in such circumstances, the Secretary of State had a duty to review the whole case.

Chapter 12

Remedies for Non-Compliance

1 Introduction

There are four statutory remedies for non-compliance relating to an actual or threatened breach of planning control. It is a criminal offence under TCPA 1990, s 179 not to comply with the requirements of an enforcement notice. This provision has been clarified and simplified by the Planning and Compensation Act 1991 but it is not a new concept. Section 178, as amended by the Planning and Compensation Act 1991, empowers the LPA to carry out default works, and related to this, ss 196A–C give the LPA rights of entry. The LPA are also now given specific powers under s 187B to seek an injunction restraining breaches of planning control.

2 Offence of non-compliance

It is an offence for the owner of land or a person who has control of, or an interest in, the land to which an enforcement notice relates to be in breach of that notice. There are two separate offences created by s 179. One relates to the owner of the relevant land, the other to a person who has control of or an interest in the land.

The owner offence

Under s 179(1), where at any time after the end of the period for compliance with an enforcement notice, any step required by the notice to be taken has not been taken or any activity required by the notice to cease is being carried on, the person who is then the owner of the land is in breach of the notice, and shall be guilty of an offence under s 179(2). There are a number of elements to this offence:

(a) *The compliance period specified in the notice must have expired*
   It is a requirement of s 173 that an enforcement notice must specify a period for compliance with the requirements of the notice (*see* Chapter 6). This relates to the steps required to be taken or the activities required to cease. An offence cannot be committed under s 179 until the specified compliance period has

expired. This does not commence until the enforcement notice has come into effect, which will be on the date specified in the notice (or on the date of the unfavourable determination or withdrawal of an enforcement appeal). The LPA must prove the date by which the notice had to be complied with and the date must be alleged in the information laid before the court (*Maltedge Ltd v Wokingham District Council* (1992) *The Times*, 22 May).

(b) *The required steps have not been taken, or the specified activities have not ceased*

The enforcement notice must specify the steps which the LPA require to be taken, or the activities which the LPA require to cease to remedy the breach (s 173, *see* Chapter 6, p 66). An offence will only be committed under s 179 if those specified steps have not been taken or those activities carried out on the land have not ceased. When the specified steps have not been taken, the offence will be complete when the compliance period has expired. However, an offence involving the continuation of activities required to cease, may be committed at any time after the expiry of the compliance period. The owner offence applies either to failure to take the required steps *or* failure to cease the specified activity after the expiry of the compliance period.

(c) *The owner of the land is in breach of the notice, and therefore guilty of an offence*

The offence is committed by the owner at the time when the compliance period specified in the notice expires. It is for the LPA to prove that the defendant is the owner of the land or was the owner at the time of the offence (*R v Epping Magistrates, ex parte Woolhead* [1994] JPL B28). The offence is not proved unless the prosecution shows that the defendant was the owner at that time (*R v Ruttle, ex parte Marshall* [1989] JPL 681).

In order to prove ownership, the LPA can rely upon an index map search in the case of registered land, replies to a requisition for information, or a response to a planning contravention notice (*see* Chapter 3) or relevant correspondence. As a matter of good practice, before issuing and serving an enforcement notice, the LPA should carry out a land registry search, a company search and serve a planning contravention notice where appropriate.

A subsequent owner who remains in breach of the enforcement notice will also be guilty of an offence under this section. The rationale behind this is that a purchaser will be aware of the existence of the enforcement notice as it will be entered in the enforcement register (s 188) and if he is not so aware, he may rely on s 179(7), as detailed below.

There are two statutory defences to the owner offence. Section 179(3) provides that it is a defence for the owner to show that he did everything he could be expected to do to secure compliance with the notice. The burden of proof is on the owner and the standard of proof on the balance of probabilities. There may be circumstances where it would be impossible for the owner to comply with the requirements of an enforcement notice, eg where the premises concerned are occupied by a tenant, or a third party is responsible for the breach and the owner has no control over such party. In these circumstances, the owner could seek to rely on the defence in s 179(3). In *Kent County Council v Brockman* [1994] JPL B27 the court held that the plain meaning of the words in s 179(3) permit the personal circumstances of the defendant to be taken into account. In that case, the defence was that the defendant was incapacitated, both financially and physically, and that it was not within his power or capability to comply with the enforcement notice. This defence was successful, although Buckley J commented that where such a defence was raised the court should be fairly rigorous in the proof which it expects or demands of a defendant, and not allow itself to be hoodwinked by protestations of impecuniosity. In addition, given that the TCPA 1990 empowered the LPA to go onto the land and correct the position itself, thereafter recovering its costs and expenses from the individual concerned, the public interest could still be protected.

In the event that the owner is prevented from taking the steps required by an enforcement notice by a third party with an interest in the relevant land, eg a tenant, he may apply to the magistrate's court for an order that such other person permit the steps to be taken under the Town and Country Planning General Regulations 1992 (SI No 1492), reg 14, made under s 178(3), applying the provisions of the Public Health Act 1936, s 289.

The second statutory defence is contained in s 179(7). Where an owner has not been served with a copy of the enforcement notice, and the notice is not contained in the enforcement register, it is a defence for him to show that he was not aware of the existence of the notice. Again, the onus is on the owner to prove that such circumstances exist. The first two elements of the defence may be shown as a matter of fact. The third element is the one that the owner must establish to the satisfaction of the court.

The person who has control of the land

The offence relating to a person who has control of or an interest in the land (other than the owner) is contained in s 179(5). Such a person must not carry on any activity which is required by the notice to cease or cause or permit such an activity to be carried on (s 179(4)). A person who does so after the expiry of the compliance period specified in the notice shall be guilty of an offence. This may be committed *at any time* after the time for compliance has expired.

A person who is not the owner, but has control of, or an interest in the land can only commit an offence under s 179 where the requirements of the notice relate to activities carried out on the land. It is the owner who will be liable where steps required by the enforcement notice have not been taken.

The circumstances in which a person causes or permits an activity to be carried on have been considered by the courts. A person can only permit another to do an act where he has:

    (a) the power to forbid him to do the act (such as the power that a landlord has over a tenant to enforce the terms of a lease), and

    (b) failed to take reasonable steps to prevent it.

In the case of *Test Valley Investments, Ltd v Tanner* (1964) 15 P & CR 279, the court held that a person might be said to 'permit' something, not only if he gave express permission, but also if he failed to take reasonable steps to prevent it. A failure to take unreasonable steps (in that case the physical removal of gypsies) could not amount to 'permitting'.

Section 179(7) provides a statutory defence to an offence under s 179 committed by a person who has control of or an interest in the land. This defence is detailed above in relation to the owner offence.

TCPA 1990, s 285

Section 285 prevents a challenge against the validity of an enforcement notice as a defence to a prosecution under s 179 on any of the grounds upon which an appeal may be made to the Secretary of State. There is a statutory exception to this contained in s 285(2) and this is dealt with in detail in Chapter 6, p 62. However, it is open to a defendant to challenge an enforcement notice on grounds other than those contained in s 174(2), eg to show that the enforcement notice is a nullity, or that it was issued fraudulently. In such a case, the defendant would be questioning the validity of the enforcement notice, but not on any of the grounds on which an appeal may be brought under s 174(2) (*Davy v Spelthorne District Council* [1984] AC 262).

In the case of *Bugg v DPP* (1993) *The Times*, 11 September, the Court of Appeal considered the circumstances in which the courts will entertain a challenge to the validity of an instrument as a defence to a prosecution based on it. It was held that the court could investigate a case of substantive invalidity which was clear on the face of the instrument, but should not investigate a case of procedural invalidity, where there has been a failure to comply with a procedural requirement in making the instrument, as this depends on evidence being called and not purely on the enabling legislation and the instrument itself.

Authority to prosecute

The full council of the LPA may delegate the authority to prosecute to either a committee or sub-committee, or to an officer. Such powers of delegation will be contained in the authority's standing orders (*see* Chapter 4). To avoid any risk of a successful challenge to the authority to prosecute, the LPA should ensure that the authorisation of the prosecution is correctly minuted, it names the party correctly, it identifies the relevant land clearly, and that the terms of the enforcement notice are properly recited.

Penalties

In terms of criminal penalties, Carnwath saw a need for the courts to have the power to impose penalties which will be a real deterrent and to take into account the financial benefit which has accrued to the offender by reason of the contravention. Parliament accepted these recommendations and the Planning and Compensation Act 1991, s 8 substituted a new s 179. In addition, Planning Policy Guidance Note 18 quotes from the Government White Paper 'Crime, Justice and Protecting the Public' (Cmd 965) which states:

> If people ignore or flout laws and regulations designed to protect the public from serious harm, they should be properly punished, and the punishment should take account of the resulting profits or savings.

Section 179(8) imposes a maximum fine on summary conviction of £20,000, and an unlimited fine on conviction on indictment. Under s 179(9), in determining the amount for any fine, the court shall have particular regard to any financial benefit which has accrued or appears likely to accrue to the person convicted of the offence because of the offence. The LPA must provide evidence to this effect. Circular 21/91 advises that

> prosecuting authorities should always be ready to give any available details about the proceeds resulting, or likely to result, from the offence, so that the court can take account of them in sentencing.

An offence under s 179 may be charged by reference to any day or longer period of time. Therefore the LPA can choose a date when the offence is alleged to have taken place eg, the date of the enforcement officer's visit. A second or subsequent offence shall be a separate offence and a person may be convicted of such an offence by reference to any period of time following the preceding conviction (s 179(6)). Evidence of a previous conviction can be given by producing a certificate of conviction, together with evidence of identity (Police and Criminal Evidence Act 1984, s 73). These provisions follow the recommendation in the Carnwath Report that it is made clear that there may be further offences following a second conviction.

Prosecutions and planning applications

Where a planning application is made, either before or after prosecution proceedings are instigated, the two matters should continue to be processed on separate but parallel tracks. However, in the case of *R v Newland* [1987] JPL 851, the Court of Appeal held that where criminal proceedings for non-compliance with the terms of an enforcement notice were brought, and a planning application for the alleged breach of planning control had been made, the criminal proceedings ought to be deferred where, as in this case, the result of the planning application could reasonably be expected in a matter of weeks. There is an argument, accepted by Counsel for the appellant in the *Newland* case, that where the appellant sought an adjournment of the criminal proceedings on the basis that a planning application had been lodged merely to delay compliance with the enforcement notice, then that adjournment should be refused.

In *R v Beaconsfield Magistrates, ex parte South Buckinghamshire District Council* [1993] JPL B53, enforcement notices were served requiring the removal of caravans from land. The LPA subsequently prosecuted for non-compliance with the notices. The defendants were waiting for the result of applications for planning permission. The court held that the magistrates must deal with the matter forthwith, unless there was a prospect that the outcome of the planning application would be known shortly. In this case, the decision of the magistrates to adjourn the case indefinitely was upheld. Although the court acknowledged that this was a very unusual course, it was justified by the circumstances that existed, namely, the age, means, state of health, and particular circumstances of the defendant, and also a very substantial period of inaction by the LPA.

In both the *Newland* and the *Beaconsfield Magistrates* cases, the court recognised the general rule that a prosecution under s 179 should proceed where an application for planning permission has been made for the same matters which constitute the breach of planning control. However, in circumstances where the outcome of the planning application will become known in the very near future, a prosecution may be adjourned.

Reinstatement or restoration

Once an enforcement notice comes into effect, it imposes a continuing obligation. Under s 181(1) compliance with the requirements of an enforcement notice does not discharge it, although, where a later planning permission is granted, the enforcement notice ceases to have effect for those parts of the buildings which are the subject of the planning permission (*R v Chichester Justices, ex parte Chichester District Council* [1990] EGCS 13). A requirement that a use of land be discontinued operates as a requirement to discontinue that use permanently and a subsequent resumption of that use shall be a contravention of the enforcement notice and an offence under s 179 (s 181(2)). In the case of *Prosser v Sharp* [1985] JPL 717, a caravan was removed from land in compliance with the requirements of an enforcement notice, but replaced with another. The court held that the enforcement notice had continuing validity, and therefore the stationing of a replacement caravan on the land was a breach of the existing enforcement notice.

An enforcement notice shall also apply to the reinstatement or restoration of buildings or works that have been removed or altered in accordance with the requirements of such an enforcement notice. If a person reinstates or restores buildings or works which have been removed or altered in compliance with an enforcement notice, he shall be guilty of an offence (s 181(5)). The offence is committed by the person who carried out the reinstatement or restoration. The owner's liability under s 179(2) is excluded by s 181(5)(*b*), where he is not the person who carried out the reinstatement or restoration.

3 Default powers

The statute gives LPAs power to enter land to which an enforcement notice relates and to carry out any required steps. This power arises where any steps required by an enforcement notice are not taken within the period specified for compliance with the notice (s 178(1)). The LPA is given a power to carry out works in default of the person on whom the enforcement notice is served. In the event of non-compliance with the requirements of an enforcement notice, the LPA may exercise the power under s 178 without prejudice to the criminal liability of the owner under s 179.

Failure to take steps

The basis of the power contained in s 178 is that the person on whom the enforcement notice is served has failed to take the required steps before the expiry of the compliance period specified in the notice. The power relates to *any* steps required by an enforcement notice. This includes:

    (a)   remedying the breach of planning control;

    (b)   steps remedying any injury to amenity which has been caused by the breach; and

    (c)   ceasing any activity on the land to which the notice relates.

The LPA may carry out works to make any development comply with the terms of any planning permission which has been granted for the land to which the enforcement notice relates. Circular 21/91 also makes it clear that the LPA may carry out steps to discontinue a use of land (including the discontinuance of mining operations, by virtue of the Town and Country Planning (Minerals) Regulations 1971 (SI No 756), reg 3), and gives the example of a storage use, where an enforcement notice requires the removal of stored items. The LPA may remove those items themselves and continue to remove such items as may appear on the land. The works that may be carried out by the LPA extend to the alteration or removal of a building, if these are the steps specified in the enforcement notice. North East Derbyshire District Council demolished a pig farm in early 1994, almost three years after having first taken enforcement action. The demolition was carried out by council staff under police protection, and was celebrated by the local residents affected.

In terms of taking steps to ensure that specified activities cease, the LPA have the power to remove any materials from any premises and to sell any such materials that are not claimed by the owner within three days of their removal (Town and Country Planning General Regulations 1992, reg 14, made under s 178(3), applying the provisions of the Public Health Act 1936, s 276). Accordingly, the LPA may effectively ensure that specified activities cease, and may also ensure the discontinuance of a use of land by removing materials from the land, eg, a caravan (*Midlothian District Council v Stevenson* [1986] JPL 913). Any proceeds from the sale of such materials must be paid to the person to whom they belonged, after the LPA have deducted the amount of any expenses.

Expiry of compliance period

An enforcement notice must specify a period for compliance with the requirements of the notice (s 173(9)). The power for the LPA to carry out default works does not arise until the compliance period has expired. The LPA have the power to extend the period allowed for compliance as part of its statutory power to waive or relax any requirement of an enforcement notice (s 173A, *see* Chapter 6, p 73), and, in such a case, the power under s 178 will not arise until such extended period for compliance has expired.

The LPA are not required to give notice of the exercise of the power under s 178 (however, *see* below). The compliance period specified in the enforcement notice should have given the person on whom it is served sufficient time for compliance with the requirements of the notice, so no further notice period need be given. However, in the case of the removal or alteration of buildings reinstated or restored in contravention of an enforcement notice, the LPA must give not less than 28 days' notice of their intention to remove or alter the buildings, using the power under s 178, to the owner and occupier of the land (s 181(4)).

Recovery of expenses

The LPA are given a statutory right to recover any expenses reasonably incurred by them in entering and carrying out default works from the owner of the land at the time of entry and carrying out of the works, (s 178(1)(*b*)). These expenses include the recovery of overheads by virtue of the Local Government Act 1974, s 36. Regulation 14(2) of the Town and Country Planning General Regulations 1992 provides that the expenses recoverable under s 178(1) are, until recovered, a charge that is binding on successive owners of the land to which the enforcement notice relates. Such charge will take effect from the date of completion by the LPA of the steps required to be taken by the enforcement notice.

If the owner is not responsible for the breach of planning control to which the enforcement notice relates, he may recover any expenses incurred by him for the purpose of complying with the notice, and recover any sums paid to the LPA for carrying out default works under s 178, from the person by whom the breach of planning control was committed (s 178(2)).

The liability of an owner who can prove that he is receiving rent from the relevant premises, merely as agent or trustee for some other person, and that he does not have, and since the date of the service of a demand for payment, has not had sufficient money to discharge the whole demand on behalf of that other person, is limited to the total amount of money he has in his hands. In these circumstances, the LPA can recover the balance from the person on whose behalf the agent or trustee receives the rent (Town and Country Planning General Regulations 1992, reg 14, made under s 178(3), applying the provisions of the Public Health Act 1936, s 294).

Offence under TCPA 1990, s 178

Any person who wilfully obstructs the LPA in exercising its powers under s 178 shall be guilty of an offence and liable on summary conviction to a fine not exceeding 'level 3' on the standard scale, currently £1,000 (s 178(6)). This provision was introduced by the Planning and Compensation Act 1991, s 7.

Exercise of the power

The LPA will need to obtain committee authority to exercise their power under s 178. The LPA do not have to serve notice on the landowner that they intend to enter on the land and carry out default works. However, the service of such a notice is good practice, and may have the effect of prompting the landowner to carry out the works himself.

A notice served on the landowner should give a date when the works are to begin. In line with the date upon which an enforcement notice comes into effect, at least 28 days' notice should be given. The notice may also provide the landowner with an estimate of the cost of the works This can be provided by the LPA copying to the landowner a number of estimates (reasonably, at least three). If these procedural arrangements are followed, there is less risk of a successful challenge being mounted against the actions of the LPA.

In some circumstances it may prove more cost effective for LPAs to take direct action and to carry out default works, rather than proceed with a criminal prosecution through the courts, which may not achieve the desired result or may result in a derisory fine (although the maximum penalties have now been increased, *see* p 163 above). In addition, where the LPA carry out default works, this may act as a deterrent to others, particularly where it is carried out accompanied by widespread publicity.

Validity of exercise of the power

A person may challenge the exercise of the power under s 178 in circumstances where a person has failed to lodge an appeal against an enforcement notice in time, but can show that one of the grounds of appeal under s 174(2) might have been made out had such an appeal been lodged. In the case of *R v Greenwich London Borough Council, ex parte Patel* [1985] JPL 851, the court expressed the view that there might be cases where a person who had not been served with an enforcement notice and who had not appealed was in a position to place facts before the LPA which tended to show that one of the grounds of appeal under the TCPA 1990 could be made out. The LPA had a duty to investigate those facts before it took action to enter and carry out works. If the LPA unreasonably refused to carry out such an investigation, the court would be entitled to review the decision to enter the land and carry out default works.

The use of force

The Royal Town Planning Institute (RTPI) has made a recommendation to the Home Office (yet to be taken) that s 178 should be supplemented to include an additional power to allow planning officials to use 'reasonable force' to enable them to enter land and carry out remedial works required by an enforcement notice. Force may be used to enter land under warrant (see below). The RTPI consider that once the increased power became established and well known, it would become a rarely used reserve power, but would be a useful supplementary power to s 178.

4 Rights of entry

Right to enter without warrant

Section 196A confers on LPAs broad powers to enter land for investigative purposes in connection with their enforcement powers. The right is limited to what is essential for the effective enforcement of planning control. It is not restricted to circumstances where the LPA actually propose to issue an enforcement notice or a stop notice. This means that LPA officers can visit a site on several occasions if necessary, and record, photograph and monitor the site with a view to building up documentary evidence to support future enforcement action, or to inform members of the situation on site.

The right of entry may be exercised to:
  (a) ascertain whether there is, or has been, any breach of planning control on the land, or on any other land;
  (b) determine whether any of the enforcement powers conferred on the LPA should be exercised in relation to the land, or any other land;
  (c) determine how any such power should be exercised; and
  (d) ascertain whether there has been compliance with any requirement imposed as a result of any such power having been exercised in relation to the land, or any other land.

It therefore covers a very wide range of matters associated with the LPA's enforcement powers. The references to 'any other land' mean that LPAs can enter neighbouring land if necessary, regardless of ownership.

There are some limits on the exercise of the power. The person exercising the power must be duly authorised in writing by the LPA, the entry onto land must be made at a reasonable hour, and there must be reasonable grounds for entering for the purpose in question (s 196A(1)). Circular 21/91 advises that 'reasonable grounds' is interpreted to mean that entering the land is the logical means of obtaining the information required by the LPA. The exercise of the right to enter under s 196A may be authorised by the Secretary of State, but only after consultation with the relevant LPA.

There is a statutory exception to entry as of right under s 196A. Section 196A(4) provides that 24 hours' notice of the intended entry must be given to the occupier of any building used as a dwellinghouse. Circular 21/91 makes it clear that such protection also applies to any residential accommodation within an industrial or commercial building (eg, a caretaker's flat). However, the notice requirement does not apply to the outbuildings or garden land in the curtilage of a dwellinghouse, unless the access to them can only be gained by going through the dwellinghouse.

Right to enter under warrant

Any person duly authorised in writing by the LPA or the Secretary of State under a warrant issued by a justice of the peace has a right to enter (s 196B). This power reinforces that contained in s 196A and allows entry to be made by force if necessary. It is therefore a useful tool for LPAs in particularly difficult or controversial cases, or where evidence as to the unauthorised development of land is deliberately concealed.

To issue such a warrant, a justice of the peace must be satisfied on sworn information in writing that:

    (a) there are reasonable grounds for entering any land for any of the purposes specified in s 196A; and

    (b) that admission to the land has been refused (it is sufficient if no reply is received to a request for admission within a reasonable period), or a refusal is reasonably apprehended, or the case is one of urgency.

Once a warrant has been issued, it authorises entry on one occasion only and that entry must be made within one month from the date of the issue of the warrant; and at a reasonable hour, unless the case is one of urgency (s 196B(3))

Compensation

The LPA are required to compensate any person suffering any damage to land (including a building) or chattels (eg, machinery, equipment or livestock) caused by the LPA in the exercise of a right of entry (s 196C(3)). Circular 21/91 advises that as the LPAs investigations for enforcement purposes will normally be confined to a visual inspection, any consequential damage should be 'most exceptional'. In cases where the right of entry is authorised by the Secretary of State, such compensation is payable by him. Any question of disputed compensation shall be referred to and determined by the Lands Tribunal in accordance with s 118.

Supplementary matters

The statute provides for a number of supplementary matters relating to the exercise of the right of entry. These are set out in s 196C. When seeking to exercise the right of entry, a person authorised to enter land must, if so required, produce evidence of his authority and state the purpose of his entry before so entering, he may take with him such other persons as may be necessary, and, if the owner is not present, on leaving the land, he shall leave it secured.

These matters are in place to provide some reassurance and protection for persons who doubt the legitimacy of the right to enter, or the person seeking to exercise the right, and persons affected should not hesitate to make use of these rights. However, a person wilfully obstructing a person properly exercising a right of entry commits an offence under s 196C(2) and is liable on summary conviction to a fine at 'level 3' on the standard scale, currently £1,000.

The Secretary of State has stated that special precautions are essential when the right of entry to agricultural land is exercised. An appendix to Annex 5 of Circular 21/91 sets out the additional precautions which must be taken before, and when, entering agricultural land. This is reproduced at Appendix 6.

There may be circumstances where a person exercising a right of entry has access to information relating to a manufacturing process or trade secret. If he discloses such information obtained by him while on the land, he will be guilty of an offence and liable on summary conviction to a fine of £5,000 or on conviction on indictment, to two years' imprisonment or an unlimited fine or both (s 196C(5) and (7)). The exception is where the disclosure is made by a person in the course of performing his duty in connection with the purpose for which he was authorised to enter the land (s 196C(6)). These provisions provide some protection for business occupiers, particularly where secret developments give rise to suspicions on the part of the LPA, which lead to the exercise of the right of entry.

5 Injunctions

Background

Before the provisions of s 187B came into effect, injunctive relief in planning law did exist, but was rarely used and difficult to obtain. One of the principle complaints contained in the Carnwath Report was the lack of urgency associated with the enforcement of breaches of planning control. Two methods for improving the situation were suggested by Carnwath. The first was a revision of the circumstances in which a stop notice may be served (*see* Chapter 7). The second remedy was the use of an injunction which Carnwath suggested 'should be recognised by the statute itself as a useful weapon in the planning armoury'.

Carnwath identified two circumstances where the ability of the LPA to apply for an injunction would be especially useful:

    (a)   it can provide an urgent remedy in cases where there is a serious threat to amenity, to deal with either a threatened breach (before a stop notice can be served) or an actual breach;

    (b)   it can provide a stronger back-up power in cases where the existing remedies have proved, or are thought likely to be, inadequate.

The recommendation given in the Carnwath Report was adopted by Parliament and forms the basis of the statutory remedy now contained in s 187B.

Local Government Act 1972, s 222

The local authority is empowered under s 222 of the 1972 Act to appear in any legal proceedings in their own name where they consider it expedient for the promotion or protection of the interests of the inhabitants of their area. This power has been used successfully by local authorities to obtain an injunction supplementing their enforcement powers. Under s 222, a local authority can obtain both a mandatory injunction, requiring a party to take some positive steps, and a restraining injunction, to restrain a party from doing an act.

In general, cases may be brought under s 222 in supplementation of the statutory enforcement powers where there has been a deliberate and flagrant flouting and a clear breach of the law (*Stoke-on-Trent City Council v B & Q*

(Retail) Ltd [1984] AC 754). However, it is not necessary for the local authority to have first exhausted their statutory remedies, or for the LPA to have instituted prosecution proceedings, particularly where such proceedings would have been slow and futile, and the effectiveness of a financial penalty would be in doubt, eg, against gypsies or a man of straw (*Runnymede Borough Council v Ball* [1986] 1 WLR 353).

It is made clear in para 4 of Annex 4 of Circular 21/91 that the availability of the injunctive provisions in s 187B is without prejudice to the LPA's power to seek an injunction under the enabling powers of s 222. However, there appears to be little merit in resorting to s 222, as s 187B is designed to be used in relation to planning control, and can be used to obtain a mandatory injunction as well as an injunction restraining a breach of planning control (*see* the *Gladden* case below).

TCPA 1990, s 187B

The statutory provisions empower the LPA to apply to the High Court or to the county court for an injunction, where they 'consider it necessary or expedient for any actual or apprehended breach of planning control to be restrained by injunction'. This application may be made whether or not the LPA have exercised, or propose to exercise, any of their other powers to enforce planning control.

The scope of the power contained in s 187B was reviewed by the Court of Appeal in two recent decisions. In *Croydon London Borough Council v Gladden and Another* [1994] EGCS 24, the court held that s 187B could be used to obtain either a mandatory or a restraining injunction. Although the wording of the statutory provision referred to restraining a breach of planning control, Dillon LJ stated that:

> ... section 187B was drawn on the statutory assumption that an actual, as well as an intended, breach of planning control could be restrained by injunction. Therefore the word 'restrained' had to be given a wider, and in the context more natural, meaning. Once that was done it was obvious that mandatory injunctions were not excluded.

In the case of *Runnymede Borough Council v Harwood* (1994) EGCS 23, the court held that s 187B granted a wider power than s 222 of the 1972 Act. The power given to the court to grant injunctions to enforce planning control applied to apprehended as well as actual breaches of planning control. In the case of an actual breach, and an application for an interlocutory injunction, the court was not confined to preserving the status quo until the trial. In this case, this would have had the effect of giving temporary planning permission for the continued use of land for which the LPA had consistently refused permission.

The exercise of the court's discretion

Under s 187B(2) an injunction may be granted 'as the court thinks appropriate for the purpose of restraining the breach'. The court therefore has a broad discretion. However, the grant of an injunction is an equitable remedy, and the court will need to consider existing judicial criteria in determining whether or not to grant injunctive relief.

The general principles relating to the exercise of a discretionary power to grant injunctive relief are set out in the case of *American Cyanamid Co v Ethicon* [1975] AC 396. The House of Lords held that the court must determine where the 'balance of convenience' lies. The two factors that must be balanced are:

(a)   the plaintiff's need for protection against the violation of his rights; and

(b)   the defendant's need for protection against injury resulting from being prevented from exercising his own legal rights.

However, the court recognised that where there was doubt as to the parties respective remedies in damages being adequate to compensate for any loss resulting from any restraint imposed on them, the status quo should be preserved. However, in the context of the enforcement of planning control, *see* the decision in the *Harwood* case detailed above.

The court will also be influenced by any delay in seeking an injunction. Generally, an injunction is sought in cases of urgency and as it is a discretionary remedy, the court will need to be convinced of the need for urgency, in addition to the other criteria detailed below.

Exercise of the power by the LPA

It will be necessary for the LPA to make a careful assessment of whether or not to seek injunctive relief by means of an application under s 187B, which provides that the power may be exercised where the LPA consider it 'necessary or expedient'. This criteria relates to the breach of control, actual or anticipated. Matters to be considered by the LPA in this context include:

(a)   the seriousness of the breach of planning control;

(b)   the urgency for remedial action;

(c)   the need to take prompt action to restrain a developer;

(d)   the circumstances of the persons against whom proceedings are contemplated; and

(e)   whether other enforcement proceedings would take too long.

Paragraph 7 of Annex 4 to Circular 21/91 provides that the following criteria should be satisfied before the court are likely to grant an injunction:

(a)   the LPA have taken account of what appear to be the relevant considerations in deciding that it is necessary or expedient to initiate injunctive proceedings;

(b)   there is clear evidence that a breach of planning control has already occurred, or is likely to occur;

(c)   injunctive relief is a commensurate remedy in the circumstances of the particular case;

(d)   in the case of an injunction sought against a person whose identity is unknown, it is practicable to serve the court's order on the person or persons to whom it will apply.

Even where all the above criteria are satisfied, the court will not necessarily grant injunctive relief, if they decide that the circumstances of the case do not, on the balance of convenience, justify granting an injunction. The court may grant an injunction and then suspend its effect until a specified later date.

The last category of the criteria listed above is relevant, as any injunction granted by the court is directed at named persons. It does not become a charge on the land, as an enforcement notice, stop notice or breach of condition notice does. Circular 21/91 advises that LPAs will need to assess the likely effect of this difference in considering whether to initiate injunctive proceedings.

The relevant considerations

The first of the criteria that the court will consider as detailed in para 7 of Annex 4 to Circular 21/91, is whether the LPA have taken account of the 'relevant considerations' in deciding that it is necessary or expedient to initiate injunctive proceedings. These considerations will include such matters as:

(a) the nature of the breach or anticipated breach of planning control;
(b) the evidence available to indicate that a breach has already occurred or is likely to occur (this will have to be sufficient to satisfy the court);
(c) whether an injunction is an appropriate remedy, given the range of alternative enforcement powers available;
(d) whether the breach of planning control is of such significance that it warrants urgent action, ie, conflict with important planning policy considerations, or the extent of controversy surrounding the breach;
(e) whether recurrence of the breach of planning control is a possibility; and
(f) the legal costs that may be involved, including damages (*see* below).

Legal costs

As with all legal proceedings, the LPA may have a costs liability arising from initiating injunctive proceedings. Paragraph 6 of Annex 4 to Circular 21/91 advises that to minimise the possibility of incurring wasted costs, the LPA will need to make their own best assessment (if necessary, by obtaining counsel's opinion) of the likely outcome of such proceedings.

Undertaking in damages

An undertaking in damages is given to the court in any injunctive proceedings. This is to protect the person against whom the injunction (if any) is granted. If that person suffers loss or damage as a result of being restrained from carrying out a development or taking some action, and the substantive proceedings are ultimately unsuccessful, ie, the developer eventually obtains planning permission, or it is shown that no breach of planning control occurred, the LPA will be required to pay those damages. It is therefore important for the LPA to make an assessment of the possible liability for damages and to make some provision in this respect, before deciding to initiate injunctive proceedings.

An undertaking in damages is not a prerequisite to seeking an injunction. The House of Lords has recently held in *Kirklees Borough Council v Wickes Building Supplies Ltd* [1992] 3 All ER 717 that, where the LPA seek an injunction to restrain a breach of planning control, and such action is taken in the public interest, the court has a discretion whether or not to require an undertaking in damages from the LPA.

Persons unknown

Section 187B(3) states that rules of court may provide for an injunction restraining a breach of planning control to be issued against a person whose identity is unknown. This provision was inserted in recognition of the fact that there may be circumstances where an injunction should be granted to prevent serious and irreparable harm from being caused and the urgency of the matter may prevent an investigation being undertaken to identify the person concerned.

Order 110 of the Rules of the Supreme Court and the County Court Rules 1981, Ord 49, r 6 make such provision in respect of injunctions to prevent environmental harm, which include injunctions under s 187B.

Guidance is given in Circular 21/91 on the type of information that may be used in support of the LPA's application to court, where an injunction is sought against a person whose identity is unknown. This includes:

(a) photographic evidence of the persons concerned;
(b) affidavit evidence sworn by the LPA's officers;
(c) reference to chattels on the land, known to belong to, or to be used by, that person (eg, a registered motor vehicle); and
(d) any other relevant evidence (such as a name by which the person is known, even though it is not his given name).

In addition, when applying to the court, Circular 21/91 states that the LPA will have to provide affidavit evidence of their inability to ascertain the identity of the person within the time reasonably available, and the steps taken in attempting to do so.

Actual or apprehended breach of planning control

Robert Carnwath QC recommended that the power to apply for an injunction should relate both to any threatened or actual breach of planning control, whether or not an enforcement or stop notice has been served. This approach was adopted by Parliament, and the power under s 187B is available to LPAs where, in the light of all the relevant circumstances, it is necessary or expedient to make such an application where a breach of planning control has not yet occurred, but it is clear to the LPA that it is threatened. In such circumstances, the LPA should remember that the court have a discretion to grant an injunction. It is therefore particularly important for the LPA to satisfy the court that there is sufficient evidence of the threatened breach, as well as the criteria set out on pp 173 and 174.

The power to restrain an apprehended breach of planning control appears to be a considerable strengthening of the powers that existed under the Local Government Act 1972, s 222. The cases where injunctions were granted under that provision in relation to a breach of planning control appear to be limited to actual breaches of planning control. In the case of *Doncaster Borough Council v William Green and Others* [1992] JPL 658, a case brought under s 222, the court refused to grant an injunction where there was an enforcement appeal pending.

Effect of an injunction

Once a person has been served with a court order, he will be in contempt of court if he continues to act in breach of the terms of the order. However, the courts have been reluctant to commit a person in contempt of an injunction granted under s 187B. In the case of *Guildford Borough Council v Valler* [1993] EGCS 78 the court held that, unless the conduct of the person in contempt of court involved a wilful or deliberate disobedience of the order, the contempt could not attract committal. It was for the court to carry out a balancing exercise as to whether a committal could be justified.

An interlocutory or interim injunction will operate to restrain the alleged breach of planning control until the issue is determined, either by an enforcement notice appeal, or by the determination of an application for planning permission, which may involve an appeal. Both may be the subject of a challenge to the High Court, and it could be some considerable length of time before the matter is concluded (*see* Chapter 9). It is important for the LPA to bear this in mind when deciding whether or not to seek an injunction, as it may affect the undertaking for damages. Alternatively, the issue may be considered by the court at a substantive hearing, either under s 222 or s 187B, following the grant of an interlocutory injunction, as in the case where the LPA have not exercised any of their other powers to enforce planning control.

Chapter 13

Lawful Development Certificates

1 Introduction

The planning status of land is an issue that is often a matter of concern both to LPAs and to landowners or developers. Prior to the Planning and Compensation Act 1991, the procedures available to a landowner or developer for establishing planning status consisted of applications for established use certificates and applications to determine whether planning permission was required for a particular type of development.

In his Report, Carnwath suggested that there should be a formal means of confirming the legality of a use or operation, based on a unified procedure. This led to the introduction of a procedure for obtaining Lawful Development Certificates (referred to in this chapter as LDC) for existing use or development and for proposed use or development.

Section 10 of the Planning and Compensation Act 1991 applies the concept of 'lawfulness' for planning purposes to all those breaches of planning control which have become immune from planning enforcement action by virtue of the time limits on taking such action (*see* Chapter 5). As a result, uses, operations or activities are either lawful or unlawful and the procedure for obtaining a LDC reflects this state of affairs.

The provisions of TCPA 1990, ss 191 to 196 detail the new procedures for establishing the planning status of land. This chapter briefly summarises the historical background relating to the introduction of the LDC and the practical means of applying for and obtaining a LDC by using the new procedures. These are a way of requiring LPAs to determine the lawfulness of existing and proposed uses, operations and activities. The popular practice of issuing letters of comfort on planning matters should now be superseded by these formal procedures.

2 Historical background

Prior to the introduction of LDCs, there were two established procedures in planning law for determining the planning status of land.

Established use

The first related to the planning status of land with regard to its established use. Under the old s 191 of the TCPA 1990 (now replaced by new s 191), any person with an interest in land could apply to the LPA for an 'established use certificate'. This provided conclusive evidence about any matters specified in it for the purposes of an appeal against an enforcement notice served subsequently. It did not confer a 'lawful use' relating to the land, but merely an 'established use', which was effective in relation to enforcement action taken by the LPA. Established use rights started as unlawful uses and, although they gained immunity in certain circumstances, they remain tainted by their origin. (*Bailey v Secretary of State for the Environment and Sedgemoor District Council* [1993] JPL 774).

Proposed development

The second related to the situation where a developer proposed to carry out an operation on land or to make any change in the use of the land. Under the old s 64 of the TCPA 1990 (now replaced by new s 192), any person could seek a determination from the LPA as to whether such proposal would constitute or involve development of the land, and if so whether an application for planning permission was required. The result of such a determination would then enable any person to proceed accordingly, as the planning status of the land would be established with regard to a proposed development.

Deficiencies

Both the above procedures were criticised in the Carnwath Report, and difficulties had become apparent to both LPAs and landowners and developers in the application of the procedures.

To obtain an established use certificate, it was necessary for an applicant to establish that a particular operation or material change in the use of land was immune from enforcement action. Under the old provisions, a material change of use became immune from enforcement action where it could be shown that the use had continued uninterrupted since the end of 1963. This was becoming increasingly difficult to establish with the passage of time.

The power to determine whether planning permission was required for a proposed development applied only to proposed uses or operations, and not to those already in existence. In addition, the LPA were confined to consideration of the proposed use or operation, without regard to background factors, such as the legality of a previous use, or the scope of an established use certificate relating to it.

It was partly as a result of these deficiencies that Carnwath made a recommendation in his report that there be a single procedure whereby the LPA could issue a certificate that any specified use or operation (whether or not instituted before the application was made) can be carried on without planning permission. Parliament adopted this recommendation and introduced a new procedure into the TCPA 1990 through the vehicle of the Planning and Compensation Act 1991.

3 Certificate of lawfulness of existing use or development

A procedure is now set out in s 191 for applying to the LPA for a certificate of lawfulness of existing use or development, or CLEUD. Any person (not just a person with an interest in the land) may make an application to the LPA to ascertain whether any:

    (a) existing use of buildings or other land is lawful;

    (b) operations which have been carried out in, on, over or under land are lawful; or

    (c) other matter constituting a failure to comply with any condition or limitation subject to which planning permission has been granted is lawful.

The form and content of an application

Section 191(1) expressly provides that an application shall specify the land and describe the existing use, operations or other matter to which the application relates. Paragraph 18 of Annex 1 to Circular 17/92 states that such existing use, operation or other activity will have to be described in reasonably precise terms in the application which must be made in writing on a form provided by the LPA. A model application form, which LPAs may like to use, is appended to Annex 1 to Circular 17/92. The information to be contained in the application is prescribed in Article 26A of the 1988 GDO pursuant to the powers contained in s 193(1). The application must specify:

    (a) whether it relates to an existing use, operation or other matter;

    (b) the date on which the existing use, operation or other matter began, or in the case of operations carried out without planning permission, the date on which those operations were substantially completed;

    (c) in the case of an existing use, the name of any use class specified in the Use Classes Order which the applicant considers is applicable to the existing use;

    (d) in the case of any matter constituting a failure to comply with any condition or limitation subject to which planning permission has been granted, sufficient details of the relevant planning permission to enable it to be identified;

    (e) the applicant's reasons, if any, for regarding the existing use, operations or other matter described in the application as lawful;

    (f) such other information as the applicant considers to be relevant to the application.

The application must also be accompanied by:

    (a) a plan identifying the land to which the application relates; and if the application relates to two or more uses, operations or other matters, indicating to which part of the land each relates;

(b) such evidence verifying the information as the applicant can provide;

(c) a statement setting out the applicant's interest in the land, the name and address of any other person known to the applicant to have an interest in the land and whether any such other person has been notified of the application.

Receipt of an application

The procedure for dealing with an application for a LDC made under s 191 is also set out in art 26A of the 1988 GDO. When the LPA receive an application, together with any fee, they shall, as soon as reasonably practicable, send an acknowledgement to the applicant in terms prescribed in Sched 3, Part I to the 1988 GDO. If the LPA subsequently determine that the application is invalid, they shall notify the applicant as soon as practicable. The LPA have an eight-week period to determine the application, beginning with the date of receipt of the application and any fee, although this period may be extended by agreement.

The evidential burden

It is for the applicant to satisfy the LPA of the lawfulness of the existing use, operations or other matter described at the time of the application. Section 191(4) provides that if the LPA are provided with information that so satisfies them, they shall issue a certificate to that effect; and in any other case they shall refuse the application. The LPA are also given the option of modifying or substituting the description in the application so as to enable them to issue the certificate on the basis of the information provided by the applicant (s 193(4)).

Guidance is given in para 20 of Circular 17/92 on the onus of proof in an application. It is recognised that in many cases the applicant will be best placed to produce information about the present and any previous activities taking place on the land to which the application relates, especially information about the history of any unauthorised activity on the land. However, the LPA are advised to co-operate with an applicant seeking information they may hold about the planning status of the land, by making records readily available, although they need not go to great lengths to show that the use, operations, or failure to comply with a condition, specified in the application, is not lawful.

The evidence given in support of the application for a LDC under s 191 must go to show that the existing use or operation is lawful, or that any matter constituting a failure to comply with any condition or limitation subject to which planning permission has been granted is lawful. In relation to an existing use or operation, the applicant must show that no enforcement action may be taken in respect of it (whether because it did not involve development or require planning permission or because the time for taking enforcement action has expired or for any other reason), and that it does not constitute a contravention of any enforcement notice then in force (s 191(2)). In relation to failure to comply with a condition the applicant must show that the time for taking enforcement action for the failure has expired, and that it does not constitute a contravention of any enforcement notice or breach of condition notice then in force (s 191(3)).

As stated in para 16 of Annex 1 to Circular 17/92, the effect of s 191(2) and (3) is that the concept of development or an activity on land in breach of condition, being 'unlawful but immune from enforcement action', ceases to apply. If the development or activity is immune from enforcement action, it is also lawful for planning purposes.

The onus of proof in showing that any of the above matters apply lies firmly on the applicant. The need to show that the existing use or operation or other matter is lawful is the primary purpose behind the information supplied with an application for a LDC under s 191. This must be borne in mind by the applicant when collating the evidence required in support of the application.

The relevant evidential test

The advice given in para 21 of Annex 1 of Circular 17/92 follows that of the courts who have held that the relevant test of the evidence on an application for a LDC under s 191 is 'the balance of probability'. The determination of the application should be based on purely legal issues. The planning merits of the use, development or other matters described in the application are irrelevant. LPAs should not refuse a LDC under s 191 because the applicant has failed to discharge the stricter, criminal burden of proof 'beyond reasonable doubt'. In addition, the applicant's own evidence does not need to be corroborated by independent evidence (*FW Gabbitas v Secretary of State for the Environment and Newham LBC* [1985] JPL 630).

It is a criminal offence for an applicant to make false or misleading statements for the purpose of obtaining a LDC (s 194(1)). The LPA are given the power to revoke a LDC where the applicant made a false statement or withheld any material information (s 193(7)). Where there is information available, either in a readily accessible form or through the particular knowledge of a third party, the applicant should produce it or risk prosecution and revocation of any LDC granted on the basis of such information (*see* p190 and 191).

Presentation of evidence

The evidence provided by the applicant may be oral, documentary or photographic. In a written application, oral evidence will take the form of a statutory declaration, and this can be used as a vehicle for presenting documentary and photographic evidence.

Oral evidence
Information that is peculiarly within the applicant's knowledge, or that of a

third party, can be presented in the form of a statutory declaration. This will state the declarant's name (it need not be the applicant himself, the knowledge may be that of a neighbour, previous landowner, or relative), his interest in the land, if any, and the information upon which the applicant is relying. A draft form of statutory declaration is reproduced in Appendix 7.

Documentary evidence

Documentary evidence is particularly useful for an application for a LDC. The LPA will need to be satisfied on the facts of the case, as well as the planning law applicable to the site, that the existing use, operation or other matter described in the application is made out.

The most usual type of documentary evidence is a statement in support of the application which may outline the factual situation, and for this purpose make reference to any statutory declaration or other evidence submitted with the application. It may also refer to the applicable planning law and annex relevant planning documentation, eg, planning permissions or enforcement notices. Other types of evidence that can be given in documentary form includes letterheads, invoices and receipts which, for example, indicate that a particular business operation has been carried out on the land for a period of time which would make that use of the land lawful within the meaning of s 191(2) or (3) .

Photographic evidence

Again, on an application for a LDC, photographic evidence can show that an existing use, operation or other matter described in an application has continued on land for a period of time. Aerial photographs may be available from local authority records, local libraries, or private sources. An application supported by such irrefutable evidence is likely to be looked upon favourably by the LPA.

Determination of the application

Under s 191(4), to grant a LDC under s 191, the LPA need to be satisfied of the lawfulness, at the time of the application, of the uses, operations or other matters described in the application for a LDC. Article 26A(8) of the 1988 GDO provides that the LPA must give written notice of their decision on an application within a period of eight weeks from receipt of the application and the appropriate fee (if any). As with an application for planning permission, the LPA may agree an extended period for determination with the applicant.

The LPA may direct the applicant to provide additional information in relation to an application for a LDC under s 191 (art 26A(7) of the 1988 GDO). In particular, para 43 of Annex 1 to Circular 19/92 indicates that the LPA may canvass evidence from a person other than the applicant who has an interest in the land, or a neighbour, where the LPA consider that such a person may be able to disprove a claim made by the applicant. However, such evidence will be limited to fact and law as the planning merits of the case are irrelevant for the purposes of the determination of an application for a LDC.

Circular 17/92 makes it clear in para 21 of Annex 1 that, if the LPA have no evidence of their own, or from others, to contradict or otherwise make the applicant's version of events less than probable, there is no good reason to refuse the application, if it is precise enough to justify the grant of a LDC.

The content of a certificate

Section 191(5) provides that a LDC granted under s 191 shall:

(a) specify the land to which it relates (normally identifying it by means of an attached, scaled site plan);

(b) describe the use, operations or other matter in question, identifying it by reference to one of the classes specified in the Use Classes Order where possible (otherwise such a description should state the characteristics of the use, operations or other matter, providing a complete definition, and not just give a title or label to the use);

(c) give the reasons for determining the use, operations or other matters to be lawful; and

(d) specify the date of the application for the certificate.

Article 26A(10) of the 1988 GDO provides that, where an application is refused, in whole or in part (including a case in which the LPA modify the description of the use, operations or other matter in the application, or substitute an alternative description), the notice of decision shall state clearly and precisely the LPA's full reasons for their decision and shall include a statement to the effect that if the applicant is aggrieved by the decision, he may appeal to the Secretary of State under s 195.

In drafting a certificate, LPAs are advised by para 22 of Annex 1 to Circular 17/92 to take particular care. The effect of a LDC is similar to the grant of planning permission (*see* p 184) and a LDC should be precisely drafted. If a use of land cannot be described by reference to a use class, it is important for the LPA to state the limits of the use at a particular date, usually the date of the application, being the date on which the evidence the LPA relied on when making their determination was available.

Examples of descriptions of uses are given in para 23 of Annex 1 to Circular 17/92 and include the:

(a) number and type or size of caravans on a caravan site;

(b) the number and size of lorries based at a haulage yard;

(c) hours of work at a site; or

(d) extent of goods stored on the site by reference to area and height above ground level.

Further detailed advice is given in Annex 1 to Circular 17/92 on uses, operations or other matters that involve a particular building on a site, a vehicle park used for a limited use, a '*sui generis*' use, and a planning unit which is in mixed or composite use.

The applicant for a LDC under s 191 should bear in mind the requirement upon the LPA to be specific with regard to the content of a LDC. Unless the evidence presented by the applicant is sufficiently specific, the LPA may be reluctant to issue a certificate, as they would not feel able to describe in sufficient detail the use, operation or other matter in question.

The scope of a LDC granted under s 191 is governed by s 193. It may be granted for the whole or part of the land specified in the application, and for all or some of the uses specified in the application (s 193(4)). This provision enables the LPA to issue a LDC of a different description from that applied for. Rather than refusing a certificate, the LPA may consider that the information provided in support of the application is sufficient for the issue of a LDC in an alternative form from that applied for, and that such a certificate would be of value to the applicant, eg a LDC may relate to a lesser area of land than that applied for.

There is a prescribed form of LDC granted under s 191 contained in Sched 6 to the 1988 GDO and this is reproduced at Appendix 8. Paragraph 44 of Annex 1 to Circular 17/92 suggests that LPAs may supplement the description in a LDC by including a cross-reference to the terms of the application and accompanying plans or drawings, eg issuing a LDC for a use of land 'as more particularly described in' or 'in accordance with' the terms of the submitted application.

The effect of a certificate

Once a LDC is issued by the LPA under s 191, the lawfulness of any use, operations or other matter for which the certificate is in force shall be conclusively presumed (s 191(6)). For the purposes of certain specified enactments, it shall have effect as if it were a grant of planning permission (s 191(7)), so as to enable a licence to be granted. These are:

    (a)   Caravan Sites and Control of Development Act 1960, s 3(3);

    (b)   Control of Pollution Act 1974, s 5(2); and

    (c)   Environment Protection Act 1990, s 36 (2)(a).

However, as pointed out in para 30 of Annex 1 to Circular 17/92, the practical consequence is that the planning merits of the matter may never have been considered, and there has been no opportunity to impose planning conditions on the development. The licensing authority may still impose conditions on the licence.

A refusal to issue a LDC does not necessarily mean that something is not lawful. A certificate may not have been granted because insufficient evidence was presented to satisfy the LPA that the use, operation or activity is lawful. The applicant may then submit an application for planning permission. There are no fee concessions, and as the fee paid on an application for a LDC (*see* p 189) is not refundable on a refusal, the applicant may find himself paying twice. The applicant may therefore consider that the submission of an application for planning permission in the first place would be faster and cheaper than risking the refusal of a LDC, and then having to submit an application for planning permission.

The description contained in a LDC must be precise. The effect of a LDC granted under s 191 is to certify that a particular use, operation or past breach of a condition or limitation is lawful. The description contained in a LDC will operate as a yardstick, specifying what was lawful at a specified date, against which any subsequent change may be measured. Any development carried out in breach of planning control may be subject to enforcement action.

It is provided by s 193(5) that a LDC shall not affect any matter constituting a failure to comply with any condition or limitation subject to which a planning permission has been granted unless that matter is described in the certificate. In the following circumstances, a LDC does not make a breach of condition lawful:

(a) where it is granted on the basis of an extant planning permission for the development;

(b) that such planning permission was granted subject to conditions;

(c) there has been, or it is intended that there will be, a breach of one or more of those conditions as a result of the development; and

(d) the LDC issued by the LPA does not describe the matter constituting the failure to comply with the condition.

Unspecified existing or future breaches of any condition or limitation attached to a planning permission will not be covered by the LDC.

Existing established use certificates

The effect and value of an existing established use certificate remains unchanged under the new provisions (art 3(2) of the Planning and Compensation Act 1991 (Commencement No 11 and Transitional Provisions) Order 1992 . They remain conclusive evidence for any matters specified in them for the purposes of an appeal against any enforcement notice, although they are not conclusive about anything which may have occurred on the land since the date specified in the certificate. As they confer immunity against enforcement action for the matters to which they relate, they confer a lawful use status on those matters by virtue of s 191(2).

An existing established use certificate can be 'converted' into a LDC on application to the LPA. This is not automatic and a LDC will still be required to confirm the lawfulness of a use, operation or other matter. There is a concessionary fee (one half of the usual fee, *see* p 189) for such an application. This concession will be removed with effect from 3 January 1995. The benefit derived from converting an existing established use certificate is that the new LDC will reflect the current lawfulness of uses or operations on the land.

For an application to convert an established use certificate, para 40 of Annex 1 to Circular 17/92 advises that the LPA will need to be satisfied that the 'established use' cited in the certificate has continued to subsist on the land without any material change, before issuing a LDC for the same use. Further evidence may need to be supplied to the LPA by the applicant for this purpose.

4 Certificate of lawfulness of proposed use or development

The provisions of s 192 replace the old provisions under s 64 for a determination as to whether a proposed use or operation would require planning permission (*see* p 178). Under s 192(1) there is a procedure for applying to the LPA for a certificate of lawfulness of proposed use or development, or CLOPUD. Any person may make an application to the LPA to ascertain whether any:

> (a) proposed use of buildings or other land would be lawful; or
> (b) operations proposed to be carried out in, on, over or under land would be lawful.

The form and content of an application

Section 192(1) expressly provides that when making an application to the LPA, the applicant must specify the land and describe the use or operations in question. As with an application under s 191, a precise description of the proposal will have to be submitted in the application, which must be made in writing. A form will be available from the LPA and a model application form, which LPAs may like to use is appended to Annex 1 to Circular 17/92. As with an application under s 191, the procedure for making an application for a LDC for proposed operations, uses or activities under s 192, is prescribed by art 26A of the 1988 GDO, pursuant to the powers contained in s 193(1). The application must specify:

> (a) whether the application relates to a proposed use of buildings or land, or to a proposed operation to be carried out;
> (b) in the case of an application for a proposed use, the use of the land at the date of the application, and the name of any use class specified in the Use Classes Order which the applicant considers applicable to the proposed use;
> (c) the applicant's reasons, if any, for regarding the use, operations or other matter described in the application as lawful;
> (d) such other information as the applicant considers to be relevant to the application.;

In addition, the application must be accompanied by:

> (a) a plan identifying the land to which the application relates; and, if the application relates to two or more proposed uses or operations, indicating to which part of the land each relates;
> (b) such evidence verifying the information as the applicant can provide; and
> (c) a statement setting out the applicant's interest in the land, and the name and address of any other person known to have an interest in the land and whether any such other person has been notified of the application.

Receipt of an application

The procedure for dealing with an application for a LDC made under s 192 is also set out in art 26A of the 1988 GDO. It is the same as that for an application made under s 191 and is detailed on p 180.

The evidential burden

The onus of proof is firmly on the applicant, as with an application made under s 191. The applicant must make it clear to the LPA exactly what is proposed and will need to describe the proposal clearly and precisely, including a written description and plans. Other information and legal submissions may be made with the application to persuade the LPA to grant a LDC.

For a proposed change of use, the applicant will need to provide the LPA with a description of the present or last use of the land, and where the lawfulness of that use is being relied upon, to provide sufficient information to satisfy the LPA. This may include a previous planning permission or certificate, or evidence as to the existence of permitted development rights under the 1988 GDO.

The relevant evidential test

As with an application under s 191, an application for a LDC under s 192 raises legal issues and the relevant test of evidence is 'the balance of probability' (*see* p 181).

Presentation of evidence

The information supplied by the applicant in support of an application for a LDC under s 192 can be presented by means of oral evidence (in the form of a statutory declaration) and documentary evidence, eg, a previous planning permission, or legal submission. The relevance and form of such evidence is set out on pp 181-2 and is equally applicable to an application made under s 192.

Determination of the application

Under s 192(2) the LPA need to be satisfied that the proposed use or operation described in the application for a LDC would be lawful if instituted, or begun at the time of the application. It is therefore a consideration of the proposal in planning terms, ie, whether the proposed use or operation would be lawful for planning purposes. Again, the LPA must give written notice of their decision on an application within a period of eight weeks from receipt of the application (art 26A(8) of the 1988 GDO). Such period can be extended by agreement with the applicant.

It appears that, once a determination is made, the LPA cannot review their decision. In a recent planning appeals decision [1993] JPL 1177, the LPA had issued a letter confirming that the stationing of anything up to four kiosks on the land involved was a lawful use of that land. This determination was made

on the basis of statements and statutory declarations put forward by the owners. The LPA accepted the claim at face value. Two structures were then erected
on the land, resulting in uproar from traders and others, and statements were
made to the LPA which suggested that the basis of the lawful use determination was incorrect. The inspector considered that by this time it was too late,
and that the LPA were estopped from saying otherwise. However, the LPA do
have powers to revoke a LDC in certain circumstances (*see* p 190).

The LPA will consider the lawfulness of the proposal by looking at the
planning history relating to the land and by determining the validity and scope
of any existing planning permission, enforcement notices or other planning
evidence. Paragraph 32 of Annex 1 to Circular 17/92 advises that

> the LPA will have to address the question whether, having regard to the detailed
> description of the submitted proposal, the facts of the site and the relevant plan-
> ning law, the proposed use or operations would be lawful if it were carried out in
> accordance with the stated terms.

The content of a certificate

The content of a LDC granted under s 192 is prescribed under s 192(3). Such
a certificate shall:
- (a) specify the land to which it relates;
- (b) describe the use or operations in question (in the case of any use
falling within one of the use classes specified in the Use Classes
Order, identifying it by reference to that class);
- (c) give the reasons for determining the use or operations to be lawful; and
- (d) specify the date of the application for the certificate.

As with a LDC granted under s 191, where the LPA refuse an application or
modify the description of the proposed use or development or substitute an
alternative description, the certificate shall state their reasons for doing so,
and shall include a statement on the applicant's right of appeal to the Secretary
of State under s 195 (*see* p 183).

Paragraph 36 of Annex 1 to Circular 17/92 provides that it is vital to ensure
that the terms of the certificate are precise and that there is no room for doubt
about what is lawful at a particular date. This is because the certificate has the
effect of indicating that it would be lawful to proceed with the proposal (*see*
below).

A certificate granted under s 192 should be issued in the prescribed form
contained in Sched 6 to the 1988 GDO. This is reproduced in Appendix 8.

The effect of a certificate

It is provided by s 192(4) that the lawfulness of any use or operation for which
a certificate granted under s 192 is in force shall be conclusively presumed
unless there is a material change, before the use is instituted or the operations
are begun, in any of the matters relevant to determining such lawfulness.

The certificate is not the equivalent in law of a grant of planning permission for the proposed development to which it relates, but it does indicate that it would be lawful to proceed with the proposal, unless any relevant factor has changed since the application date specified in the certificate. Paragraph 38 of Annex 1 to Circular 17/92 gives examples of such a change as the removal of permitted development rights contained in the 1988 GDO, on which the proposal relied for its lawfulness, or the revocation of a planning permission on which the proposal relies.

5 Fees for the application

The appropriate fee must be paid to the LPA on an application for a LDC. The fee is prescribed by the Town and Country Planning (Fees for Applications and Deemed Applications Regulations 1989 (SI No 193) (as amended), and is broadly linked to the national fee scale for planning applications. Fees are payable for an application for a LDC, regardless of the fact that the subject matter of the application may prove to be lawful for any reason.

No fee is payable where an application is made for a LDC within 12 months of an earlier application which has been withdrawn before the notice of decision was issued, or has been refused, or is the subject of an appeal to the Secretary of State. However, the subsequent application must relate to the same site, or part of that site, it must relate to the same description of use, operation or other matter, the fee for the earlier application must have been paid, and the application must not be already exempted from the requirement to pay a fee.

There are certain specified exceptions, exemptions and maximum charges prescribed. The main ones are, where a use specified in an application:

(a) is a use as one or more separate dwelling houses;
(b) is an 'established' use (*see* p185);
(c) is made under s 191(1)(*a*) or (*b*) and under s 191(1)(*c*);
(d) relates to access for disabled people; or
(e) relates to applications made by parish or community councils.

The detail relating to these main exceptions and exemptions is contained in reg 10A of the Town and Country Planning (Fees for Applications and Deemed Applications) Regulations 1989 (as amended).

The fee due must accompany the application for a LDC when it is lodged with the LPA. It will be refunded if the application is rejected as invalid.

A fee is also payable for a deemed application for a LDC in consequence of an enforcement notice appeal, where the Secretary of State issues a certificate under s 191 in accordance with s 177(1)(*c*) (*see* p 191 below).

6 Publicity

As the LPA will determine an application for a LDC on matters of evidential fact and law, not the planning merits, there are no requirements for an application for a LDC to be notified to other owners or publicised. However, LDC applications and decisions should be entered in the planning register (art 27(4) of the 1988 GDO, applied by s 193(6)).

The information to be contained in the register in respect of every application for a LDC under s 191 or s 192 is the:

(a)   name and address of the applicant;
(b)   date of the application;
(c)   address or location of the land to which the application relates;
(d)   description of the use, operations or other matter included in the application;
(e)   decision (if any) of the LPA on the application and the date of such decision; and
(f)   reference number, date and effect of any decision of the Secretary of State on an appeal about the application.

7 Revocation of a LDC

The LPA now has statutory power to revoke a LDC. This is available where the LPA discover that on the application for the LDC, a statement was made, or document used, which was false in a material particular, or any material information was withheld. Article 26A(12) to (14) of the 1988 GDO, provides a statutory procedure which LPAs should follow in giving notice of revocation and carrying out the revocation itself. These provisions are made pursuant to s 193(8).

Where the LPA propose to revoke a LDC, they shall, before they revoke the certificate, give notice of that proposal to the owner and occupier of the affected land, and to any other person who will in their opinion be interested. Where a certificate is issued by the Secretary of State under s 195, notice shall also be given to the Secretary of State.

The decision whether to revoke a LDC is entirely for the LPA, even where the certificate has been issued by the Secretary of State. However, the LPA must take into account any representation made by a person on whom a notice of proposed revocation is served before they make their decision. The LPA may be estopped from changing a lawful use determination (Planning Appeals Decision [1993] JPL 1177, *see* p187).

A person served with notice of a proposed revocation shall be invited to make representations to the LPA within 14 days and the LPA shall not revoke the certificate until the expiry of that period. Once a certificate is revoked, written notice shall be given to every person on whom notice of the proposed revocation was served.

In the event of a revocation, no compensation is payable and there is no right of appeal to the Secretary of State, although the decision to revoke may be challenged by application to the High Court for judicial review.

8 Offences

Section 194 provides that it is a criminal offence for any person, for the purpose of procuring a particular decision on an application (whether by himself or another) for the issue of a LDC to:

    (a) knowingly or recklessly make a statement which is false or misleading in a material particular;

    (b) use any document which is false or misleading in a material particular with intent to deceive; or

    (c) withhold any material information with intent to deceive.

The offence is not restricted to the applicant for a LDC. By virtue of the wording in parenthesis, it applies equally to any third party, including an officer or member of the LPA.

On summary conviction, the maximum penalty is a fine of £5,000, and on conviction on indictment, it is an unlimited fine, or imprisonment for two years, or both. Section 194(3) dispenses with the provisions of the Magistrates' Courts Act 1980, s 127 which provides for a six-month limitation period, from the date of the commission of the offence, within which information must be laid in the court. This is because evidence of the offence under s 194 may not emerge for some time, and an offender should not escape prosecution in these circumstances.

9 Issue of a LDC by the Secretary of State

On an enforcement notice appeal made under s 174 , the Secretary of State has a discretionary power to determine whether, on the date on which the appeal was made,

    (a) any existing use of land was lawful;

    (b) any operations carried out were lawful, or

    (c) any matter constituting a failure to comply with any condition subject to which planning permission was granted was lawful.

If he so determines, he may issue a certificate under s 191 (s 177(1)(c)). The power can be exercised where an enforcement notice appeal succeeds on grounds (c) or (d) of s 174(2).

Paragraph 64 of Annex 1 to Circular 17/92 provides that 'it is anticipated that this power will only be exercised in exceptional circumstances.' The power is not exercised automatically, it is necessary for the appellant to specifically request the issue of a LDC, before the date on which the appeal is determined, where the enforcement notice appeal succeeds on grounds (c) or (d) of s 174(2). However, it must be remembered that the power to issue a LDC is a discretionary power and it may still be refused.

As the LDC procedure is intended to be administered primarily by LPAs, 'In most circumstances, where an enforcement appeal succeeds on grounds (c) or (d), the notice will be quashed, the "deemed application fee" refunded by the Secretary of State (and, where applicable, by the LPA) and the appellant advised that it is open to him to apply to the LPA for a LDC under section 191' (para 65, Annex 1, Circular 17/92). It will be unusual for the Secretary of State to exercise his discretion to issue a LDC. He will not be in the best position to identify all the relevant details about a use, operation or activity which may need to be specified in a LDC.

10 Right of appeal

The applicant for a LDC has a statutory right of appeal to the Secretary of State against the refusal or partial refusal of an application for a LDC, or failure by the LPA to give the applicant notice of their decision within the prescribed period of eight weeks (or agreed extended period) from the making of the application (s 195(1)). The right of appeal relates to a partial refusal of an application for a LDC and therefore can be exercised by the applicant where the LPA issue a LDC in terms different from those applied for. The LDC should contain a statement advising the applicant of his right of appeal (*see* pp 183 and 188).

An appeal must be made in writing within six months of the notification of the LPA's decision. Appeal forms are available the DoE. All appeals made under s 195 will be determined by the Secretary of State as he has not yet exercised the power to transfer such appeals to inspectors as was the case in appeals against established use certificates.

Determination of an appeal

Where the Secretary of State is satisfied that the LPA's refusal is not well-founded, or where no notice of the decision has been given, that if the LPA had refused the application, their refusal would not have been well-founded, he shall grant the LDC. He is also given the power to modify a LDC granted by the LPA in the case of a refusal in part (s 195(2)). A refusal in part includes a modification or substitution of the description in the application of the use, operation or other matter in question. Where the Secretary of State is satisfied that the LPA's refusal is, or would have been well-founded, he shall dismiss the appeal (s 195(3)).

There is no deemed application for planning permission on an appeal relating to a LDC. The Secretary of State is not being asked to determine the planning merits of the case, but merely to assess the evidential fact and law relating to the use, operation or other matters described in the application. This reflects the powers of the LPA on the determination of an application for a LDC.

Where evidence as to the facts submitted in support of an application for a LDC is in issue, the Secretary of State will normally direct that a local inquiry be held (s 196(1)) with evidence taken on oath if necessary and witnesses subject to cross-examination. Paragraph 56 of Annex 1 to Circular 17/92 advises that 'where the appeal simply involves the interpretation of agreed facts and statute or judicial authority, the written representations procedure will suffice'. The Town and Country Planning (Enforcement) (Inquiries Procedure) Rules 1992 (SI No 1903) apply to local inquiries into LDC appeals (*see* Chapter 10).

Planning permission may be applied for in the normal way, and in some instances, this may be a quicker and cheaper way of proceeding (*see* p 184). Where such an application is refused, or the LPA fail to give a decision, an applicant may appeal to the Secretary of State, and both the LDC appeal and the planning appeal may be determined at the same time. Although there is no requirement for the planning application fee to be refunded if the LDC appeal is successful it would be good practice for the LPA to pay such a refund, as explained in para 28 of the Annex to Circular 5/89.

Costs on appeal

The costs of a LDC appeal do not follow the event. The parties are normally responsible for their own costs. However, where a party has behaved 'unreasonably' in the appeal process, costs may be awarded against him, whether the appeal is dealt with by way of public inquiry or written representations procedure. To that extent the costs position on a LDC appeal follows that of an enforcement appeal (*see* Chapter 9, p 128).

Appeal to the High Court

There is a further right of appeal to the High Court against the Secretary of State's decision on a LDC appeal (s 288). However, such an appeal can only be made on a point of law. Commentary on the right of appeal to the High Court is contained in Chapter 11.

Chapter 14

Listed Buildings and Conservation Areas

1 Introduction

Enforcement powers in relation to certain types of planning control are distinct from those contained in Part VII of the TCPA 1990, although there is some overlap in the applicable method of control. This chapter deals with enforcement powers for listed buildings and conservation areas, where there is a direct criminal liability for breaches of planning control. It contains only a brief outline of the special powers available. For further information on the enforcement of listed building control, see *Listed Buildings and Conservation Areas* Mynors (Longman) 1994, 2nd Edn.

The enforcement provisions relating to listed buildings and conservation areas are contained in the Planning (Listed Buildings and Conservation Areas) Act 1990 (referred to in the remainder of this chapter as 'the Listed Buildings Act'). The relevant sections of the Listed Buildings Act were amended by s 25 and Sched 3 of the Planning and Compensation Act 1991. These amendments bring listed building enforcement and enforcement in conservation areas broadly into line with the enforcement powers contained in the TCPA 1990.

Where there is a breach of planning control that affects a listed building, the LPA may take enforcement action under the TCPA 1990 and the Listed Buildings Act. In these circumstances, the person on whom the respective notices are served must ensure that he deals with both notices, either by complying with the required steps, or by appealing against the notices.

2 Criminal liability

There is one important difference between the enforcement regime relating to listed buildings and that which is contained in Part VII of the TCPA 1990. Criminal liability arises under the Listed Buildings Act, s 9 for the unauthorised demolition of a listed building, or its alteration or extension in a manner affecting its character as a building of special architectural or historic interest, or for failure to comply with any condition attached to a grant of listed building consent. This liability arises independently of the power to take enforcement action contained in the Listed Buildings Act, Part I, Chapter IV.

Under the Listed Buildings Act, s 7, there is a straight prohibition on unauthorised works to a listed building. There are some specific exceptions to this general rule, eg, ecclesiastical buildings. Works for the alteration or extension, or demolition of a listed building are authorised only if they have the benefit of a listed building consent granted by the LPA and are executed in accordance with the terms and conditions of that consent (Listed Buildings Act, s 8).

The offence

The offence under the Listed Buildings Act, s 9 relates to a contravention of the provisions of s 7. There are three types of offence under s 9:

    (a) unauthorised demolition of a listed building (s 9(1));

    (b) unauthorised alteration or extension of a listed building in a manner affecting its character as a building of special architectural or historic interest (s 9(1)); and

    (c) failure to comply with any condition attached to a grant of listed building consent (s 9(2)).

Any person who carries out any of the above shall be guilty of an offence and liable to a fine or imprisonment, or both. The maximum penalty on summary conviction is £20,000 or six months' imprisonment, or both. On conviction on indictment, the maximum penalty is an unlimited fine or two years' imprisonment, or both. As with an offence committed in relation to a breach of planning control under the TCPA 1990, Part VII in determining any fine, the court shall have regard to any financial benefit which has accrued or appears likely to accrue to the offender in consequence of the offence (s 9(5)).

The criminal liability arising under s 9 is an immediate liability and therefore it is not necessary for there to be a provision for the stop notice procedure to be used as an enforcement tool in relation to listed buildings. As a result, there is no provision in the Listed Buildings Act which equates to the provision in the TCPA 1990, s 183 (*see* Chapter 7).

It should be noted that the offence under s 9 is one of strict liability. It doesn't matter whether the person who carried out the unauthorised works, or failed to comply with any condition attached to a grant of listed building consent knows that the building was listed or not (*R v Wells Street Metropolitan Stipendiary Magistrate (ex parte Westminster City Council*) [1986] 1 WLR 1046).

Statutory defence

There is a statutory defence to criminal liability available under the Listed Buildings Act, s 9(3). For the defence to be made out, the defendant must show that:

    (a) the works carried out were urgently necessary in the interests of safety or health, or for the preservation of the building;

    (b) it was not practicable to secure safety or health or to preserve the building by works of repair;

(c) the works were limited to the minimum measures immediately necessary; and

(d) notice in writing, justifying in detail the carrying out of the works, was given to the LPA as soon as possible.

These circumstances would need to be established to the satisfaction of the court. If the works are urgently necessary, it is unlikely that notice can be given to the LPA before the works have taken place, but this should be given as soon as possible. The timing will be a question of fact, but whether it is sufficient to satisfy the requirements of the defence will be a question of judgment for the court.

3 Power to take enforcement action

Exercise of the power

The LPA has the power to issue a listed building enforcement notice where it appears that works have been, or are being executed to a listed building in their area, and the works contravene the provisions of s 9(1) and (2) of the Listed Buildings Act. The LPA may 'if they consider it expedient to do so having regard to the effect of the works on the character of the building as one of special architectural or historic interest', issue a listed building enforcement notice (Listed Buildings Act, s 38). There is no limitation period on the issue of a listed building enforcement notice.

When exercising the power to take enforcement action in relation to a listed building, the LPA is not specifically required to have regard to the provisions of the development plan and any other material considerations as they are when exercising the power to take enforcement action under the TCPA 1990, Part VII. The primary criterion for the exercise of the power is the effect of the unauthorised works on the building itself.

The LPA can act independently. There is no requirement for it to consult with English Heritage. Whereas, if the Secretary of State wishes to exercise his reserve powers to issue a listed building enforcement notice under s 46 of the Listed Buildings Act, he must first consult with the LPA *and* English Heritage.

Failure to keep a listed building in repair is not a matter for enforcement action under the Listed Buildings Act, s 38. The LPA has very limited powers for the prevention of deterioration and damage to a listed building under Part I, Chapter V of the Listed Buildings Act. In general, it is up to the owners to keep a listed building in good repair. There is a separate offence contained in the Listed Buildings Act, s 59 relating to damage caused to a listed building.

Content of a listed building enforcement notice

Section 38 of the Listed Buildings Act provides that a listed building enforcement notice shall specify the alleged contravention and require such steps as may be specified in the notice to be taken for:

(a) restoring the building to its former state;
(b) executing such further works as the LPA considers necessary to alleviate the effect of the unauthorised works (listed building consent shall be deemed granted for such works executed as a result of compliance with such requirements, s 38(7)) if restoration is not reasonably practicable or is undesirable; or
(c) bringing the building into a state in which it would have been had the terms and conditions of a listed building consent been complied with.

A listed building enforcement notice must also specify the date upon which it is to take effect and specify the compliance period for the requirements of the notice. Different periods may be specified for different steps required by the notice.

Service of a listed building enforcement notice

As with the enforcement of planning control under the TCPA 1990, Part VII the issue and service of a listed building enforcement notice are separate. The service requirements in the Listed Buildings Act, s 38 are similar to those for the service of an enforcement notice relating to a breach of planning control under the TCPA 1990, Part VII.

Service must be effected not more than 28 days after the issue of the listed building enforcement notice, and not less than 28 days before it takes effect (*see* Chapter 6). The LPA must serve the owner, the occupier, and any other person having an interest in the building 'which in the opinion of the LPA is materially affected by the notice' (s 38(4)).

Failure to comply with a listed building enforcement notice

As with a planning enforcement notice, failure to comply with the requirements of a listed building enforcement notice within the specified compliance period is an offence (Listed Buildings Act, s 43(1)). The maximum penalty on summary conviction is a fine of £20,000, and on conviction on indictment, an unlimited fine. The court is entitled to have regard to any financial benefit that has accrued, or appears likely to accrue to the offender in consequence of the offence.

The person guilty of the offence is the owner at the time the notice is issued, unless he has ceased to be the owner before the expiry of the compliance period specified in s 43(2). In these circumstances he is given the benefit of a procedure by which on laying of information before the court and giving not less than three days clear notice to the prosecutor, he is able to exonerate himself by saying that it was not his responsibility that the required steps had not been taken, but that of a subsequent owner.

There is a statutory defence available to the owner under s 43(4). The defendant must either show that he did everything he could be expected to do to secure that all the steps required by the notice were taken or that he was not served with a copy of the listed buildings enforcement notice and was not aware of its existence. This defence may be appropriate where the owner does not have day-to-day control of the building, such as in a landlord and tenant situation.

Default works

Under the Listed Buildings Act, s 42 the LPA have power to enter the land and carry out the required works at the owner's expense, if the steps required to be taken by the listed building enforcement notice are not taken within the compliance period. The LPA can then recover reasonable expenses from the person who is then the owner of the land.

As with the power to carry out default works associated with a planning enforcement notice (*see* Chapter 12), the LPA can also recover their overheads by virtue of the Local Government Act 1974, s 36. In addition the Public Health Act 1936, ss 276, 289 and 294 are applied by the Planning (Listed Buildings and Conservation Areas) Regulations 1990 (SI No 1519), reg 11. Under reg 11(2) the expenses recoverable by the LPA are, until recovered, a charge binding on the land.

4 Appeal against a listed building enforcement notice

Right of appeal to the Secretary of State

Any person having an interest in the building to which a listed building enforcement notice relates, or a relevant occupier of that building, has a right of appeal to the Secretary of State against the notice on specified grounds. A 'relevant occupier' is defined in the Listed Buildings Act, s 39(7) as an occupier by virtue of licence, either written or oral, who continues to occupy when an appeal is brought.

The specified grounds of appeal are set out in the Listed Buildings Act, s 39(1). They are similar to the grounds upon which an appeal against a planning enforcement notice may be based, as set out in the TCPA 1990, s 174 with appropriate substitutions (*see* Chapter 9). However, there are three further grounds that are applicable to an appeal against a listed building enforcement notice. These are that the:

    (a) steps required by the notice for the purpose of restoring the character of the building to its former state would not serve that purpose (ground (i));

    (b) steps exceed what is necessary to alleviate the effect of the works on the character of the building as a building of special architectural or historic interest (ground (g));

    (c) steps exceed what is necessary to bring the building into the state it would have been in if the terms and conditions of the listed buildings consent had been complied with (ground (g)).

The procedure for an appeal against a listed building enforcement notice is contained in the Town and Country Planning (Enforcement Notices and Appeals) Regulations 1991 (SI No 2804). The Listed Buildings Act, s 39 requires that an appeal be made in writing and provides for the effect of a listed building enforcement notice to be suspended until the final determination or withdrawal of the appeal. These provisions reflect those relating to a planning enforcement appeal and are dealt with in more detail in Chapter 9.

Powers of the Secretary of State on appeal

As with a planning enforcement appeal, the Secretary of State has the power to correct any defect, error or misdescription in a listed building enforcement notice, or to vary the terms of the notice, if he is satisfied that it will not cause injury to the appellant or to the LPA (Listed Buildings Act, s 41). Commentary in relation to these matters so far as they are applicable to planning enforcement appeals is contained in Chapter 9.

In addition, in determining a listed building enforcement appeal, the Secretary of State may:

(a) grant listed building consent for the whole or part of the works to which the listed building enforcement notice relates (if listed building consent is granted, the enforcement notice ceases to have effect in so far as it requires those steps to be taken (Listed Buildings Act, s 44));

(b) discharge any condition or limitation subject to which listed building consent has been granted and substitute any other condition; or

(c) remove the listed building from the statutory list, subject to prior consultation with English Heritage and other bodies or persons who appear to him appropriate.

Right of appeal to the High Court

An appeal may be made to the High Court against a decision of the Secretary of State on an appeal against a listed building enforcement notice (Listed Buildings Act, s 65). This is substantially the same as the right of appeal to the High Court against a decision of the Secretary of State on an appeal against a planning enforcement notice contained in s 289 (*see* Chapter 11). On an appeal to the High Court, the court has power only to remit the appeal against the listed building enforcement notice for redetermination by the Secretary of State. As with a planning enforcement appeal, it is necessary to apply to the court for leave to appeal.

5 Injunctions

The LPA is given the power to apply to the court for an injunction as part of their enforcement powers in relation to listed buildings (Listed Buildings Act, s 44A). This power corresponds s 187B (*see* Chapter 12). To make a successful application, the LPA needs to show some special reasons why the power of the court to grant an injunction should be used to reinforce the statutory system of remedies. However, as unauthorised works to a listed building may result in irreparable damage, in practice the courts are more than happy to grant an injunction in circumstances where the LPA can show that a listed building requires immediate protection. This is particularly so as there is no stop notice procedure available in relation to listed building enforcement action.

6 Validity of a listed building enforcement notice

In a parallel provision to that contained in the s 285 the Listed Buildings Act, s 64 provides that the validity of a listed buildings enforcement notice shall not, except by way of an appeal under s 39, be questioned in any proceedings whatsoever on any of the grounds on which such an appeal may be brought (for further detail on the parallel provision of s 285 *see* Chapter 11, p 154).

A distinction between the TCPA 1990, s 285 and the Listed Buildings Act, s 64 is that there is no statutory defence contained in s 64 that is equivalent to s 285(2) (*see* Chapter 6, p 62). Criminal liability under the Listed Buildings Act, s 43 only attaches to the person on whom a copy of the listed building enforcement notice was served, so the protection conferred by s 285(2) is not applicable to s 43.

7 Right to enter land

The LPA have a right to enter land for the purpose of surveying it in connection with a proposal by the LPA to issue a listed building enforcement notice (s 88(2)(*a*)). This right is supplemented by the right to enter by warrant. Under the Listed Buildings Act, s 88A a warrant may be issued by a justice of the peace on the basis of sworn information, in writing, that there are reasonable grounds for entering the land for any of the purposes set out in s 88 and that admission to the land has been or is likely to be refused or the case is one of urgency.

Such a warrant will authorise entry on one occasion only. The right to enter must be exercised within one month from the date of issue of the warrant and must be made at a reasonable hour, unless the case is one of urgency (this can be particularly useful where there is a strong suspicion that unauthorised works are about to be carried out on a listed building).

Under the Listed Buildings Act, s 88B(3) any person who wilfully obstructs the exercise of the right to enter shall be guilty of an offence and liable to a fine not exceeding 'level 3' on the standard scale (currently £1,000).

The effect of the Listed Buildings Act, ss 88, 88A and 88B is to provide separate but identical rights of entry for listed building enforcement purposes as exist under the TCPA 1990, Part VII. For planning enforcement purposes (*see* Chapter 12).

8 Conservation areas

The demolition of unlisted buildings in a conservation area is an offence (listed buildings are of course covered by the above provisions). Under the Listed Buildings Act, s 74 the demolition of a building in a conservation area requires the consent of the LPA. This is known as a 'conservation area consent'.

In terms of enforcement, the Listed Buildings Act, s 38 is applied to a breach of conservation area consent by reg 12 and Sched 3 of the Planning (Listed Buildings and Conservation Areas) Regulations 1990 (SI No 1519). This is effected by the substitution of the terms 'conservation area consent' for 'listed building consent', 'conservation area enforcement notice' for 'listed building enforcement notice', and 'the character or appearance of the conservation area in which the building is situated' for 'the character of the building as one of special architectural or historic interest'. Other enforcement powers contained in the Listed Buildings Act are also applied, with the exception of the right of entry contained in s 88 and detailed above.

Chapter 15

The Control of Minerals Planning

1 Introduction

The minerals planning authority (referred to in the remainder of this chapter as the 'MPA') is responsible for minerals planning. The MPA for a particular area is usually the county council who is responsible for planning control relating to county matters (*see* Chapter 4). Unauthorised mineral workings can cause particular problems for MPAs as damage can be irreparable and can be caused very quickly. Carnwath considered the enforcement controls that exist in relation to development involving minerals and came to the conclusion that no special amendments to the enforcement code were required to deal with such development.

Minerals planning control is well established as part of the planning system. Under the TCPA 1990, s 171A the carrying out of building, engineering, *mining* or other operations in, on, over or under land without the required planning permission, or failure to comply with any condition or limitation which relates to the carrying out of such operations and subject to which planning permission has been granted in relation to that land, constitutes a breach of planning control. The enforcement powers contained in the TCPA 1990, Part VII govern the control of such breaches and therefore encompass unauthorised mineral workings. However, certain minerals operations have the benefit of a planning permission granted by virtue of Sched 2, Part 23 to the 1988 GDO, and to that extent are not open to enforcement action.

TCPA 1990, s 315 allows the provisions specified in Sched 16, Parts I and II to be modified or adapted in relation to minerals. The Town and Country Planning (Minerals) Regulations 1971 (SI No 756) prescribe the modifications and adaptations relevant to the control of minerals planning.

2 Relevant definitions

As explained in Chapter 2, p 12 there is no statutory definition of 'mining operations'. However, the term 'minerals' is defined in s 336(1) as including 'all substances of a kind ordinarily worked for removal by underground or surface working, except that it does not include peat cut for purposes other than sale'. This definition is extended to include the removal of material of any description from a mineral working deposit or from other deposits and the extraction of minerals from a disused railway embankment (s 55(4)). A 'mineral working deposit' is defined by s 336 as meaning 'any deposit of material remaining after minerals have been extracted from land or otherwise deriving from the carrying out of operations for the winning and working of minerals in, on or under land.'

A fuller definition of 'mining operations' is contained in reg 1(3) of the Town and Country Planning (Minerals) Regulations 1971. For the purposes of the regulations, 'mining operations' means 'the winning and working of minerals, other than excepted minerals in, on or under land, whether by surface or underground working'. Regulation 1(3) also provides that 'excepted minerals' means minerals

(a) won or worked on land held or occupied with land used for the purposes of agriculture, which are reasonably required for the purpose of that use, and

(b) vested in the British Coal Corporation, which are specified land to which any provisions of the TCPA 1990 relating to operational development of statutory undertakers apply by virtue of regulations made under s 317.

3 Policy guidance

Minerals Planning Guidance

Paragraph 6 of MPG 1 provides that the basis of the control of mineral development is contained in the TCPA 1971 (now superseded by the TCPA 1990) and that one of the key elements of control is the enforcement of planning control to prevent unauthorised development and to ensure compliance with planning permissions.

In relation to the imposition of conditions, para 63 of MPG 1 gives guidance on the need to pay attention to the possibility of enforcement. MPAs should consider the ease of detecting the breach of a particular condition, and whether, in the event of a breach of condition, enforcement action will be practicable. A condition that can only be worded in a positive form is likely to be difficult to enforce. A condition worded in a negative way, eg, that the working of the site is not to commence until an adequate access has been provided, is preferable to a condition worded in a positive form, eg, that an adequate access is required as part of the initial development.

More detailed guidance on the use of enforcement powers in relation to unauthorised minerals development is given in paras 42 to 51 of MPG 4. The main points arising from that guidance are as follows:

(1) An enforcement notice for non-compliance with any condition or limitation subject to which permission for mining operations was granted may be served at any time within four years after the non-compliance *has come to the knowledge of the mineral planning authority* (Town and Country Planning (Minerals) Regulations 1971, reg 4, *see* Chapter 5, p 55).

(2) Mining operations constitute a continuing development, and for the purposes of the time limit referred to above, each shovelful is a fresh act of development (*David Thomas (Porthcawl) Ltd v Penybont Rural District Council* [1972] 1 WLR 1526, see Chapter 5, p 48).

(3) The requirements stated in an enforcement notice may include the cessation of a use of land, and the reclamation of the land. The carrying out of mining operations are a use of land for this purpose and references to the continuance or discontinuance of a use of land shall include the continuance or discontinuance of mining operations (Town and Country Planning (Minerals) Regulations 1971, reg 3).

(4) The right of appeal to the Secretary of State and to the High Court apply equally to enforcement action taken in relation to minerals development as they do to enforcement action taken in relation to other development (*see* Chapters 9 and 11).

(5) The statutory provisions relating to the power to serve stop notices applies to all unauthorised minerals development for which an enforcement notice has been issued (*see* Chapter 7).

Circular 21/91

Paragraph 38 of Annex 2 to Circular 21/91 contains further specific guidance in relation to the enforcement of planning control involving unauthorised minerals development. Particular advice is given to MPAs. The main points are as follows:

(1) Damage caused by unauthorised workings is sometimes irremediable and can be caused very quickly, so MPAs need to be able to stop unauthorised activity as soon as it is detected. They are directed to the provisions of TCPA 1990, s 184(3) which enable a stop notice to be made immediately effective where special reasons justify it (*see* Chapter 7, p 81);

(2) In relation to the non-observance of planning conditions imposed on minerals permissions, either where operators have failed to meet restoration conditions or where they have ignored requirements to protect the local environment while working is taking place, eg, screening banks, noise levels, MPAs are reminded that an enforcement notice for non-compliance with any condition or limitation subject to which permission for mining operations was granted may be issued at any time within four years after the non-compliance has come to the knowledge of the MPA (*see* Chapter 5, p 55).

(3) Although formal enforcement action will be considered necessary where unauthorised mineral working is taking place or where planning conditions are not being observed, MPAs are advised that it remains preferable for liaison and contact between MPAs and operators to be sufficiently good to avoid breaches of planning control and to resolve any problems by discussion and co-operation.

Planning Policy Guidance note 18

The guidance given in paras 19 to 21 of PPG 18 essentially reiterates that given in Circular 21/91. It is noted that the general policies and principles applicable to planning enforcement apply equally to minerals cases, and that some of the new powers should be helpful to MPAs to prevent damage which would otherwise be virtually or totally irremediable either to the site itself or to its surroundings.

PPG 18 refers to the benefit of effective liaison and contact between MPAs and minerals operators and the need to stop an unauthorised activity as soon as it is detected, eg, an operator moving soil materials in contravention of clear planning conditions so as to jeopardise the restoration and aftercare of the site, or where unauthorised excavation outside the permitted boundary causes irremediable damage, or endangers the safety and stability of the surrounding land. PPG 18 also reminds MPAs that the planning injunction provisions of s 187B are available for unauthorised minerals development (*see* Chapter 12).

4 Default works

The Minerals Workings Act 1985 contains enabling powers for the LPA to carry out default works for a breach of minerals planning control. Under s 8 of the 1985 Act, LPAs acting under the National Parks and Access to the Countryside Act 1949, s 89(2), may enter on former mining land and carry out restoration works without first obtaining the owner's consent. This power may be used where works of restoration are urgently required. In certain circumstances the LPA must apply to the Secretary of State for a decision as to whether or not works under s 89(2) of the 1949 Act may be carried out without the consent of all persons interested in the land. This is supplemental to the power to carry out default works contained in s178 (*see* Chapter 12).

5 Orders controlling minerals workings

Discontinuance orders

MPAs may by order require the discontinuance of the use of land for mineral workings, or as a means of imposing restoration and aftercare conditions upon existing mineral workings. This power is conferred on MPAs by the TCPA 1990, Sched 9, para 1. A discontinuance order may be made by the MPA if, with regard to the development plan and to any other material considerations, it appears to the MPA that it is expedient in the interests of the proper planning of their area (including the interests of amenity) to make such an order. The exercise of this power may arise as a result of a review of the terms on which minerals operations are being or have been carried out. A statutory duty is imposed upon MPAs under s 105 to undertake periodic reviews about the winning and working of minerals in their area. The MPA may specify that certain steps must be taken for the alteration or removal of buildings, works, plant or machinery used with the mineral workings.

Prohibition orders

Where it appears to the MPA that mineral development has occurred, but has permanently ceased, it may by order prohibit a resumption of the mineral workings. This power is conferred on MPAs by Sched 9, para 3. A prohibition order may impose a requirement to:

(a) alter or remove plant and machinery;

(b) take specified steps to remove or alleviate any injury to amenity (other than injury due to subsidence); or

(c) comply with a condition subject to which planning permission has been granted.

The MPA may assume that the mineral working has permanently ceased when no workings have occurred to any substantial extent, for a period of at least two years, and it appears to the MPA on the evidence available to them when they make the order, that the resumption of any substantial mineral working at the site is unlikely.

Suspension orders

The TCPA 1990, Sched 9, para 5 allows the MPA to make an order requiring that steps be taken for the protection of the environment where mineral working has been temporarily suspended. The MPA might assume that mineral working has ceased temporarily where no working has occurred to any substantial extent at the site for a period of at least 12 months, and it appears, on the evidence available to it at the time it makes the order, that the resumption of such workings to a substantial extent is likely.

What constitutes 'steps for the protection of the environment' is defined in Sched 9, para 5 as steps for the purpose of preserving the amenities of the area during the period of suspension, protecting the area from damage during that period, or preventing any deterioration in the condition of the land during that period. At any time during which a suspension order is in effect, the MPA may make a supplementary suspension order adding to or substituting any of the required steps in the original order, or replacing the original suspension order.

Compensation

Compensation is payable for minerals discontinuance orders, prohibition orders, suspension orders and supplementary suspension orders. Details as to the assessment of any compensation entitlement in such cases are set out in reg 4 of the Town and Country Planning (Compensation for Restriction on Mineral Working) Regulations 1985 (SI No 2224) made under the TCPA 1971 and saved by the Planning and Compensation Act 1991, Sched 1, para 16(2) to have effect as if made under the TCPA 1990, s 116.

Making a claim

A claim for compensation must be made to the LPA within the time and in the manner prescribed by the 1985 regulations. This claim may be made by a person interested in the land to which the order relates, or a person without an interest in the land itself but who has an interest in the minerals in, on or under it, for expenditure, loss or damage resulting from the provisions of the order.

The basis of a claim

The person making a claim for compensation must show that he has incurred expenditure in carrying out work which is rendered abortive by the provisions of the order (this must include preparation of plans for the purposes of any work and other similar preparatory matters), or has otherwise sustained loss or damage which is directly attributable to the provisions of the order. These provisions reflect those relating to compensation for the revocation or modification of planning permissions

In calculating loss or damage consisting of depreciation of the value of an interest in land, it shall be assumed that planning permission would be granted for development of the land of any class of development falling within the TCPA 1990, Sched 3, paras 1 and 2. Guidance is given in reg 4(3) of the 1985 regulations as to what constitutes loss or damage directly attributable to the provisions of the order. Expenditure incurred by any person who carried out works for the purpose of removing or alleviating any injury to amenity caused by the winning and working of minerals on land to which the order relates, or for the purpose of restoring land after the extraction of minerals, under an agreement in writing with the LPA entered into before the order takes effect, shall be treated as constituting loss or damage directly attributable to the provisions of the order. Regulation 4(4) provides that in the case of a prohibition order, no account shall be taken of the value of any mineral in, on or under the land which cannot be won or worked in consequence of the order.

Compensation may be assessed on a reduced basis where the mineral compensation requirements are satisfied. Detailed calculations for the assessment of compensation are set out in regs 5, 6 and 7 of, and Scheds 1 and 2 to the 1985 regulations. For further detail on any compensation entitlement *see Boynton's Guide to Compulsory Purchase and Compensation* (Longman) 1994, 7th edn.

Enforcement

Any person who uses land in contravention of a discontinuance order, resumes mineral working in contravention of a prohibition order, contravenes a requirement of a discontinuance order or a suspension order or a supplementary suspension order shall be guilty of an offence (s 189). A statutory defence is provided in s 189(4) for a person charged with an offence to prove that he took all reasonable measures and exercised all due diligence to avoid committing the offence. If it is alleged that the offence was committed through the act or default of another person, the defence in s 189(4) can only be relied upon where notice in writing is given to the prosecutor, within a period ending seven clear days before the hearing, identifying the other person.

In addition to the power to prosecute, the MPA may enter upon land and carry out any step required to be carried out by a minerals discontinuance order, a prohibition order, a suspension order or a supplementary suspension order (s 190). The MPA is entitled to recover the expenses of so doing from the present owner of the land (s 189(3)).

Chapter 16

Tree Preservation

1 Introduction

The TCPA 1990 recognises the importance of trees and the contribution that they make to the general amenity and environment of an area, particularly urbanised areas. Provision is made for the protection of trees by s 197, which imposes a duty on LPAs to ensure, whenever it is appropriate, that in granting planning permission for any development, adequate provision is made by the imposition of conditions for the preservation or planting of trees. LPAs also have special power under s 198 to make tree preservation orders for specific trees or woodlands in their area, where it appears to them that it is expedient in the interests of amenity to make such an order. The procedure for the making of a tree preservation order is governed by the Town and Country Planning (Tree Preservation Order) Regulations 1969 (SI No 17) which contains a prescribed form of order.

Policy guidance on the application of tree preservation orders, tree preservation order procedures and trees in conservation areas is contained in Circular 36/78 — Trees and Forestry.

2 The offence

Once a tree preservation order comes into effect, it is an offence to breach its prohibition of topping, lopping, or felling the specified trees or woodland without consent. There are certain exemptions from the requirement to obtain consent. These are included in the Second Schedule to the form of order prescribed by the 1969 Regulations. These exemptions include work immediately required for the purposes of carrying out development, specified work carried out by or at the request of a statutory undertaker, an electricity company, a water company or drainage board, work on trees which obstruct the safe and efficient use of an airfield or defence installation, and work on fruit trees so long as they are cultivated for fruit production.

Section 210(1) provides that if any person, in contravention of a tree preservation order 'cuts down, uproots or wilfully destroys a tree, or wilfully damages, tops or lops a tree in such a manner as to be likely to destroy it, he shall be guilty of an offence'. A direct criminal liability arises from the breach of the provisions of a tree preservation order. This differs from the position in relation to a breach of planning control, which is not a criminal offence (*see* Chapter 1).

The Planning and Compensation Act 1991 introduced a substantial increase in the penalties for the offence. The maximum fine on summary conviction is now increased to £20,000. As stated in para 43 of Annex 2 to Circular 21/91, this takes account of the fact that illegal felling or destruction of trees protected by a tree preservation order can lead to substantial profit for the offender. Section 210(3) gives the court power, in determining the amount of any fine, to have regard to any financial benefit which has accrued or appears likely to accrue to the offender as a result of the offence. The LPA has the power to seek conviction on indictment where the court may impose an unlimited fine. This power is likely to be used where the offence is particularly serious

3 The consequences of tree removal

The consequences of tree removal are dealt with in the TCPA 1990, Part VIII. Section 206 imposes a duty on the owner of land to replace any tree for which a tree preservation order is in force where the removal is:

    (a) in contravention of the tree preservation order (this is also a criminal offence, *see* above); or

    (b) required as the tree(s) that is/are the subject of the tree preservation order is dying or dead or has become dangerous.

The duty to replace requires the owner of the land to plant another tree of an appropriate size and species at the same place as soon as he reasonably can. This duty transfers to the new owner where the land in question changes hands. The requirement to replant in the same place means that the replacement tree should be planted in the position referred to in the relevant tree preservation order (*Bush v Secretary of State for the Environment* [1988] JPL 108). However, s 206(3) provides that, for woodland trees, it is sufficient to replace the trees removed by planting the same number of trees on or near the land where the original trees stood or on such other land as may be agreed with the LPA. The relevant tree preservation order will then apply to the replacement tree as it applied to the original tree (s 206(4)).

An owner can apply to the LPA for the duty to be dispensed with (s 206(2)). This may be appropriate where a replacement tree may cause a danger to persons or property, or where an owner intends to make provision elsewhere and the exact location of a replacement tree is not critical. In such circumstances, the owner would need to show to the LPA's satisfaction that the duty could be dispensed with.

4 Replacement enforcement notice

The requirements of s 206 can only be enforced by means of a replacement enforcement notice served on the owner of the land under s 207. This notice may be served by the LPA where it appears that the provisions of s 206, are not complied with (s 207(1)(*a*)). This is an exclusive enforcement system for the replacement duty imposed by s 206.

A replacement enforcement notice can also be served under s 207 where it appears to the LPA that any conditions of a consent given under a tree preservation order which require the replacement of trees are not complied with. Once a tree preservation order comes into effect, the consent of the LPA will be required for any person to remove, top, lop, uproot, wilfully damage or wilfully destroy any tree covered by the order. This consent may be granted subject to conditions requiring the replacement of trees. In circumstances where it appears to the LPA that such conditions are not complied with, the LPA may serve the owner of the land with a replacement enforcement notice.

Section 207 requires that a replacement enforcement notice shall specify:
  (a) the period within which the replacement shall take place;
  (b) the size and species of trees that are to be planted; and
  (c) a period at the end of which it is to take effect, which shall be not less than 28 days after the date of service of the notice.

The power given to the LPA to serve a replacement enforcement notice is restricted by a time limit. Section 207(2) provides that this notice may only be served within four years of the date of the alleged failure to comply with the provisions of s 206 or the conditions attached to a consent granted under a tree preservation order. After that period the owner will be immune from enforcement action of the type provided for in s 207.

5 Appeals against a replacement enforcement notice

A person on whom a replacement enforcement notice is served has a statutory right of appeal to the Secretary of State. The grounds of appeal set out in s 208(1) state that:
  (a) the provisions of s 206, or the conditions attached to a consent granted under a tree preservation order are not applicable, or have been complied with;
  (b) in all the circumstances of the case, the duty imposed by s 206 should be dispensed with;
  (c) the requirements of the notice are unreasonable in respect of the period or the rise or species of trees specified in it;
  (d) the planting of tree(s) in accordance with the notice is not required in the interests of amenity or would be contrary to the practice of good forestry;
  (e) the place on which the tree(s) is required to be planted is unsuitable for that purpose.

As with an appeal against an enforcement notice lodged under the TCPA 1990, s 174, the appeal against a replacement enforcement notice must indicate the grounds of appeal and state the facts on which such an appeal is based. An appeal must be made by giving written notice to the Secretary of State before the requirements of the notice take effect. Where a notice of appeal is sent to the Secretary of State in a properly addressed pre-paid letter, it shall be valid if, in the ordinary course of post, it would be delivered to him before the date on which the notice is due to take effect (s 208(2)). It is likely that the case law relating to the time limit for an appeal against a planning enforcement notice will apply equally to the time limit applicable to an appeal against a replacement enforcement notice (*see* Chapter 9).

Section 208 also provides for the appeal to be dealt with by public inquiry or informal hearing, and the procedure would be the same as that relating to planning enforcement notice appeals (*see* Chapters 9 and 10). In addition, where such an appeal is brought, the replacement enforcement notice shall be of no effect pending the final determination or the withdrawal of the appeal (s 208(6)).

The Secretary of State is also given power to correct any defect, error or misdescription in the notice or to vary any of its requirements, if he is satisfied that the correction or variation will not cause injustice to the appellant or to the LPA (s 208(7)). Paragraph 40 of Annex 2 to Circular 21/91 provides that, as with enforcement notices, 'This power does not extend to the correction of notices so fundamentally defective that they must be quashed, and LPAs should therefore continue to prepare such notices thoroughly'.

6 Default works

Failure to comply with a replacement enforcement notice served under s 208 is not a criminal offence. The only means of enforcing the requirements of the notice is for the LPA to enter the land and plant the trees and to recover its reasonable expenses from the person who is the owner of the land at that point (s 209). The power to enter does not arise until the compliance period specified in the replacement enforcement notice has expired, although, where the circumstances justify it, the period initially specified in the notice can be extended by the LPA (s 209(1)).

There is provision in s 209(3) and (5) for regulations to be made applying ss 276, 289 and 294 of the Public Health Act 1936, and to make any expenses recoverable by the LPA in exercising its right under s 209 a charge on the land. Regulation 14 of the Town and Country Planning General Regulations 1992 (SI No 1492) applies these sections to notices issued under s 207(1). (*See* Chapter 12 for the application of these powers in respect of planning enforcement notices.)

Any person who wilfully obstructs the LPA from exercising the right to enter the land and plant the trees shall be guilty of an offence and liable on summary conviction to a fine not exceeding 'level 3' on the standard scale (currently £1,000). This correlates with the penalty for obstructing the carrying out of default works in relation to a planning enforcement notice (*see* Chapter 12).

7 Rights of entry

As with planning enforcement notices, the LPA are given statutory rights of entry for protected trees. These powers were introduced by the Planning and Compensation Act 1991, and are contained in TCPA 1990, ss 214B–D.

Section 214B gives the LPA right to enter land without a warrant for specified purposes, including determining whether an offence has been committed under s 210 (*see* above, p 207), or whether a replacement enforcement notice under s 207 should be served on the owner of the land (*see* above, p 208). There must be reasonable grounds for entering for the purpose in question. Advance notice of such entry for these purposes need not be given to the occupier of the land, except for any building used as a dwellinghouse (s 214B(7)), although entry must be made at a reasonable hour (s 214B(8)).

The power in s 214B is supplemented by the right to enter under warrant provided for in s 214C. A warrant to enter land may be issued by a justice of the peace on the basis of sworn information in writing that there are reasonable grounds for entering land for any of the purposes set out in s 214B and that a request for admission has been refused or is likely to be refused or the case is one of urgency. Where a warrant is issued, it authorises entry on one occasion only, and the entry must be made within one month and at a reasonable hour, unless the case is one of urgency.

The provisions as to the right to enter without a warrant or under warrant are substantially the same as those applying in relation to the exercise of planning enforcement powers under TCPA 1990, Part VII (*see* Chapter 12). Any person who wilfully obstructs the exercise of either right of entry shall be guilty of an offence, and liable on summary conviction to a fine not exceeding 'level 3' on the standard scale (currently £1,000) (s 214D(3)).

8 Injunctions

LPAs have the power (contained in s 214A) to apply to the court for an injunction, where they consider it necessary or expedient for an actual or apprehended offence under s 210 (*see* above) or s 211 (*see* below) to be restrained by injunction. This power is similar to that conferred by s 187B in relation to the enforcement of breaches of planning control (*see* Chapter 12) and specifically adopts subs (2)–(4) of s 187B, which relate to the jurisdiction of the court and the application of the rules of the court.

9 Conservation areas

Trees in conservation areas are subject to a blanket tree preservation order (s 211). This is in recognition of the special contribution that trees can make to the character and appearance of a conservation area.

The statutory requirements in relation to the preservation of trees in a conservation area relate to the need to serve notice on the LPA of an intention to cut down, top, lop, uproot, damage or destroy trees in a conservation area. Such an act can be carried out with the consent of the LPA, or after the expiry of six weeks, and within two years, from the date of the notice of intention (s 211(3)). Otherwise, to carry out such an act is an offence.

There is an automatic replanting duty contained in s 213 if any tree to which s 211 applies is removed, uprooted, or destroyed in contravention of that section. However, the owner can apply to the LPA for the requirement contained in s 211 to be dispensed with. The provisions of s 213 may only be enforced by the service of a replanting enforcement notice in accordance with the provisions of s 207 (*see* above).

Chapter 17

Hazardous Substances Control

1 Introduction

Section 4 of the Planning (Hazardous Substances) Act 1990 requires that a hazardous substances consent be obtained if a hazardous substance is present on land in a controlled quantity. This is granted by the hazardous substances authority, which is usually the LPA. Enforcement against breaches of control generally follow the planning enforcement provisions contained in TCPA 1990, Part VII. However, the critical difference is that a contravention of hazardous substances control is a criminal offence.

There are two independent courses of enforcement action available to deal with a contravention of hazardous substances control. These are contained in the Planning (Hazardous Substances) Act 1990 (referred to in the remainder of the section as 'the HSA') and the Planning (Hazardous Substances) Regulations 1992 (SI No 656). Guidance on the application of these provisions is set out in Circular 11/92.

The first relates to criminal liability which arises under the HSA, s 23 upon the contravention of hazardous substances control. There is no provision for the stop notice procedure as there is in relation to planning enforcement, as this is not necessary where immediate criminal liability arises independently. The second relates to contravention action under the HSA, s 24 which is entirely independent from and additional to the liability under s 23. The contravention procedures under s 24 are intended to be remedial.

2 The criminal offence

A contravention of hazardous substances control is an offence under the HSA, s 23. There are two types of offence:

(1) Where a quantity of hazardous substances equal to, or exceeding the controlled quantity, is or has been present on, over or under land and there is no hazardous substances consent for the presence of the substance, or there is a hazardous substances consent for its presence, but

the quantity present exceeds the maximum quantity permitted by the consent. This offence may be committed by any person in control of the relevant land or who knowingly caused or allowed the substance to be present.

(2) Where there is failure to comply with a condition subject to which a hazardous substances consent has been granted. This offence may only be committed by a person in control of the land.

The maximum penalty on summary conviction is a fine of £20,000. On conviction on indictment, the maximum penalty is an unlimited fine.

The unauthorised presence of a hazardous substance could have serious and immediate consequences, and the provisions of s 23 enable a hazardous substances authority, where satisfied that a contravention of control has knowingly been committed, to bring the offender to court relatively quickly, should this be in the public interest.

There are statutory defences to the offence contained in the HSA ss 23(5)-(7). These are:

(a) that the defendant took all reasonable precautions and exercised all due diligence to avoid the commission of the offence; or

(b) that he could only avoid the offence by a breach of a statutory duty.

A further defence is that the defendant did not know and had no reason to believe that the elements of the offence were present.

3 Contravention action

Power to take enforcement action

Where it appears to the hazardous substances authority that there has been a breach of hazardous substances control, it has the power to issue a hazardous substances contravention notice specifying the steps to be taken to rectify the contravention of control. Section 24(1) of the HSA provides that where a hazardous substances authority has identified a breach of control it should, before issuing a hazardous substances contravention notice, consider whether it is expedient and appropriate to do so, having regard to any material considerations.

The provisions of s 24 are modelled on the TCPA 1990, ss 172 and 173. The hazardous substances authority is empowered to serve a hazardous substances contravention notice requiring the owner or person otherwise in control of the land to take such steps as are specified in the notice, within such time as may be specified, to remedy the contravention. The notice must also specify the date on which it is to take effect and, by virtue of the Planning (Hazardous Substances) Regulations 1992, Sched 4 which apply the TCPA 1990, s 179, an offence is committed if a hazardous substances contravention notice is not complied with after it has taken effect.

The guidance given in para A85 of Circular 11/92 states that:

since the controlled quantities of hazardous substances have been set at amounts at or above which it is considered that major hazards could arise to persons in the surrounding area, authorities should be mindful of the serious risks that may arise if prompt and effective action is not taken.

For more serious breaches of control, hazardous substances authorities may consider that direct prosecution under s 23, or injunctive proceedings under the HSA, s 26AA should be taken.

Right of appeal

There is a right of appeal against the issue of a hazardous substances contravention notice. The provisions that apply to appeals against such notices, and to the determination of those appeals are contained in the Planning (Hazardous Substances) Regulations 1992, made under the HSA, s 25. These follow closely those procedures which apply to planning enforcement notices.

An appeal may be made by any person having an interest in the land to which the contravention notice relates, or a relevant occupier, whether or not a copy of the notice has been served on him. A 'relevant occupier' includes a person who occupies by virtue of a licence, either written or oral. The appeal must be made before the notice takes effect and must be made on grounds specified in Sched 4, para 1(b) of the Planning (Hazardous Substances) Regulations 1992.

As with a planning enforcement appeal, an appeal against a hazardous substances contravention notice suspends the effect of a notice until the final determination or withdrawal of the appeal (*see* Chapter 9, p 109 for further commentary).

Injunctive proceedings

The HSA, s 26AA confers express power on the hazardous substances authority to seek an injunction from the court in support of its enforcement functions. This power is parallel to the power conferred by the TCPA 1990, s 187B (*see* Chapter 12). The use of the power to seek an injunction is governed by s 26AA and rules of the court.

Section 26AA provides that the hazardous substances authority may apply to the court for an injunction where they 'consider it necessary or expedient for any actual or apprehended contravention of hazardous substances control to be restrained by injunction'. This can be made whether or not they have exercised, or are proposing to exercise, any of their other powers under the HSA. On an application by the hazardous substances authority, the court may grant such injunction as it thinks appropriate for the purpose of restraining the contravention. These provisions reflect the powers of the LPA to seek an injunction and the powers of the court to grant an injunction under the provisions of the TCPA 1990, Part VII.

Chapter 18

Advertisement Control

1 Introduction

The system of advertisement control is largely governed by a self-contained set of regulations. These are the Town and Country Planning (Control of Advertisements) Regulations 1992 (SI No 666) (referred to in the remainder of this chapter as 'the 1992 Regs'). The following sections deal with the provisions in the regulations relating to the enforcement of advertisement control. However, there may still be circumstances where it is appropriate to rely on other enforcement powers in relation to advertisement control. For example, where advertisements are fixed to listed buildings, it may be more appropriate to rely upon the enforcement powers that are available in relation to listed buildings (*see* Chapter 14).

2 The statutory framework

The power to make regulations controlling the display of advertisements is contained in the TCPA 1990, ss 220 and 224. The 1992 Regs were made under these sections and identify exempt classes of advertisements that are not subject to control, eg, advertisements on packaging or vehicles. They also identify those classes of advertisements for which there is a deemed planning consent eg, temporary advertisements and advertisements on business premises.

Development

The display of advertisements constitutes development under the TCPA 1990, s 55(5), which provides that the use of the external part of a building for the display of advertisements shall be treated as involving a material change in the use of that part of the building. However, under the TCPA 1990, s 222, where the advertisement is displayed in accordance with the 1992 Regs, planning permission for that development shall be deemed to be granted, and no planning application shall be necessary.

The statutory offence

The enforcement of control as to advertisements is governed by the 1992 Regs made under the TCPA 1990, s 224. However, s 224(3) also provides that, without prejudice to the 1992 Regs, any person who displays an advertisement in contravention of the 1992 Regs shall be guilty of an offence and liable on summary conviction to a fine not exceeding 'level 3' on the standard scale (currently £1,000), and a continuing fine for each day during which the offence continues after conviction.

Paragraph 8 of Circular 5/92 provides that the Secretary of State considers that it would often be reasonable for LPAs to invite a person who appears to be contravening the regulations to remove the advertisement or to apply for consent, before proceeding to prosecute. However, in cases of blatant, deliberate or repetitive displays of advertisements, immediate prosecution may be the more appropriate course to secure the early removal of an unlawful advertisement.

A person shall be deemed to display an advertisement for the purposes of s 224(3) if he is the owner or occupier of the land on which the advertisement is displayed, or the person whose goods, trade, business or other concern the advertisement gives publicity to (s 224(4)). A statutory defence is contained in s 224(5) where a person deemed to display an advertisement in accordance with s 224(3) proves that it was displayed without his knowledge or consent.

3 Enforcement under the 1992 Regs

There are three courses of action open to the LPA in relation to the display of advertisements. The first, and probably the most common means of enforcement is the power to take discontinuance action, the second is a means of dealing with unauthorised advertisements or fly-posting, and the third is the power to remove or obliterate advertisements.

Discontinuance action

Under reg 8 of the 1992 Regs, the LPA may serve a notice requiring the discontinuance of the display of an advertisement, or the use of a site for the display of an advertisement for which deemed consent is granted under reg 6 of the 1992 Regs 'if they are satisfied that it is necessary to do so to remedy a substantial injury to the amenity of the locality, or a danger to members of the public'. This is known as a discontinuance notice. There is also power for the Secretary of State to initiate discontinuance action after consultation with the LPA (reg 23(1)).

A discontinuance notice should be served on the advertiser, the owner and occupier of the site, and, if the LPA think fit, on any other person displaying the advertisement. Where the LPA are unable to identify any of the parties to be served, Circular 5/92 gives detailed advice on how the authority should proceed.

Regulation 8 of the 1992 Regs provide that a discontinuance notice must:

(a) specify the advertisement or the site to which it relates;
(b) specify the period within which the display or the use of the site is to be discontinued; and
(c) contain a full statement of reasons why action has been taken under reg 8.

The notice must also specify the date upon which it takes effect which must be at least eight weeks after the date upon which the notice is served. A discontinuance notice will not take effect on this date where an appeal has been made to the Secretary of State under reg 15 of the 1992 Regs (*see* below), or where it is withdrawn by the LPA before it takes effect, or where the LPA have extended the period within which it is to take effect.

Paragraph 19 of Circular 5/92 advises that LPAs should always consider the particular circumstances and allow reasonable time for discontinuing a display, especially where discontinuance action is likely to have serious financial consequences for a particular advertiser. The LPA may consider that a modified display would be more acceptable in a particular location. If so, an approach should be made to an advertiser on this basis before a discontinuance notice is served. Alternatively, the LPA could enter into negotiations with an advertiser and withdraw a discontinuance notice or extend the period within which it is to take effect, in order to enable such negotiations to take place. The threat of action or the existence of a discontinuance notice may enable any such negotiations to proceed more effectively.

A discontinuance notice can be issued in relation to a particular advertisement or a site being used for the display of an advertisement. The power to issue a discontinuance notice in relation to a site can be of use for whole sites where temporary advertisements, eg, window stickers are to be discontinued. When using the power in regard to an entire site to which the notice relates, para 18 of Circular 5/92 advises that LPAs need to define precisely the site to which the notice relates, so as to avoid discontinuing the display of any advertisements which are considered acceptable, and to be satisfied that complete removal of deemed consent rights for a defined area of land is fully justified in the interests of amenity or public safety.

There is a right of appeal to the Secretary of State against a discontinuance notice contained in reg 15 of the 1992 Regs. The Secretary of State may deal with the appeal as if the appellant had applied for an express consent under the 1992 Regs, the LPA had refused consent, and the applicant had appealed to the Secretary of State.

Unauthorised advertisements

Advertisements displayed without the site owner's permission can be dealt with by LPAs. The display of these types of advertisements is commonly known as fly-posting. Where it is entirely unauthorised, it entails liability on the person responsible, the owner of the site, and on the person benefiting from the display. The LPA can prosecute under the TCPA 1990, s 224 for unauthorised advertisements of this type. A statutory defence is available where the defendant can prove that the fly-posting was done without his knowledge or consent (s 224(5)). This may assist the owner of the site who would be liable under s 224.

Paragraph 52 of Circular 5/92 gives advice to LPAs on procedures to be adopted in relation to fly-posting:

(1) The enforcement officers duties should include keeping a regular watch for any new fly-posting.
(2) The enforcement officer should note all new fly-posting sites, photograph them (and date the photographs) and, where possible, remove a copy of the illegal poster for exhibition in court.
(3) The LPA should take positive steps to find the person benefiting from the poster, including making a personal call on the person or attending the venue of any event advertised by the poster.
(4) A preliminary warning about prosecution should be given to the person responsible followed by the LPA allowing a reasonable time for removal of the poster.

Removing advertisements

Section 225 of the TCPA 1990 gives power to the LPA to remove or obliterate placards or posters displayed in contravention of the 1992 Regs. There is no definition of 'placard' or 'poster' in s 225. This is a matter for the LPA and eventually the court to decide on the particular facts of the case. Where it is possible to identify the person who displayed the placard or poster, or caused it to be displayed, the LPA must give notice in writing to that person that they intend to remove the placard or poster within a specified period. Paragraph 54 of Circular 5/92 provides that two clear days after the date when the notice is served must be allowed before the LPA proceed to remove or obliterate the display.

This advance notice procedure enables anyone who genuinely believes that the poster or placard is being displayed with deemed consent or express consent under the 1992 Regs to inform the LPA that this is the case and to ask them to reconsider their intention to remove the placard or poster.

Under s 324(3) , the LPA are given power to enter land or premises for the purpose of exercising the power in s 225, provided that the land or premises are unoccupied and it would be impossible to exercise the power without entering the land.

Chapter 19

Crown Land

1 Introduction

Crown development benefits from a general immunity from enforcement. However, the Government has indicated that it intends to remove Crown exemption from the planning system as soon as a suitable legislative opportunity arises. A consultation paper on the proposal was issued in November 1992. In response to comments received, it is intended to provide an informal appeal mechanism to deal with disputes between LPAs and Crown bodies in relation to alleged breaches of planning control. Such remedy would be in addition to the power to obtain a High Court declaration. In the meantime however, Crown development retains a general immunity from enforcement, although there are limited circumstances in which enforcement action can be taken in relation to Crown land. The Planning and Compensation Act 1991 did not amend the provisions of the TCPA 1990, ss 294 and 295 which apply to the control of development on Crown land.

2 Special enforcement notices

Introduction

The only circumstances in which an enforcement notice can be issued under s 172 for development carried out on Crown land, is where such development is carried out, otherwise than by or on behalf of the Crown, at a time when no person is entitled to occupy the land by virtue of a private interest (s 294). In effect, control in relation to unauthorised development on Crown land can only be exercised where such development is carried out on Crown land by a person with no interest in the land, eg, the stationing of a mobile snack bar or refreshment van on highway verges by a trespasser. A person entitled to occupy Crown land by virtue of a licence in writing shall be treated as having an interest in that land for the purposes of s 294 (s 293(4)).

In such circumstances, where it appears to the LPA that development of Crown land has taken place in its area, and having regard to the provisions of the development plan and to any other material considerations, it considers it expedient, it may issue a special enforcement notice (s 294(3)). The consent of the appropriate Crown authority (defined in s 293(2)) to the issue of a special enforcement notice is required. However, para 2 of Annex 6 to Circular 21/91 provides that 'Government Departments and other Crown bodies do not unreasonably withhold their consent where the land is being occupied without their written permission'.

Content

Subsections 294(5), (6) and (7) of the TCPA 1990 set out the requirements for the content of special enforcement notices. A special enforcement notice must specify the:

(a) matters alleged to constitute development;
(b) steps which the LPA require to be taken for:
  (i) restoring the land to its previous use; or
  (ii) discontinuing any use of the land instituted by the development;
(c) date on which the notice is to take effect; and
(d) period within which any required steps are to be taken, and different periods may be specified for the taking of different steps.

A model special enforcement notice is contained in the Appendix to Annex 6 of Circular 21/91 and is reproduced at Appendix 9.

Issue and service

A special enforcement notice must be issued, then served. Service must take place not more than 28 days after the date of issue of the notice and not less than 28 days before the specified date (s 295(1)). This is the same as the service requirements for an enforcement notice under s 172 (*see* Chapter 6, p 61). A copy of the special enforcement notice must be served on the person who carried out the development alleged in it, on any person who is occupying the land when the notice is *issued*, and on the appropriate Crown authority (s 295(1)). Where the LPA are unable, after reasonable inquiry, to identify or trace the person who carried out the development, they need not serve a copy of the notice on such person (s 295(2)).

Right of appeal

Any person on whom a copy of the special enforcement notice is served (other than the appropriate Crown authority) may appeal against the notice to the Secretary of State, whether or not he was served with a copy of it. An appeal may be made on the ground that the matters alleged have not taken place, or do not constitute development to which s 294 applies (s 295(3)).

Examples of circumstances where the matters alleged in the notice do not constitute development to which s 294 applies are give in para 5 of Annex 6 to Circular 21/91. They are that:

(a) development took place before 12 April 1984 (the date on which the special enforcement notice procedure was introduced;

    (b) the land is not Crown land;

    (c) there is a private interest in the land; or

    (d) the matters alleged in the notice did not constitute development.

It is made clear in Circular 21/91 that the planning merits of the development are irrelevant for the purposes of an appeal against a special enforcement notice. There is no deemed application for planning permission as there is with an enforcement notice appeal made under s 174.

The Secretary of State has received very few appeals against special enforcement notices. Annex 6 of Circular 21/91 provides that the Secretary of State does not intend to apply formally to special enforcement notices and appeals the relevant provisions of the Enforcement Notices and Appeals Regulations 1991 and the Inquiries Procedure Rules 1992 (*see* Chapters 9 and 10). Instead, he will act in accordance with those provisions, as far as is practicable, as though they applied to special enforcement notices, and will expect the same of LPAs and appellants. To that end, LPAs are requested to enclose appeal forms and 'Notes for Appellants' with every copy of a special enforcement notice they serve. Copies are contained in the Appendices to Annex 6 of Circular 21/91.

3 The Town and Country Planning (Special Enforcement Notices) Regulations 1992

Certain provisions of the TCPA 1990 are expressly applied to special enforcement notices by s 295(5). These are ss 174(3)–(5), 175(1)–(4), and 176(1)–(4). Other provisions of the TCPA 1990 are applied to special enforcement notices by regulations made by the Secretary of State. The current regulations are the Town and Country Planning (Special Enforcement Notices) Regulations 1992.

The provisions applied to special enforcement notices by the regulations are:

    (a) power for the Secretary of State to make regulations for the content of enforcement notices and informing the persons served with a copy of the notice of the right of appeal against the notice (s 173(10));

    (b) variation and withdrawal of enforcement notices (s 173A);

    (c) restrictions on right to claim in proceedings that an enforcement notice has not been duly served and awards of costs at appeals (ss 175(5) and (7), 322 and 322A);

    (d) penalties for non-compliance with an enforcement notice (s 179);

    (e) effect of planning permission on enforcement notice (s 180);

    (f) enforcement notice to have effect against subsequent development (s 181);

    (g) power to serve stop notices and to provide compensation (ss 183, 184, 186, and 187);

    (h) register of enforcement and stop notices (s 188);

    (i) restriction on right to question validity of notices otherwise than by way of appeal to the Secretary of State (s 285(1) and (2)); and

    (j) appeals to the High Court (s 289).

Appendix 1

Model Planning Contravention Notice

MODEL NOTICE
IMPORTANT—THIS COMMUNICATION AFFECTS
YOUR PROPERTY

.... Council (a)

TOWN AND COUNTRY PLANNING ACT 1990 (as amended by the
PLANNING AND COMPENSATION ACT 1991)

PLANNING CONTRAVENTION NOTICE

.... (b)

1. It appears to the   (a) Council ('the Council'),
being the local planning authority for the purposes of section 171C of the Town and
Country Planning Act 1990 ('the Act'), that there may have been a breach of planning
control in respect of the land described in Schedule 1 below ('the land').

2. The breach of planning control which may have occurred is specified in Schedule
2 below. (c)

3. This notice is served on you as a person who—
    (1) is the owner or occupier of the land or has any other interest in it;
        or
    (2) is carrying out operations in, on, over or under the land or is using it for any
        purpose.

4. In exercise of their powers under section 171C(2) and (3) of the Act the Council
require you, so far as you are able, to give them the following information in writing
within twenty-one days, beginning with the day on which this notice is served on you:

(1)
                    Specify the information required,
(2)*   having regard to the terms of sec-
                    tion 171C(2) and (3)
(3)*

* delete where not required

*5.   If you wish to make—
   (a)   an offer to apply for planning permission, or to refrain from carrying out any
         operations or activities, or to undertake remedial works; or
   (b)   any representations about this notice,
the Council, or representatives of the Council, will consider them on
                              (d) at   (e),
when you will be able to make any such offer or representations in person at that time
and place.

Dated 19   Signed ....
                                                        Council's authorised officer.

SCHEDULE 1

Land to which this notice relates

(Address or description of the parcel of land,
by reference to an attached plan where necessary)

SCHEDULE 2

Suspected breach of planning control (c)

WARNING

1.   It is an offence to fail, without reasonable excuse, to comply with any requirement
of this notice within twenty-one days beginning with the day on which it was served
on you. The maximum penalty on conviction of this offence is a fine of £1,000. Continuing failure to comply following a conviction will constitute a further offence.
2.   It is also an offence knowingly or recklessly to give information, in response to
this notice, which is false or misleading in a material particular. The maximum penalty
on conviction of this offence is a fine of £5,000.

ADDITIONAL INFORMATION

3.   If you fail to respond to this notice, the Council may take further action in respect
of the suspected breach of planning control. In particular, they may issue an enforcement notice, under section 172 of the 1990 Act, requiring the breach, or any injury to
amenity caused by it, to be remedied. (f)
4.   If the Council serve a stop notice, under section 183 of the 1990 Act, section
186(5)(b) of the Act provides that should you otherwise become entitled (under section 186) to compensation for loss or damage attributable to that notice, no such compensation will be payable in respect of any loss or damage which could have been
avoided had you given the Council the information required by this notice, or had you
otherwise co-operated with the Council when responding to it.

*delete where not required

Notes for the LPA

(a) Insert the Council's name.

(b) Insert the address of the land, or the description by which it is commonly known.

(c) It is helpful, but not essential, to specify the suspected breach. If it is not possible to do so on the information available, paragraph 2 and Schedule 2 should be omitted.

(d) Insert the date and time.

(e) Insert the address where the person served with the notice may be heard.

(f) Substitute any other 'likely consequences', in accordance with section 171C(5)(a) of the 1990 Act, if appropriate.

Appendix 2

Matters Which Constitute 'County Matters'

What constitutes a 'county matter' is defined in TCPA 1990, Sched 1, para 1 as the following:

    (a) the winning and working of minerals in, on or under land (whether by surface or underground working) or the erection of any building, plant or machinery-

        (i) which it is proposed to use in connection with the winning and working of minerals or with their treatment or disposal in or on land adjoining the site of the working; or

        (ii) which a person engaged in mining operations proposes to use in connection with the grading, washing, grinding or crushing of minerals;

    (b) the use of land, or the erection of any building, plant or machinery on land, for the carrying out of any process for the preparation or adaption for sale of any mineral or the manufacture of any article from a mineral where-

        (i) the land forms part of or adjoins a site used or proposed to be used for the winning and working of minerals; or

        (ii) the mineral is, or is proposed to be, brought to the land from a site used, or proposed to be used, for the winning and working of minerals by means of a pipeline, conveyor belt, aerial ropeway, or similar plant or machinery, or by private road, private waterway or private railway;

    (c) the carrying out of searches and tests of mineral deposits or the erection of any building, plant or machinery which it is proposed to use in connection with them;

    (d) the depositing of mineral waste;

    (e) the use of land for any purpose required in connection with the transport by rail or water of aggregates (that is to say, any of the following, namely—

        (i) sand and gravel;

        (ii) crushed rock;

        (iii) artificial materials of appearance similar to sand, gravel or crushed rock and manufactured or otherwise derived from iron or steel slags, pulverised fuel ash, clay or mineral waste),

    or the erection of any building, plant or machinery which it is proposed to use in connection with them;

    (f) the erection of any building, plant or machinery which it is proposed to use for the coating of roadstone or the production of concrete or of concrete products or artificial aggregates, where the building, plant or machinery is to be erected in or on land which forms part of or adjoins a site used or proposed to be used—

    (i)   for the winning and working of minerals; or

    (ii) for any of the purposes mentioned in paragraph (e) above;

(g)   the erection of any building, plant or machinery which it is proposed to use for the manufacture of cement;

(h)   the carrying out of operations in, on, over or under land, or a use of land, where the land is or forms part of a site used or formerly used for the winning and working of minerals and where the operations or use would conflict with or prejudice compliance with a restoration condition or an aftercare condition;

(i)   the carrying out of operations in, on, over or under land, or any use of land, which is situated partly in and partly outside a National Park;

(j)   the carrying out of any operation which is, as respects the area in question, a prescribed operation or an operation of a prescribed class or any use which is, as respects that area, a prescribed use or use of a prescribed class.

Appendix 3

Model Enforcement Notices

MODEL ENFORCEMENT NOTICE—OPERATIONAL DEVELOPMENT

IMPORTANT—THIS COMMUNICATION AFFECTS YOUR PROPERTY

TOWN AND COUNTRY PLANNING ACT 1990 (as amended by the Planning and Compensation Act 1991)

ENFORCEMENT NOTICE

ISSUED BY: [name of Council]

1.   THIS IS A FORMAL NOTICE which is issued by the Council because it appears to them that there has been a breach of planning control, under section 171A(1)(a) of the above Act, at the land described below. They consider that it is expedient to issue this notice, having regard to the provisions of the development plan and to other material planning considerations.

2.   THE LAND AFFECTED

Land at [address of land], shown edged red on the attached plan.

3.   THE BREACH OF PLANNING CONTROL ALLEGED

Without planning permission, the erection of a brick-built, single-storey building, and the construction of a driveway leading to it, in the approximate position marked with a cross on the attached plan.

4.   REASONS FOR ISSUING THIS NOTICE

It appears to the Council that the above breach of planning control has occurred within the last four years. The building in question was substantially completed less than four years ago. The building looks like, and appears to have been designed as, a dwellinghouse. The site lies within the approved Green Belt where, with certain exceptions which do not apply in this case, there is a strong presumption against any development. The building appears as an intrusion in this otherwise mainly open, rural landscape. It is contrary to development plan policies and harmful to the visual amenities of the area. The Council do not consider that planning permission should be given, because planning conditions could not overcome these objections to the development.

5. WHAT YOU ARE REQUIRED TO DO

   (i)   Remove the building and the driveway.
                  Time for compliance: 12 weeks after this notice takes effect.
   (ii) Remove from the land all building materials and rubble arising from compli-
         ance with the first requirement above, and restore the land to its condition
         before the breach took place by levelling the ground and re-seeding it with
         grass.
                  Time for compliance: 24 weeks after this notice takes effect.

6. WHEN THIS NOTICE TAKES EFFECT

This notice takes effect on [specific date, not less than 28 clear days after date of
service], unless an appeal is made against it beforehand.

Dated: [date of issue]

Signed: [Council's authorised officer]

on behalf of

[Council's name and address]

                                                                        ANNEX

YOUR RIGHT OF APPEAL

You can appeal against this notice, but any appeal must be received, or posted in time
to be received, by the Secretary of State before [the specified effective date]. The
enclosed booklet 'Enforcement Appeals—A Guide to Procedure' sets out your rights.
Read it carefully. You may use the enclosed appeals forms. One is for you to send to
the Secretary of State if you decide to appeal. The other is for you to keep as a duplicate for your own records. You should also send the Secretary of State the spare copy
of this enforcement notice which is enclosed.

WHAT HAPPENS IF YOU DO NOT APPEAL

If you do not appeal against this enforcement notice, it will take effect on [the specified effective date] and you must then ensure that the required steps for complying
with it, for which you may be held responsible, are taken within the period[s] specified
in the notice. Failure to comply with an enforcement notice which has taken effect can
result in prosecution and/or remedial action by the Council.

MODEL ENFORCEMENT NOTICE—MATERIAL CHANGE OF USE

IMPORTANT—THIS COMMUNICATION AFFECTS YOUR PROPERTY

TOWN AND COUNTRY PLANNING ACT 1990 (as amended by the Planning and
Compensation Act 1991)

ENFORCEMENT NOTICE

ISSUED BY: [name of Council]

1. THIS IS A FORMAL NOTICE which is issued by the Council because it appears
to them that there has been a breach of planning control, under section 171A(1)(a) of

the above Act, at the land described below. They consider that it is expedient to issue this notice, having regard to the provisions of the development plan and to other material planning considerations.

2. THE LAND AFFECTED

The dwelling and associated land at [address of land], shown edged red on the attached plan.

3. THE BREACH OF PLANNING CONTROL ALLEGED

Without planning permission, change of use of the garage and adjoining land from private domestic use to use for a vehicle repair business.

4. REASONS FOR ISSUING THIS NOTICE

It appears to the Council that the above breach of planning control has occurred within the last ten years. The unauthorised use is not suitable for this residential area. It disturbs the neighbours through noise, traffic movement and car parking and is unsightly in such an area. The Council do not consider that planning permission should be given, because planning conditions could not overcome these problems.

5. WHAT YOU ARE REQUIRED TO DO

(i)   Stop using the garage and adjoining land for repairing or maintaining motor vehicles on a commercial basis.
                         Time for compliance: 30 days after this notice takes effect.
(ii)   Remove from the land all machinery and installations brought onto the land for the purpose of repairing or maintaining motor vehicles on a commercial basis. (You may keep any equipment which you use solely for the maintenance of your own private vehicles.)
                         Time for compliance: 6 months after this notice takes effect.

6. WHEN THIS NOTICE TAKES EFFECT

This notice takes effect on [specific date, not less than 28 clear days after date of service], unless an appeal is made against it beforehand.

Dated: [date of issue]

Signed: [Council's authorised officer]

on behalf of

[Council's name and address]

ANNEX

YOUR RIGHT OF APPEAL

You can appeal against this notice, but any appeal must be received, or posted in time to be received, by the Secretary of State before [the specified effective date]. The enclosed booklet 'Enforcement Appeals—A Guide to Procedure' sets out your rights. Read it carefully. You may use the enclosed appeals forms. One is for you to send to the Secretary of State if you decide to appeal. The other is for you to keep as a duplicate for your own records. You should also send the Secretary of State the spare copy of this enforcement notice which is enclosed.

WHAT HAPPENS IF YOU DO NOT APPEAL

If you do not appeal against this enforcement notice, it will take effect on [the speci-fied effective date] and you must then ensure that the required steps for complying with it, for which you may be held responsible, are taken within the period[s] specified in the notice. Failure to comply with an enforcement notice which has taken effect can result in prosecution and/or remedial action by the Council.

MODEL ENFORCEMENT NOTICE—
BREACH OF CONDITION

IMPORTANT—THIS COMMUNICATION AFFECTS YOUR PROPERTY

TOWN AND COUNTRY PLANNING ACT 1990 (as amended by the Planning and Compensation Act 1991)

ENFORCEMENT NOTICE

ISSUED BY: [name of Council]

1.   THIS IS A FORMAL NOTICE which is issued by the Council because it appears to them that there has been a breach of planning control, under section 171A(1)(b) of the above Act, at the land described below. They consider that it is expedient to issue this notice, having regard to the provisions of the development plan and to other mate-rial planning considerations.

2.   THE LAND AFFECTED

The restaurant and associated land at [address of land], shown edged red on the at-tached plan.

3.   THE BREACH OF PLANNING CONTROL ALLEGED

On [date of planning permission] planning permission was granted for the use of this land as a restaurant, subject to conditions. One of those conditions is that members of the public should not be permitted to enter the premises for the consumption of food, or for the purchase of food for consumption off the premises, after 2200 hours on any day. It appears to the Council that the condition has not been complied with fully, because the premises have been open for the sale of food for consumption off the premises after 2200 hours on most Fridays and Saturdays.

4.   REASONS FOR THIS NOTICE

It appears to the Council that the above breach of planning control has occurred within the last ten years. The area is in mixed business and residential use. It contains a number of residential properties, including many flats above the shops and other business premises. The sale of 'takeaway' food from the restaurant, late at night, attracts large numbers of people to the area both on foot and in vehicles. The noise made by these customers, the banging of their car doors and the noise of car engines stopping and re-starting late at night, is causing serious disturbance to nearby residents at a time when the area would otherwise be relatively peaceful. The Council do not consider that there should be any relaxation of the condition in question, which already permits such sales up to a reasonable hour in the evening.

5.   WHAT YOU ARE REQUIRED TO DO

Stop selling for consumption off the premises after 2200 hours on any day.

Time for compliance: 21 days after this notice takes effect.

6.   WHEN THIS NOTICE TAKES EFFECT

This notice takes effect on [specific date, not less than 28 clear days after date of service], unless an appeal is made against it beforehand.

Dated: [date of issue]

Signed: [Council's authorised officer]

on behalf of

[Council's name and address]

ANNEX

YOUR RIGHT OF APPEAL

You can appeal against this notice, but any appeal must be received, or posted in time to be received, by the Secretary of State before [the specified effective date]. The enclosed booklet 'Enforcement Appeals—A Guide to Procedure' sets out your rights. Read it carefully. You may use the enclosed appeals forms. One is for you to send to the Secretary of State if you decide to appeal. The other is for you to keep as a duplicate for your own records. You should also send the Secretary of State the spare copy of this enforcement notice which is enclosed.

WHAT HAPPENS IF YOU DO NOT APPEAL

If you do not appeal against this enforcement notice, it will take effect on [the specified effective date] and you must then ensure that the required steps for complying with it, for which you may be held responsible, are taken within the period[s] specified in the notice. Failure to comply with an enforcement notice which has taken effect can result in prosecution and/or remedial action by the Council.

Appendix 4

Model Stop Notice

IMPORTANT—THIS COMMUNICATION AFFECTS YOUR PROPERTY

Town and Country Planning Act 1990 (as amended by the Planning and Compensation Act 1991)

.... Council

To .... (name of intended recipient of the notice).

Whereas:

(1) The .... Council, being the local planning authority for the land to which this notice relates, have issued an enforcement notice (dated ....) under section 172 of the Town and Country Planning Act 1990, alleging that there has been a breach of planning control on the land described in Schedule 1 to this notice; and

(2) The Council consider it expedient that a relevant activity required by the enforcement notice to cease should cease before the expiry of the period allowed for compliance with the requirements of the enforcement notice;

Notice is hereby given that the Council, in exercise of their power in section 183 of the 1990 Act, now prohibit the carrying out of the activity specified in Schedule 2 to this notice.

A copy of the related enforcement notice, issued under section 172 of the 1990 Act, is annexed to this notice. This notice shall take effect on .... (date) when all the activity specified in Schedule 2 to this notice shall cease.

Dated   Signed

Address of Council   Council's authorised officer

SCHEDULE 1

The land or premises to which this notice relates comprises land at .... (address or brief identifying details of the land), shown edged in red on the annexed plan.

SCHEDULE 2

The activity to which this notice relates is [a breach of]* [part of a breach of]* planning control, consisting of .... [without the required planning permission;] [the continuing breach of condition No. .... imposed on the planning permission granted on .... (date)]*.

*Delete and complete as appropriate.

Appendix 5

Model Breach of Condition Notice

IMPORTANT: THIS COMMUNICATION AFFECTS YOUR PROPERTY

TOWN AND COUNTRY PLANNING ACT 1990 (as amended by the
Planning and Compensation Act 1991)

BREACH OF CONDITION NOTICE

Issued by: [name of Council]

1.   This is a formal notice which is issued by the Council, under section 187A of the
above Act, because they consider that [a condition] [conditions] imposed on a grant of
planning permission, relating to the land described below, [has] [have] not been complied with. They consider that you should be required to [comply] [secure compliance]
with the condition[s] specified in this notice.

2.   The land affected by the notice

The [restaurant and associated land] at [address of land], shown edged in red on the
attached plan.

3.   The relevant planning permission

The relevant planning permission to which this notice relates is the permission granted
by the Council on [insert date of issue of permission] for the change of use of land
[from an office use to a restaurant] [Council's reference number].

4.   The breach of condition

The following condition[s] [has] [have] not been complied with—

(1)

(2)   [State the terms of each condition which has
         not been complied with.]

(3)

5.   What are you required to do

As the person responsible for the breach[es] of condition specified in paragraph 4 of
this notice, you are required to [comply] [secure compliance] with the stated condition[s]
by [taking the following steps]—

(1)
(2)   [State clearly the steps to be taken in order to
(3)   secure compliance with the
      condition[s] in paragraph 4 above.]

[and] [ceasing the following activities]—

(1)
(2)   [State clearly the activities which must cease
(3)   in order to secure compliance with the
      condition[s] in paragraph 4 above.]

Time for compliance: 30 days beginning with the day on which this notice is served on you. [This assumes that there is only one compliance period for all the required steps.]

6   When this notice takes effect

This notice takes effect *immediately* it is served on you or you receive it by postal delivery.

Dated: [date of issue]

Signed:[Council's authorised officer]

On behalf of: [Council's name and address]

Warning

There is no right of appeal against this notice.

It is an offence to contravene the requirements stated in paragraph 5 of this notice after the end of the compliance period. You will then be at risk of **immediate prosecution** in the Magistrates' Court, for which the maximum penalty is £1,000 for a first offence and for any subsequent offence. If you are in any doubt about what this notice requires you to do, you should get in touch *immediately* with [Council's nominated officer to deal with enquiries, address and telephone number].

If you need independent advice about this notice, you are advised to contact urgently a lawyer, planning consultant or other professional adviser specialising in planning matters. If you wish to contest the validity of the notice, you may only do so by an application to the High Court for judicial review. A lawyer will advise you on what this procedure involves.

Do not leave your response to the last minute.

Appendix 6

Appendix to Annex 5 to Circular 21/91

Entry to Agricultural Land

Animal health

1.When there is an outbreak of serious disease in animals (such as foot-and-mouth disease or anthrax), notices giving warning of the outbreak will be placed strategically by Diseases of Animals Inspectors on the edge of farmland. This would warn any unexpected or casual visitors (such as a local authority Enforcement Of ficer) of the dangers and should effectively prevent them entering the land and thus being responsible for spreading the disease. However, there are other instances (such as during a TB/brucellosis outbreak) where there is no requirement to place notices warning of the dangers, but entry to the land could nevertheless cause the spread of disease. LP A officers should therefore contact the MAFF or WOAD Divisional Veterinary Officer at the local Animal Health Offices to check that there are no animal health movement restriction orders in force (or other animal health problems) on the farm they intend to visit.

Plant health

2. Similarly, where there is serious plant disease (eg rhizomania of sugar beet), access to land may be strictly controlled under the Plant Health (Great Britain) Order 1987 (SI No 1758). With soil-borne diseases, there is a distinct risk that infested soil could be spread on footwear to an unaffected part of the farm or even to another location. LPA officers *should not* rely on a sign being present on such land and should instead make inquiries with the local MAFF or WOAD Divisional Office, so that a check can be made with the local Plant Health and Seeds Inspectorate that there is no plant health restriction in force on the land to be visited.

Appendix 7

Draft Form of Statutory Declaration

I (declarant) of (address) do solemnly and sincerely declare that:

(set out statements of facts to be proved in numbered paragraphs)

[1. State interest in the land to which the application relates.

2. Set out the relevant information that is peculiarly within the declarant' s knowledge, eg, history of ownership of the land, history of development on the land (including applications for planning permission, any refusals of planning permission, any planning agreements), details of the history of the use of the land.]

AND I make this solemn declaration conscientiously believing the same to be true and by virtue of the Statutory Declarations Act 1835.

DECLARED at ..... }
this ..... day of }   (signature of declarant)
.... }

Before me
....
(signature of person before whom declaration is made)

Commissioner for oaths/ Solicitor empowered to administer oaths

Documentary evidence in support of the information contained in the statutory declaration can be exhibited to the statutory declaration.

(a) A deed may be exhibited using the following wording, where the letters AB represent the initials of the declarant' s name:

'This deed is now produced and shown to me and marked ["AB 1"]'

(b) A plan may be exhibited using the following wording, where the letters CD represent the initials of the declarant' s name:

'A plan of the land, which is to the best of my knowledge and belief accurate is now produced and shown to me and marked ["CD 1"]'

Each exhibit to be numbered consecutively.

The exhibit itself must also be identified as the exhibit referred to in the statutory declaration. The following memorandum should be endorsed on the face of the exhibit, using the reference given in the body of the statutory declaration:

'This is the deed/ plan marked ["AB 1"]/["CD 1"] referred to in the annexed declaration of (declarant) declared before me this .... day of .... (signature of person before whom declaration is made)'

Appendix 8

Prescribed form of Lawful Development Certificate granted under TCPA 1990, ss 191 or 192

TOWN AND COUNTRY PLANNING ACT 1990: SECTION 191 AND 192
(as amended by section 10 of the Planning and Compensation Act 1991)

TOWN AND COUNTRY PLANNING GENERAL DEVELOPMENT ORDER
1988: ARTICLE 26A

CERTIFICATE OF LAWFUL USE OR DEVELOPMENT
The (a) _____
Council hereby certify that on (b) _____ the
use*/operations*/matter* described in the First Schedule hereto in respect of the land
specified in the Second Schedule hereto and edged*/hatched*/coloured* (c)
_____ on the plan attached to this certificate, was*/would have
been* lawful within the meaning of section 191 of the Town and Country Planning Act
1990 (as amended), for the following reason(s)

_____
_____
_____
_____

Signed _____ (Council' s authorised officer).

On behalf of (a) _____ Council

Date _____

First Schedule

(d)

Second Schedule

(e)

Notes
1   This certificate is issued solely for the purpose of section 191*/192* of the Town
and Country Planning Act 1990 (as amended).

2   It certifies that the use*/operations*/matter* specified in the First Schedule taking
place on the land described in the Second Schedule was*/would have been* lawful, on
the specified date and, thus, was not*/would not have been* liable to enforcement
action under section 172 of the 1990 Act on that date.

3   This certificate applies only to the extent of the use*/operations*/matter* described
in the First Schedule and to the land specified in the Second Schedule and identified
on the attached plan. Any use*/operations*/matter* which is materially dif ferent from
that described or which relates to other land may render the owner or occupier liable to
enforcement action.

*4   The effect of the certificate is also qualified by the proviso in section 192(4) of
the 1990 Act, as amended, which states that the lawfulness of a described use or operation is only conclusively presumed where there has been no material change, before
the use is instituted or the operations begun, in any of the matters relevant to determining such lawfulness.

* delete where inappropriate

Insert:

   (a)   name of Council
   (b)   date of application to the Council
   (c)   colour used on the plan
   (d)   full description of use, operations or other matter , if necessary, by reference
         to details in the application or submitted plans, including a reference to the
         use class, if any, of the Use Classes Order within which the certificated use
         falls
   (e)   address or location of the site

Appendix 9

Model Special Enforcement Notice

IMPORTANT—THIS COMMUNICATION AFFECTS YOUR PROPERTY

.... Council
TOWN AND COUNTRY PLANNING ACT 1990
SPECIAL ENFORCEMENT NOTICE
.... (address)

WHEREAS

(1)   It appears to the ....Council ('the Council'),
being the local planning authority for the purposes of section 294 of the Town and
Country Planning Act 1990 ('the Act') in this matter, that development of Crown land
has been carried out, otherwise than by or on behalf of the Crown, at a time after 1 1
April 1984 when no person is entitled to occupy it by virtue of a private interest (including a licence in writing).

(2)   The land or premises ('The land') is described in Schedule 1 below .

(3)   The matters alleged to constitute development are described in Schedule 2 below.

(4)   The Council consider it expedient, having regard to the provisions of the development plan and to any other material considerations, to issue this notice (a 'special
enforcement notice') in exercise of their powers in section 294 of the Act [for the
reasons set out in the Annex to this notice].

NOTICE IS HEREBY GIVEN that the Council require that the steps specified in Schedule 3 below be taken in order to [restore the land to its condition before the development took place] [discontinue any use of the land which has been instituted by the
development] within [the period of .... days/months from the date on which this
notice takes effect] [the period specified in respect of each step in that Schedule].

THIS NOTICE SHALL TAKE EFFECT, subject to the provisions of section 175(4),
as applied by section 295(5) of the Act, on ....

issued ....   signed ....
(Council's address)   (Council's authorised officer)

SCHEDULE 1

Land or premises to which this notice relates

SCHEDULE 2

The matters alleged to constitute development of the land

SCHEDULE 3

Steps required to be taken

[ANNEX

Reasons why the Council consider it expedient to
issue the special enforcement notice]

Index